Numerology: Key to the Tarot

A good name is better than
precious ointment.

The Bible
Ecclesiastes VII, 1

Numerology
Key to the
Tarot

Para Research
Rockport
Massachusetts

Numerology: Key to the Tarot
by Sandor Konraad

Library of Congress Catalog Card Number: 83-060062
International Standard Book Number: 0-914918-45-1

Typeset in 10 pt. Paladium on Compugraphic 7500
Printed by Alpine Press, Inc.
on 55-pound Surtone II Antique
Edited by Shaun Levesque and Marah Ren
Cover design by Robert Killam and Ralph Poness
Cover photograph by Dave Watroba
Graphics by Robert Killam
Typeset by Anne Drueding and Jean King

Published by Para Research, Inc.
Whistlestop Mall
Rockport, Massachusetts 01966

Manufactured in the United States of America

First Printing, April 1983, 5,000 copies

Contents

Foreword

Over the ages people have asked themselves the question, "Is there Purpose in the universe?," or more specifically, "What, if any, is the purpose of my life?"

There are various ways of obtaining concrete answers to this existential question, but among the more helpful are the age-old practices of the Tarot and numerology. In one form or another both have offered guidance since the beginning of civilization. Their very survival is a testament to their validity. Through the centuries, seekers have learned that they can tune in to the cosmos by learning the language of these ancient disciplines.

Quite frankly, this is a "how to" book and in these pages the individual in search of self will find precise directions for setting up an astro-numeric chart and for throwing and reading Tarot spreads. The reader may come to feel, as the author does, that there is a cosmic connection between the two; he or she will learn that the Tarot takes on a new and exciting dimension when used in conjunction with one's own numerical chart.

Included in this book are nine distinctive spreads, which should be of interest to students of the Tarot at all levels of evolution. Each one is accompanied by a transcribed reading of an actual consultation.

The author supports the proposition that the central value of both numerology and the Tarot is to provide signposts along the way for all seekers after the Light.

This work is gratefully dedicated to

Kevin Quinn Avery

Teacher and numerologist *par excellence*, and
a Number 1 in anyone's book

and to that other vessel of light

Rolla Nordic

A gracious soul, perennial Queen of Wands,
and *The* Empress of the Tarot

1

East Is East: The Numbers

Our study of numerology properly begins with the first nine numbers. These are known as root numbers. The numbers 1 to 9 actually comprise all the numbers in the world, for those that follow—the compound numbers—are merely variations of these nine root numbers. The zero eludes easy classification as technically it is not considered a number and becomes one only when combined with a root number.

Numbers are really diverse symbols. Each has different sets of values attributed to it and how a given number will be read depends on several factors. Our introduction to numbers, however, will be centered on how they apply to people.

There exists a quaint tradition among some numerologists, who pretend all numbers are equally benevolent. This is demonstrably not the case. Perhaps their hearts are in the right place even if their heads are not, for it appears that they are simply misinforming their clients. Certainly, they are not providing a service, but rather, a profound disservice by attempting to gloss over the facts of a chart. For it is the major purpose of an astro-numeric chart to point out to an individual *both* strengths and weaknesses so that he or she can better work with the unique characteristics provided by nature. In some cases it is possible to modify negative characteristics. But the client is not going to be interested in doing that unless he or she understands that there are characteristics that in some way limit what he or she is capable of achieving.

One thing to note about numbers at the outset is that there is a correspondence between them and the signs of the zodiac in that the odd numbers represent one type of force—for the most part—and the even numbers represent another. The odd-numbered Sun signs are Aries, Gemini, Leo, Libra, Sagittarius and Aquarius. When one looks at natives of these signs in contrast to the even-numbered signs of Taurus, Cancer, Virgo, Scorpio, Capricorn and Pisces, one comes to a realization that there is a reason why the odd-numbered signs are considered active and positive while the even-numbered signs are thought of as passive and negative. So, too, with numbers: The Odds are considered the active citizens, while the Evens assume a more passive role. As with any generalization, there are exceptions. Seven, for example, is untypical of the Odds in that it tends to the passive, and for an Even, 8 is more than a little aggressive.

Making distinctions is not the same as making a moral judgment. One number is not necessarily better or worse than another but there are differences and it is important to understand these differences. If, for example, you are running for Generalissimo of the Armies and you have a passive Sun sign and a numerical chart overloaded with Evens, you would be well advised to change either your occupation or your name.

As this work is concerned with the correlation between numerology and the Tarot, the destination for our numerical journey will be 22, which is also the number of cards in the Major Arcana. The Major Arcana defines the twenty-two cards of greater importance in the deck; the Minor Arcana defines the fifty-six cards of secondary importance. Since the first deck of Tarot cards appeared in the fourteenth century, the word *Arcana* has been used to indicate the mysterious knowledge represented by the cards and known only to an initiate. The singular, *Arcanum*, represents this knowledge in an individual card (e.g. Arcanum X, or the tenth card of the Major Arcana, The Wheel of Fortune). In addition to the natural division between the root and the compound numbers, there is a further subdivision, for the numbers 10, 11 and 22 are considered to be in a unique category; the latter two being called Master Numbers, and 10 the bridge between the roots and the compounds. Information for finding "your numbers" is given in Chapter 3. You may wish to read that chapter first so that when you read the descriptions of the numbers that follow, you will know which of them properly applies to you.

1

Tarot—The Magician   Planet—The Sun
Zodiac—Aries   Element—Fire

In the golden days of radio and kidhood all self-respecting, red-blooded youths would never fail to be in tuning distance on Monday,

Wednesday and Friday evenings when they would hear the thrilling strains of the William Tell Overture, followed by the dulcet-toned announcer repeating his ritual words of power: "A cloud of dust, a hearty cry of 'Hi yo, Silver, huhhhway' and the Lone Ranger rides again!"

The Lone Ranger was a Number 1. One-people ride tall in the saddle and you will seldom see them traveling in packs for they believe one travels swiftest when one travels alone. They like to give orders rather than take them and often they are a law unto themselves. Ones are frequently loners and choose vocations, such as literature, where they are set off from what they might call "the common herd." Ones are natural leaders. They possess considerable creative energy. They may often be found in the communications field for they are particularly capable of expressing themselves via the written or spoken word.

In the Tarot the Number 1 card of the Major Arcana is The Magician, who might be seen as the God-Man, brimming with ego and confidence, master of all he surveys. The first sign of the zodiac is Aries—the sign of the executive, the innovator, the pioneer. The active element for 1 is fire and the first-ranking planet is the Sun, representing the Life Force and creative energy.

A Number 1 likes to be right, but would rather be President.

KEY: INDEPENDENCE, ORIGINALITY, LEADERSHIP

2

Tarot—The High Priestess   Planet—The Moon
Zodiac—Taurus   Element—Water

Tonto is a 2. Two's say, "Kemosabe," "Yes, ma'am" and "No sir." they speak when they are spoken to and do what they are told. Ones find their places in life by being oh-so-smart or oh-so-independent. Two's find theirs by being oh-so-nice. Usually, they are friendly, agreeable and cooperative, although they can be somewhat on the sensitive side. Ones lead; 2s follow. Sometimes, like Avis, they do try harder. Actually, Avis is not a Number 2, it is a Number 6. The problem is that it is a wishy-washy Even rather than a go-getter Odd. Hertz, of course, is an Odd—a forceful 5.

The first card of the Tarot, The Magician, is dominant and assertive. The Number 2 card, however, is detached and submissive. The Magician stands out in the world; the High Priestess is seated and cloistered away in a hidden chamber.

The planet that is second in the heavenly hierarchy is the Moon, symbolizing femininity and moodiness. Its element is water, which is associated with feelings, and if 2s lack the fervor of 1s, they are, nonetheless, still waters that run deep.

KEY: COOPERATIVE, SUBSERVIENT, SENSITIVE

3

Tarot—The Empress	Planet—Jupiter
Zodiac—Gemini	Element—Fire

In Hegelian terms, if 1 could be considered the Thesis, and 2 the Anti-Thesis, 3 would be the Synthesis. It is the product of the marriage of 1 and 2, and it turns out to be a joyful union indeed. In human terms, Adam is the 1, Eve, the 2, and the result of their union is humanity. Thus, 3 is a number of creation. And 3s tend to be highly fertile individuals. Whether they create fleshly progeny or new concepts, shapes and sounds in the arts and sciences, they delight in self-expression, particularly music.

If 3 is a number of creation, it is also a number of completion. Ancient religions in the East often had a deity that was three-fold in nature. Christianity, the inheritor of a school of beliefs stretching back to the remotest ages, continued to carry on the tradition of this sacred number in the Holy Trinity of Father, Son and Holy Ghost. For Christians, as for others who had come before, 3 described the differing aspects of the creator.

In the system of personality devised by Sigmund Freud, 3 is again a number of completion expressed in the terms ego, id and superego. Three, then, is a number of completion for both the divine and the human, and on both levels the trinity of the universe could be seen to represent Mind, Body, and Spirit.

Perhaps the key to this number is its association with the planet Jupiter, which in astrology is known as The Greater Fortune. Those who have "a good Jupiter" in their natal charts have their paths smoothed out for them.

Threes are "Jupiter people" in that they attract all kinds of good things without having to work very hard for them. They are highly expressive and their ideas just seem to flow. In addition, they tend to be popular, sparkling conversationalists, and, in general, find life a rather pleasant experience. On the negative side, they can be overly concerned with pleasing others or content to trade on their charm. Also, they can be somewhat adolescent in their approach to life situations. By and large, 3s lead full, active lives, make good marital partners, and are as creative in their marriages as their careers.

The dual themes of completion and creation are expressed in the third card of the Tarot, The Empress. She might be seen as mistress of the creative forces of Nature, and while her creativity is further symbolized by the fact that she is heavy with child, she is also completed by the fourth card of the Tarot, the Emperor, who is her husband.

KEY: CREATIVE, SELF-EXPRESSIVE, GREGARIOUS

4

Tarot—The Emperor	Planet—Earth, Sun
Zodiac—Cancer	Element—Earth

Four is associated with 1 in that both numbers are said to be of the House of the Sun. The association is not merely theoretical for the two numbers actually do attract one another and it is interesting to note how often 1s will have 4s for friends or mates. Perhaps the chief characteristic is for 1 people to live at 4 addresses—that is, a house number that is a 4 or a compound number that reduces to 4 such as 301 (3 + 0 + 1 = 4). But while 4 is associated with 1, it is a decidedly poor relation. It expresses the negative aspects of the Sun. Perhaps the major difficulty is that it is associated with the Earth and therefore the desires and strivings of the 4-type tend to be overly materialistic.

Unlike the carefree, easygoing 3, 4 is a grind and a drudge and each day anew finds that he or she must earn their daily bread by the sweat of their brow. They labor long and hard, but more often than not, they discover that their vines bear rotten grapes. Fours can be born losers, but more often than not, their complaining will make you think they are losers, even when they are coming out ahead.

The card of the Tarot associated with 4 is The Emperor. The Emperor is not a "bad" card; the Emperor's problem is that he is overly concerned with temporal power and material things.

Perhaps it might be well to pause and to point out at this juncture that our discussion of numbers is concerned with archetypes. And in numerology, as in astrology, relatively few people are archetypes. When someone says, "I'm a Capricorn," or "I'm an Aries," they generally mean only that their Sun is in Capricorn or in Aries. When the total weight of planetary configuration is taken into account, however, they might well be something else. Numbers work much the same way. What is important in a chart is where the number appears, how often it is repeated, and what the overall configuration is. To have a 4 in a strategic spot such as the Expression, Birth or Path number (all of which will be explained shortly) does not necessarily make for an archetype. From the viewpoints of both the astrologer and the numerologist, most people are not "pure" types, but combinations of two, three or more signs or numbers.

It is the attitude and free will of the individual that determines whether a number is "good" or "bad." The number 4 might be likened to the sign of Virgo in that the key to both is work. But whether that work is making mountains out of molehills or doing something grand, noble or heroic will rest to a large extent on the individual's self-image in relation to the universe.

KEY: WORK, WORRY, PRACTICALITY

5

| Tarot—The Hierophant | Planet—Mercury, Mars |
| Zodiac—Leo | Element—Air |

On a numerical grid comprised of the root numbers from 1 to 9, it can be seen that 5 is the solar center of the number system. This aspect of 5 is also echoed in Leo, the fifth sign of the Zodiac, for Leo is the only sign ruled by the Sun, and Leos usually manage to be the center of their personal solar system.

Five is the number of the senses and thus the number of humanity. Fives like to live life to the fullest, they like to be in the center of things, they like to be physically involved. It is the number of the adventurer, the explorer, the merry rover. On the negative side, 5s can be restless and leave behind them a pile of unfinished projects and broken love affairs in their endless quest for fresh adventures.

The fifth card of the Major Arcana is The Hierophant, associated with Taurus, the sign of earthly pleasures. The Hierophant is offering spiritual counsel to his disciples and this suggests that life can be lived fully on both the physical and spiritual levels. It also suggests that we can transcend our humanity and move from the level of sensuality to the level of the spirit.

This transcendant aspect of the card is further reinforced by the other associations: The planets Mercury and Mars represent knowledge and martial energy. Mercury may represent spiritual knowledge. The Hierophant is associated with Taurus, an earth sign, but the element associated with 5 is air, suggesting that 5s can choose to remain rooted on earth or ascend to the very heavens. Fives can go either way.

KEY: ADVENTURE, INVOLVEMENT, TRANSCENDENCE

6

| Tarot—The Lovers | Planet—Venus |
| Zodiac—Virgo | Element—Earth, Air |

Six is influenced strongly by Venus and so is a child of grace with a highly developed love nature. On one level there is love and affection for family and friends; on another level it is a love for fine things with a home designed for living. Sixes are generally rather pleasant people and exude a compelling kind of magnetism. For that reason they make very good salespeople or succeed at any occupation that is dependent upon personal appeal. Six is active in civic affairs and has a very keen sense of responsibility in all matters affecting family and community.

Essentially, 6s are "home bodies" and nothing pleases them more than to spend a cheery evening by the fireside surrounded by a circle of loved ones.

In Arcanum VI of the Tarot, a man must choose between two women, an older and a younger one. In the case of 6, the younger one could be said to represent adventure in the form of a creative calling and the older one, security in an established company or job in commerce. Since 6 is associated with Virgo, a practical earth sign, it will often opt for security and later compensate by becoming a collector of art and other things of beauty.

KEY: AFFECTIONATE, STABLE, CONSERVATIVE

7

Tarot—The Chariot   Planet—Neptune, the Moon
Zodiac—Libra   Element—Water

As 1 and 4 are associated with the House of the Sun, so 2 and 7 are also kin, both being members of the House of the Moon. This is also borne out in the Tarot as Arcanum VII, The Chariot, is associated with the sign of Cancer, which is said to be ruled by the Moon.

Seven is thought by many to be a "lucky number." This is reinforced by the card of The Chariot, which is said to symbolize great victory. But there is something curious both about the card and the number. Closer study of the chariot card reveals that while it is associated with Cancer and the Moon, the charioteer is said to symbolize Apollo, who drives the Chariot of the Sun through the heavens. Because of this, there is a duality about the card. That this duality affects the number as well is indicated by its association with the seventh sign of the zodiac, Libra, symbolized by the scales. Libra's challenge is to neutralize the polarities in its nature, and at best, it maintains a precarious balance.

So, too, 7s have the challenge of maintaining a fine and delicate balance. This balance takes many forms, but is most thoroughly felt as a pull from one side by material forces, and on the other side by spiritual forces.

Seven is also the product of the numbers 3 and 4—4 representing Earth and material things, 3 representing the number of the Holy Trinity and the kingdom of Spirit. Seven-people know they have a special task to perform. This helps to account for the fact that they are often more self-involved than they are interested in other people. Their mission is to explore the underlying meaning of life, so 7 is the number of religion, research, and all things occult. Above all, 7's task is to find the Holy Grail and the road leading back to The Great All.

KEY: INTROSPECTIVE, SECRETIVE, SPIRITUALLY ATTUNED

8

Tarot—Justice	Planet—Saturn
Zodiac—Scorpio	Element—Earth

(See page 28 for an explanation of why the Tarot cards numbered VIII (8) and XI (11) are reversed.) Eight might be considered the do-or-die number. It is the central power number—the others being 7 and 9—and there are mighty forces at work here. When 8s want something they want it NOW and they will stop at nothing to obtain it. An 8 wants wealth, power and authority and usually finds ways to get them—or perishes in the attempt.

While 8 is a number of achievement, 8s are not always sure what they want. Nor are they necessarily happy when they achieve it. One of 8's problems is that it is composed of two ciphers, which on one level represent eternity, and on the other, nothingness. An 8 is also made up of two 4s and if one 4 has problems, two of them can produce utter defeat and misery.

Eight is the strongest of the Evens but not always for the better. It is associated with the planet Saturn, and while Saturn is connected in the Tarot to the card of The World, it is also known as the planet of severity and limitation. Eight is also associated with Scorpio, the sign of both regeneration and death.

In the Tarot, Arcanum VIII is the card of Justice, symbolized by the scales. But do not despair, for if 8s make an honest effort to find and maintain the proper balance they can rise to the top; otherwise they are doomed to destruction.

Fours and 8s have a curious magnetism for each other, but this joining of forces can make for a highly explosive nature or situation. For example, a 4 will often marry an 8 or live at an 8 address. For some people, neither 4 nor 8 is a particularly fortunate number and to combine them in any form is usually asking for trouble.

It would, however, be a vast oversimplification to say that 4s and 8s are "bad" numbers, or to attempt to shun them completely. In fact, there are times when they can be quite benevolent. This applies particularly to a business or career, for 4 is the number of work, and 8 is the number of success in business. It is always best to examine the total configuration of numbers in a chart before making any kind of change. However, more often than not, clients are well advised to locate themselves at either a 4 or 8 business address or one that reduces to 4 or 8 such as 211 or 62.

KEY: AMBITIOUS, SUCCESSFUL, SELF-DESTRUCTIVE

9

| Tarot—The Hermit | Planet—Uranus |
| Zodiac—Sagittarius | Element—Fire |

As 1 is the first of the root numbers, so 9 is the last. In the beginning the 1 entered the world stage as an individual concerned only with self and ego. The 9 has now grown in wisdom and is concerned with all of humanity. This development is echoed in the Tarot by the first card of The Magician, who is all youthful ego, and The Hermit, heavy with years and learning.

Nine is the apex of the power numbers, but as in the case of the sorcerer's apprentice, power can be misunderstood, and the user may become overwhelmed by the very forces which have been set in motion. There is nothing small about 9; 9 is a dreamer and a doer. Associated with the sign of Sagittarius, 9 is a visionary; life is a quest and all the world is 9's canvas. One of the ironies is that while 9 has but one dream—to serve Humanity—Humanity does not always understand this. And so 9 becomes defensive and obstinate, often attempting to force its ways upon the world or turn away from the world altogether.

Nine, like its Tarot counterpart, The Hermit, is forever going forth into the wilderness to seek self-knowledge and learn the secret of right living. But what is done with this knowledge will depend upon the 9's free will and stage of evolution: Nine will either remain in the wilderness hoarding knowledge, or will elect to show The Way to others, beaming a lantern aloft and thus letting the light shine before all.

KEY: EMOTIONALLY CHARGED, HUMANITARIAN, UNIVERSAL

The Compound Numbers

In an astro-numeric chart, the most relevant numbers are found by reducing the name and birth numbers from compounds to roots. It is from the analysis of these that we can examine a person's character and destiny. The individual is influenced by the compound numbers as well as the final product found in the roots. Two people, for example, could have a 3 Birth Path, but in one case the compound behind it might be 12, and in the other, 21. This would suggest that the 3/12 person would have a lot more hardships to contend with than the 3/21 individual. As stated earlier, the numbers 10, 11 and 22 will be treated separately so our discussion of the compound numbers will begin with the number 12:

12

Tarot—The Hanged Man   Zodiac—Pisces

An examination of the root numbers within a compound number provides a clue to the meaning. Twelve is made of 1 and 2. One is the number of the Sun, the masculine principle; 2 represents the Moon and the feminine principle. This is reinforced by the Tarot, for Arcanum I is The Magician, which represents an active force, while Arcanum II is The High Priestess, which represents a passive force.

Twelve is a number of polarities. Pisces, the twelfth sign of the zodiac, is symbolized by two fish, one swimming upstream, the other downstream. The twelfth card of the Tarot is The Hanged Man, a card that suggests conflict and suspension of activities.

The challenge for 12 is synthesis. When this is accomplished, 1 and 2 become 3, a number of perfection and completion.

KEY: SACRIFICE, CONFLICT, INERTIA

13

Tarot—The Reaper

Thirteen is often considered an unlucky number. This is no more valid than to say that 7 is "lucky." It is true that 13 reduces to 4 (1 + 3 = 4), but the number itself is neither lucky nor unlucky. After the American Revolution, the founding fathers of the new republic certainly did not think it unlucky. They caused it to be represented several times on the Great Seal of the United States. That seal can be seen on the reverse side of a one-dollar bill. Significantly, a number of these men were Masons and well knew that 13 was traditionally a number of good fortune.

The thirteenth card of the Tarot is The Reaper, which is neither fortunate nor unfortunate. As in the case of the card, the number is primarily one of change, and much depends on the person's attitude toward the change, and what preparations have been made for it.

Examining the root numbers 1 and 3 it can be seen that 1 is the number of individuality and 3 is the number of creativity and spirit. The combination of the two can produce not only a change but a transmutation.

KEY: CHANGE, TRANSFORMATION, REBIRTH

14

Tarot—The Angel of Time

There is a natural harmony in this number as it contains the related numbers 1 and 4 of the House of the Sun. The Tarot card, The Angel of

Time, or Temperance, depicts a woman pouring waters of the past and present together, suggesting self-integration following a major change.

Because it contains the number 4, however, there is always the possibility of negative influences, particularly a petty or mean outlook on changes that have occurred.

KEY: HARMONY, INTEGRATION, DIFFICULTY IN ACCEPTING CHANGE

15

Tarot—The Devil

Many cards in the Tarot are neither good nor bad; much depends on the total configuration of a spread. This is not true of The Devil—it is an unfortunate card whenever and wherever it appears. The same could be said for the number 15. The combination of the numbers 1 and 5 is a heady one for 15 contains the negative aspects of both, the ego of 1, with the sensuality of 5.

KEY: TEMPTATION, FEAR, MISUSE OF POWER

16

Tarot—The Lightning-Struck Tower

This is not one of the fortunate numbers for it is akin to accident and catastrophe. This is dramatically illustrated by Arcanum XVI of the Tarot, which shows two figures falling out of a building that has just been hit by lightning.

One and 6 are both materialistic numbers but added together they produce 7, the number of spirit. Spirit is the plane all must eventually come to, but for those too concerned with the world, the change from material to spiritual will not be an easy one. It may, in fact, come as a thunderbolt hurled from the heavens.

KEY: SUDDEN CHANGE, ACCIDENT, DISASTER

17

Tarot—The Star

The combination of 1 and 7 is a rather fortunate one for it is the individual (1) plus spirit (7). Out of this grows a heightened feeling for all things in earth and heaven. An 8 derived from this combination of 1 and 7 is much more favored than some other type of 8, such as one drawn from 2 and 6. In the Tarot, The Star is considered a most happy card, for it represents renewal and hope.

KEY: SHINING OUTLOOK, HOPE, FAITH RENEWED

18

Tarot—The Moon

One and 8 joined together make for a formidable combination, but certainly not for the better. In 17 individuality had united with spirit (the fusion of 1 and 7) and out of this grew hope and faith. But the individual will (1) joined with power-hunger (8) can only make for an explosive and destructive combination. In the Tarot, Arcanum XVIII, The Moon, is always an unfortunate card.

KEY: DECEPTION, ILLUSION, TREACHERY

19

Tarot—The Sun

Nineteen might be considered the "born again" number, for it begins with a 1 and ends with a 9. It thus encompasses the entire spectrum of root numbers. When 1 and 9 are added together the result is 10, which might be seen as a return to the godhead and finally rebirth as a 1 (1 + 0 = 1). The number 19 contains both the individual (1) and humanity (9) and together they find spiritual rebirth. Arcanum XIX, The Sun, is perhaps the single most fortunate card in the Tarot. It is a card of great freedom and happiness.

KEY: SPIRITUAL REBIRTH, HAPPINESS, FULFILLMENT

20

Tarot—Day of Judgment

Twenty is similar to 19 in that it is also a number of rebirth. This is graphically depicted in the Tarot for Arcanum XX shows people rising up out of a coffin. They have heard the call from on high and are ready to return to their place on The Path. The fact that there are three figures is significant. This could be interpreted as a rebirth for the trinity of God, Humanity and the Universe.

**KEY: SPIRITUAL REAWAKENING, FULFILLING OF ONE'S DESTINY,
RETURN TO THE PATH**

21

Tarot—The World

This is a number of advancement and success. In the Tarot, Arcanum XXI shows a dancing figure. Everything about the card suggests unity, fulfillment and happiness. It is the last numbered card of the Major Arcana, and so this number indicates that one has successfully undergone a particular state of being or doing. And, because 2 and 1 reduce to 3, it is a number of completion and creation.

KEY: JOY, HARMONY, SELF-INTEGRATION

The "Special" Numbers

The numbers 10, 11 and 22 are placed in a different category from the other numbers. This is because 10 is the bridge between the root and the compound numbers, and 11 and 22 are often considered Master Numbers. While this type of labeling can be helpful in gaining a fuller understanding of these numbers, it can also be misleading. In actuality, any number that is operating at the top level of its vibration is capable of achieving "Special" or "Master" status. Conversely, a Master Number can be "demoted" when someone under its influence fails to live up to the high potential of its vibration.

There is actually no hard or fast rule about Master Numbers and numerologists are not in entire agreement as to what they are or what they mean, although most would concur that 11 and 22 qualify for Master status. Essentially they are numbers of very high vibration and indicate a person with a special mission to perform *provided he or she live up to their potential*. It is the same in astrology. The highly evolved nature of Aries will build empires; the unevolved one will continue to butt his or her head into a stone wall. As it is not always known whether or not a person is living up to their potential, in doing a chart, the Master Number is written as a compound over a root—$1\frac{1}{2}$ or $2\frac{2}{4}$. Which level the person is operating at depends upon the person and the quality of thought and mode of action that has been attained.

10

Tarot—Wheel of Life   Zodiac—Capricorn

To paraphrase Shakespeare, the valiant are born many times before their death; the clod tastes of life but once. Ten, which is the first compound number, is actually the rebirth of 1. Only this time, 1 is no longer standing alone, but is accompanied by a zero. To some, a zero means nothingness, but as a symbol of the world, it can also mean allness. A zero is a mandala, a primal symbol and perfect figure.

In the Tarot, Arcanum X depicts a mandala of the Wheel of Life and Death and Re-Birth. Capricorn, the tenth sign of the zodiac, is symbolized by the Goat. This sure-footed creature is capable of climbing the highest mountains. But the Goat may be so concerned with getting to the top that he or she keeps his or her eyes only on the earthly path, and fails entirely to see the view of the heavens from the majestic heights.

The 10 has undergone an entire cycle of experience starting with Self (1) and going through the various stages of human development to the All (9). Having become spiritually enlightened as 7 and following involvement with humanity as 9 and rebirth on a higher plane, this person's individuality has been retained and a partnership with the world has been formed.

If unevolved, this number can be interpreted as a 1 rather than a 10 (which is 1 *plus* 0), and as such, will be a leader and a forceful figure, but more concerned with ego than with the soul.

KEY: AS 1 IS SELF-SEEKING; A 10 IS SELF-AWARE

11

Tarot—The Enchantress   Zodiac—Aquarius

(See page 28 for an explanation of why Tarot cards VIII (8) and XI (11) are reversed.) As usual, the Tarot provides the primary clue, for Arcanum XI shows a poised young woman calmly closing the jaws of a lion. As in most cases, the card must not be taken too literally. The closing of the lion's jaws could symbolize many things. What should be noted is that the woman has the *strength* to do something that needs to be done, and does what she has to do in confidence and apparent tranquility. Also important is that the card, which is also known as Strength, is associated with the sign of Leo, the single sign ruled by the Sun. Leo's workshop is the world. One part of Leo is content to bask in the Sun of the backyard, but the higher self of Leo knows that the true place in the Sun is on the world's stage, serving as a leading actor in the human drama. Considering the association with Leo and the Sun, 11s may be considered Messengers of Light. The world may not always be ready for their message, but their task is to let their light shine forth—whatever the consequences might be. Eleven is a number that suggests leadership. However, hardship, sacrifice and even martyrdom may be involved. Failure to meet the 11 challenge will result in a downward descent to the negative 2 path.

The path of 11 is not an easy one, but those selected for it must follow it if they are to evolve ever higher.

KEY: TWO SWEEPS THE STAGE; 11 PERFORMS ON IT

22

Tarot—The Fool

The highest of vibrations, 22 is the master who must go out into the world and share knowledge, wisdom and love—the first of these being love.

The 22 vibrations are high indeed and only the true master can cope with them and function effectively. If the 22 fails, then like The Fool, the final card of the Major Arcana, the 22 must start over from scratch. Beginning again may be considerably more difficult to face than the lot of The Fool, who is about to step over a yawning chasm and defy certain death. The 22 who betrays that great potential falls to the negative 4 path and builds not shining empires, but only anthills and misery.

KEY: FOUR TAKES THE WORLD TO HEART; 22 TAKES HEART TO THE WORLD

2

. . . And So Is West: The Tarot

The Tarot is considered by many occultists to be the greatest unbound book of wisdom in the world. Less well known perhaps is that it serves also as the bible of numerology. And when used in conjunction with the numbers of one's own chart, it provides an illustrated guide to the life.

As stated earlier, the thrust of this book is to show the relationship of the Tarot to numerology. The interested student should read everything on the Tarot related to the origins, mythology and symbology of the cards, both for knowledge and as an aid in meditation, which is quite possibly the most profound value of the Tarot. For our present purposes, however, the discussion will center on the meanings of the cards in divination. Succeeding chapters will contain Tarot spreads that may be employed in relation to numerology—specifically the reader's own chart.

No two books on the Tarot offer quite the same interpretation of the cards. In fact, they are sometimes poles apart. No one need pretend that there is one and only one set of meanings that is valid, but if the Tarot is to be taken as a kind of cosmic language, then the symbols representing the vocabulary should be more or less standard. How one writer, for example, can say that Arcanum XV, The Devil, "is love in all its forms," is to be totally contrary to all logic, tradition and experience. This is equivalent to saying, "Black is white."

Tarot interpretation is both a science and an art, and through experience in working with the cards, each reader will re-fashion the meanings in his or her mind. But that is hardly the same thing as saying there are no rules. One is reminded of Humpty Dumpty's theory on language, for it was his claim that words meant anything the user wanted them to mean; it was simply a question of who was to be master.

Manufacturers of Tarot decks do a fairly lively business, but quite possibly, next to Winston Churchill's history of the Second World War, the Tarot may be one of the greatest unread books of the age. Probably the main reason for this is the apparent Herculean effort that one would need to expend in order to learn the meanings of the cards. The would-be Tarot reader gets the deck home only to find that in order to do a "reading," the meanings of each of the seventy-eight cards in the Tarot must be learned. If this is not a deterrent, one learns after a little further study that the cards mean one thing right side up but have a different meaning when reversed. So it is not seventy-eight meanings the reader has to memorize but 156. If he or she is still hanging in there, it probably won't be for long when they discover that each card has not a single meaning but several. Some authors, who apparently strive to be definitive, will list a dozen or more meanings for each card, thus making the task of learning all the more difficult. There are few souls who will have the endurance to commit close to a thousand meanings to memory and it is about this time that the cards find their way to a closet shelf.

But if the truth be told, learning the cards is much less formidable than some writers would have you believe. There are, for one thing, relationships among the cards—particularly numerical relationships. And once these patterns are understood, the task is much less awesome.

The student of numerology has a distinct advantage in learning the Tarot, for that student will discover that the cards of the Major Arcana bear a striking resemblance to their related numbers. In fact, numbers may be the major key to finding one's way through the maze of a Tarot deck.

Before we can operate the Tarot key, it is necessary to understand how a Tarot deck is constructed. We know that the deck contains seventy-eight cards, but in actuality there are two decks in one, for there is the Major Arcana consisting of twenty-two cards and the Minor Arcana with fifty-six cards. In the Minor Arcana there are four suits—Coins (or Pentacles), Wands (or Rods), Cups (or Chalices), and Swords.

Over time the Major Arcana, with the exception of The Fool, were dropped from what is now popularly accepted as a deck of playing cards. These "modern" decks have only fifty-two cards. There is a distant correspondence between the suits of the Minor Arcana and the suits of a modern deck. The ancient symbols have become diamonds (Coins or Pentacles), clubs (Wands or Rods), hearts (Cups or Chalices), and spades (Swords). The court cards of King and Queen remain in the modern deck. The Knight and Page have been combined as the Jack, and the Fool survives as the Joker, still considered outside the deck or a wild card.

Looked at another way, it can be seen that the Tarot is not two decks but three, for the sixteen Court Cards—Kings, Queens, Knights and

Pages—of the four suits of the Minor Arcana are a unique grouping. The reason for this is that they are the cards which represent people. Interestingly enough, in an average seven- or ten-card spread, against all laws of chance, one or more of these Court Cards will come up. The reason is not difficult to fathom as these are cards that have to do with people and most consultants' questions have to do with people. (The person asking the question is known as the *consultant*. The one actually doing the reading is known as the *reader*.)

The first pattern to note is what each of the three decks—Major Arcana, Minor Arcana and Court Cards—deal with. As mentioned above, the Court Cards deal primarily with *people*. The other forty cards of the Minor Arcana, the cards numbered from Ace to ten in each of the four suits, have to do largely with *material events*. The twenty-two cards of the Major Arcana can, on occasion, represent people or material events, but in general, they are "cards of the psyche"—that is, they are more concerned with *psychological* or *spiritual* matters. So, if in a given spread, a preponderance of Major Arcana cards comes up, it would indicate that the consultant is in control of what goes on around him or her. Conversely, if a majority of Minor Arcana cards appear, it would suggest—for better or worse—that the consultant is at the mercy of events. A heavy weighting of Court Cards would indicate questions dealing with friends, relations, loved ones or business associates.

Another general pattern that it is helpful to recognize is the meaning of the four suits of the Minor Arcana—Coins, Wands, Cups and Swords. One school of thought has it that the suits are related to the four seasons—Coins/spring, Wands/summer, Cups/autumn and Swords/winter. A study of the symbols on the cards, coupled with a bit of historical reflection, would suggest that Coins, symbols for money and material things, go with spring. In an earlier age, spring was the time when Renaissance merchants would undertake journeys for the purpose of buying and selling. Wands go with summer for they symbolize the peasantry whose major work would fall at that time of year. Autumn is the time for cups which held the wine that would be generously sampled after the harvest had been gathered. This invariably became a season for feasting and merry-making. Swords are associated with winter for that time of year symbolizes the often-painful completion of a cycle.

The picture begins to come into focus: The suit of Coins deals mainly with matters of money and material things. Wands is the suit of business, career and creative endeavors. Cups is the suit of glad tidings and affairs of the heart. The suit of Swords tells of strife, accident or affliction. If, in a given spread, for example, there proved to be a heavy showing of Coins, it would suggest that the consultant was concerned with money matters. On the other hand, a Cups emphasis would reveal a question about love, marriage or family matters.

However, we are now ready for the one key that, more than any other, will unlock the door leading to the mystery of the Tarot. That key is provided by numerology. With numbers in mind, we look through the seventy-eight-card deck and the pattern leaps out at us: Each of the root numbers from 1 to 9 appears not only in the cards of the Major Arcana, but is repeated four times in the suits of the Minor Arcana.

Our primary task is to see if a relationship exists between the numbers as we have discussed them and the Major Arcana cards wearing those numbers. If we are successful, it may prove that there is an extended relationship to the Minor Arcana so that all 1s (or Aces) would stand for a certain order of ideas or events, all 2s would represent another set of concepts, and so on. If this theory can be demonstrated in practice, our task will be greatly facilitated, for we can apply our knowledge of numbers—at least, the root numbers—to over half of the Tarot deck.

Writers on the Tarot often begin by discussing the twenty-two cards of the Major Arcana and then each suit of the Minor Arcana in turn. With our number plan in mind, we shall depart from that custom. After taking up a card from the Major Arcana, we will go immediately into an examination of the cards with the same number in the Minor Arcana.

But before we do, let us attempt to establish one additional pattern. We look through the twenty-two cards of the Major Arcana noting that there is a numerical sequence from 1 to 21, with one unnumbered card, and our initial impression is that there is little if any relationship of one card to another. Why then are the Major Arcana cards numbered at all? And, more significantly, why is one of them, namely The Fool, not numbered? Is it possible that there is a hidden meaning to the numerical sequence? This has mystified Tarot scholars for centuries. Let us attempt a radical premise and start with the assumption that the twenty-two Major Arcana cards deal not with twenty-two separate things or people, but rather, relate the odyssey of a single individual traveling along life's road from roughly the time of late adolescence. This is not necessarily a "true" statement, but if it will help us to learn the cards, it may prove to be a useful construct.

Every card in the Major Arcana is associated with an astrological sign, planet or element, which in each case will be listed. With regard to reversed cards, the meanings will be given, but it is not absolutely essential to learn them. A good working rule is that in most cases the meaning is lessened rather than opposite.

Tarot decks differ somewhat in the treatment of the symbols. All descriptions in this chapter apply to the cards of the Rider deck, designed by Pamela Colman Smith, under the direction of Arthur Edward Waite. **Note:** For reasons best known to himself, Waite transposed the cards of Arcana VIII and XI in the Rider Tarot. Although contrary to tradition, Arcanum VIII in this deck is Strength and Arcanum XI is Justice. There is no logical reason to follow that arrangement so the cards will be discussed in their customary sequence: Arcanum VIII—Justice and Arcanum XI—Strength, or The Enchantress.

Saga of the Fool

THE FOOL.

The Unnumbered Card—The Fool
Astrology: Air

Although The Fool is unnumbered, he is often seen as the beginning card of the Major Arcana. He can, however, also be considered the ending card. The card of The Fool is unique in that there are two sets of meanings attributed to it, one as the beginning and the other as the ending card of the Major Arcana. This duality is reflected in The Fool's journey. It is often a journey of discovery in which The Fool has to discover one or both of the two sides of his nature.

When interpreted as the beginning card, The Fool is depicted as taking a journey. He appears not to have a care in the world. At the moment we meet him, he is in a rather precarious position for there is a dog nipping at his heels and he is about to step over a precipice. Quite obviously, he is not wise in the ways of the world and the journey he is taking may prove to be a painful learning experience, and it could well be a complete disaster. From all appearances, it doesn't look at if The Fool is a very good life insurance risk.

As an unnumbered card, The Fool could be seen in this position as a cipher that contains both everything and nothing. Again, this is a reflection of The Fool's dual nature.

Because The Fool is the first card in the Major Arcana, we shall go on the assumption that "the Tarot story" is about his adventures. We shall further assume that each human figure on the twenty-one numbered cards of the Major Arcana is The Fool in various guises at different stages of his life. If there is a story, it should be his story, for The Fool is both the first and last to appear.

Our discussion of the cards of the Major Arcana will center on the wanderings of The Fool.

DIVINATION:

The Fool has become the Joker in modern playing card decks and like the Joker is best treated as a wild card. Everything really depends on where the Fool appears in a spread and what the surrounding cards are. When the card of The Fool appears at or near the beginning of a spread, it means confusion, conflict or the undertaking of an enterprise based upon shaky premises and for which adequate mental and/or material preparation has not been made.

Reversed—Inability to begin a project or enterprise due to conflicting drives.

THE MAGICIAN.

Arcanum I—The Magican
Astrology: Mercury

In Arcanum I, The Fool has become a man and he is starting his career as The Magician. He appears to be successful. The secret of his success is his powerful will, which he uses to master himself and others. In The Magician's right hand is a wand, which is raised toward heaven. He is pointing toward earth with his left hand. He represents the God-Man, the bridge between heaven and earth.

The wand that The Magician holds in his right hand could be seen as a symbol for the number 1. He seems to be placing stress on the fact that he is a 1—a leader, pioneer, original—and this will be his trademark. As a 1, The Fool is assertive, active and highly independent. His initial uncertainty has been resolved and he has begun his journey.

DIVINATION:

Will power. Persuasive individual. Inspirational teacher.
Reversed—Indecisive person. Misuse of will for selfish ends.

As The Magician could be said to be beginning his career, the Number 1 cards in the Minor Arcana—the Aces—refer to:

BEGINNINGS

Ace of Coins—New financial venture.
Ace of Wands—Start of program of study, job, career, or news of same.
Ace of Cups—Beginning of romance. Letter from loved one.
Ace of Swords—Failure of something to materialize. Bad news.

THE HIGH PRIESTESS

Arcanum II—The High Priestess
Astrology: The Moon

As The High Priestess, The Fool is undergoing an identity crisis. At an earlier stage of his life he was highly extroverted, assertive and active. Now, however, he appears introverted, retiring and passive. Essentially, he is attempting to cope with the duality in his nature. It is, on one hand, a conflict between masculine and feminine drives. On the other hand, as The High Priestess has a scroll in her lap, and there is a crescent moon at her feet, there also appears to be a conflict between reason and emotion. The polarity is further reinforced by two pillars on either side of The High Priestess, one black, the other, gray. On the black pole is the letter "B," and on the gray one, the letter "J." Numerology is instructive here, for the number values of the letters are 1 for J and 2 for B, further suggesting the rift between masculine and feminine instincts.

The Fool is following the vibrations of the numbers for as 1 he was vital and masterful; as 2 he appears insecure and subservient.

DIVINATION:

Duality. Woman who is moody or critical.
Reversed—Confusion.

In the Minor Arcana, 2 is a number of:
CONFLICT
2 of Coins—Conflict in money matters.
2 of Wands—Conflict over career or with business associates.
2 of Cups—The "Love Conquers All" card. Conflict has been resolved by patience and affectionate cooperation.
2 of Swords—Conflict on several levels. Inability to resolve conflict.

THE EMPRESS.

Arcanum III—The Empress
Astrology: Venus

As The Empress, The Fool has been successful in reconciling the differing parts of his personality—id, ego and superego—into an integrated whole. The Magician was all motion, and The High Priestess, emotion. The Empress has fused them together and the result is a vibrant, sharing and creative person. The Magician held up the wand of pure power in his right hand. In the right hand of The Empress, the wand has become a sceptre, capped with a mandala. As a 3, The Fool is everything that the number represents—creative, expressive and gregarious. A 3 is a person who is usually happily married and that is also true of The Empress, whose consort is The Emperor. Once a person has become partners with him- or herself, he or she is ready to share a life with another.

DIVINATION:

Marriage. Launching of a creative enterprise.
Reversed—Divorce. Failure to start something one desires to do.

Three is a number of self-expression, creativity and sharing. In the Minor Arcana it takes the form of:
CAREER
3 of Coins—A job. Business partnership. Marriage for financial gain.
3 of Wands—A marriage based upon mutual interests. Position in education or the arts.
3 of Cups—A marriage based upon deep affection.
3 of Swords—Divorce or separation.

Arcanum IV—The Emperor
Astrology: Aries

Now grown to glorious middle age, The Fool has reached the pinnacle of material success. He has employed his will, mind, emotions and creative talents to achieve everything that mortals aspire to—wealth, position and power. For a fool, he has come a long way.

As a 4, it is possible that he has fallen prey to the "People Race." The Fool is overly concerned with working to maintain his position and fearful of failure. Because he is associated with material success, The Emperor is generally considered a positive card in divination, but as in the case of real-life emperors, there can be problems with maintaining one's private empire.

DIVINATION:

Achievement. Marriage. Excessive concern with material things.
Reversed—Failure to realize something one has worked for. Divorce.

In the Minor Arcana, 4 is the number of:
ATTAINMENT
4 of Coins—Success in career through one's own efforts.
4 of Wands—Promotion. Financial windfall.
4 of Cups—A lover, friend, or "little stranger" comes into one's life in a
    sudden or unexpected fashion.
4 of Swords—Loss. Illness requiring hospitalization.

Arcanum V—The Hierophant
Astrology: Taurus

As The Magician, The Fool demonstrated will power; as The High Priestess, mental and emotional power; as The Empress, creative power; and as The Emperor, material power. Now on a higher plane in Arcanum V, he has become imbued with spiritual power.

Two other figures appear on the card and appear to be disciples receiving his instruction. This card is sometimes known as The Pope, but Hierophant of the Eleusinian mysteries in ancient Egypt seems more descriptive. The Hierophant was considered "the revealer of sacred things." The Fool has not only acquired spriritual knowledge, but wishes to share it with others.

Five is the number of involvement in the world and of self-transcendence. As a 5, The Fool appears to have become less concerned with his own selfish desires and more with the problems of others. He will need to learn other lessons before this one will stick, but this will prove a profoundly important one and the highest stage of his evolvement to date.

DIVINATION:
Spiritual fulfillment. Wise counselor. Period of introspection.
Reversed—Loss of faith. Identity crisis.

The Spiritual growth tends to lead to fruition in all things and so in the Minor Arcana, 5 is a number of:

FULFILLMENT
5 of Coins—Financial fulfillment.
5 of Wands—Fulfillment in career.
5 of cups—Fulfillment in love.
5 of Swords—There will be problems but matters are in control of the Spirit Guides.

THE LOVERS.

Arcanum VI—The Lovers
Astrology: Gemini

This might be called the "Adam's apple" card, for the lovers could be seen as Adam and Eve. The apple that Adam ate was not necessarily an apple; it was the fruit of "the tree of the knowledge of Good and Evil." In psychological terms, the point of the story is that Adam and Eve, if they are to develop as human beings, have to defy authority and learn what evil is so that they may learn to exercise their free will in choosing the good. The cost was a painful one for it meant expulsion from the Garden of Eden and the security the garden represented. However, at the same time, it means that Adam and Eve will be free to choose what their fate will be.

In one way or another, each individual has to make the choice of whether or not to take Adam's apple. It is really a question of advancement over inertia in personal development. In order to advance, one will have to go against parental desires or flout some other authority figure. Lesson 6 of the Tarot is not an easy one, but failure to take this step will result in the psychological impoverishment of the individual. In other words, like Adam and Eve, an individual's ability to grow is linked to his or her ability to make free and informed choices.

The primary decision that 6 has to make has to do with career and in Arcanum VI, The Fool has to decide between the job that offers him security or the more creative and adventurous one.

DIVINATION:

Time of decision.

Reversed—A block in making an important decision.

In the Minor Arcana also, 6 is a number of:

DECISION

6 of Coins—Decision concerning an organization or group of people. A wedding.

6 of Wands—Decision concerning the theatre, art, music, the occult.

6 of Cups—Decision concerning love or marriage.

6 of Swords—Warning card. Person is unable to make a decision and this card warns that a decision *must* be made if one is ever to have peace of mind.

Arcanum VII—The Chariot
Astrology: Cancer

In ancient Rome, there was a tradition known as the Roman Triumph. The warrior who had bested his enemies in battle was covered with laurels and as he rode through the triumphal arch was received with honor. This is akin to the happy fate of The Fool at this stage of his life for he has succeeded in making the decision required in Arcanum VI. Now as The Charioteer, he is in full control of his chariot of personality. The Chariot is pulled by two sphinx-like creatures. In the drama of *Oedipus Rex*, the Sphinx is the entity who poses the riddle of man, suggesting that The Charioteer has solved that enigma for himself. The fact that one sphinx is black, the other, white, indicates that the problem was of a Freudian nature, dealing with conflicting id and ego impulses.

As a 7, The Fool can be misunderstood. He may have to work alone to a certain extent for the need now is to explore the self and the mysteries of the spirit. The Charioteer does not seem disturbed by the prospect of solitude for he has acquired inner strength and harmony.

DIVINATION:

Victory.

Reversed—Dark victory. Defeat.

A victory of any kind is usually accompanied by change and in the Minor Arcana, 7 is a number of:

CHANGE

7 of Coins—A change in business or career, usually for the better. Business trip.

7 of Wands—A change concerning a student, teacher, or writer.

7 of Cups—Change in residence. A home visit to or from lover, friend
or relative.

7 of Swords—Warning card. This is a more serious warning card than
the 6 of Swords for it indicates that the person may be
on the edge of a breakdown. Also a warning against
accident. Both the 6 and 7 of Swords in the same spread
would indicate severe depression, possibly even thoughts
of suicide, and in fact, probable contemplation if either
card is reversed.

Arcanum VIII—Justice
Astrology: Libra

The balance held in the left hand of Justice is the
lesson of Arcanum VIII. The Fool has reached a
stage where his life is precariously unbalanced. He
must find a way to balance it. The fact that Justice
wields a sword in her right hand suggests that the
lesson will be a painful one.

What has brought the imbalance about is not
difficult to comprehend for as an 8, The Fool has,
in effect, doubled the problem he had in Arcanum
IV as The Emperor. Once again he has become
overly ambitious. In Arcanum V, he began to
develop the spiritual side of his nature, but as an 8,
he has been overwhelmed by his materialistic yearnings. But Justice, in the
form of conscience, has intervened.

We hope that Justice will set The Fool back on The Path. For if she does
not, The Fool is destined to suffer a terrible penance.

Please remember that in the Rider-Waite Deck, Arcanum VIII and
Arcanum XI have been reversed.

DIVINATION:

Balance or imbalance depending upon surrounding cards in spread.
Reversed—Much the same meaning, only slightly less so.

In the Minor Arcana, 8 is the number of:

IMBALANCE

8 of Coins—Imbalance in financial affairs.

8 of Wands—Imbalance in business affairs. Need for discretion. A
politician.

8 of Cups—Imbalance in one's family or love life.

8 of Swords—General imbalance in one's affairs.

THE HERMIT.

Arcanum IX—The Hermit
Astrology: Virgo

The card of The Hermit echoes the starting card of the Major Arcana. Once again The Fool is setting out on a journey. The earlier one was undertaken as an innocent youth in bright sunlight, but this one is begun as an aging man in the blackest midnight.

He begins what is known in the terminology of psychology as a "night journey." This is essentially a form of self-analysis, usually undergone without a conscious awareness that it is taking place. It generally occurs around twilight, or during the dark hours, and takes place simultaneously with an actual journey that one is taking over land, sea or air. The significance of the night journey, however, is that it is primarily a journey into the self. In literature the classic imagery to signal the onset of a night journey is white-on-black. During the course of a night journey a person explores the deepest levels of being and in Jungian terminology confronts a personal "shadow"—the shadow being the secret self that is usually hidden from the world—and ourselves.

A night journey consists of three stages: the descent into the darkness of one's shadow self, arrival at the heart of darkness and "the moment of truth," and—if the journey is successful—the upward ascent and return to light. Again, in literature, the white-on-black imagery is repeated at or near the end of the night journey, signaling its completion.

The shining lantern that The Hermit bears aloft provides the initial white-on-black imagery.

As a 9, The Fool has gained a wider vision of the world and humanity. And as 9 he completes the sequence of root numbers. The Fool, under the 9's vibrations, is ending one stage of his life.

The night journey of Arcanum IX is an emotionally turbulent stage, so The Hermit is not a particularly favorable card in divination.

DIVINATION:

The "Wilderness Card"—a time of searching or spiritual renewal. A person who is fearful and cautious.

Reversed—Rashness. Lack of control.

The journey of The Hermit is echoed in the Minor Arcana for 9s refer to:

A NEW PATH

9 of Coins—Unexpected costs in the way of money or emotions.
9 of Wands—New friends or environment.
9 of Cups—The "Wish Card"—a dream is realized.
9 of Swords—Deep personal loss.

WHEEL of FORTUNE.

Aracanum X—The Wheel of Fortune
Astrology: Jupiter

The bizarre creatures on this card could be likened to entities from the id that The Fool encounters during his night journey. At the top of the wheel reposes a sphinx-like beast, again suggesting the riddle of man that The Fool must answer. In the lower recesses, a scarlet demon lies in wait, suggesting the hidden dangers of the night journey.

As the number 10 is really the rebirth of 1, so too is The Fool undergoing a psychological rebirth.

The night journey marks a forward stage in The Fool's development. It is the beginning of self-knowledge. That, along with the card's association with Jupiter—"the Greater Fortune"—makes it a favorable one.

DIVINATION:

A turn in one's fortunes for the better.
Reversed—The beginning of an unhappy or unlucky period.

At the Gaming Table of Life, fortune's wheel favors some, but not others and this is true also in the Minor Arcana. Ten is thus the number of:

WINS AND LOSSES

10 of Coins—The Wall Street Card. It is the big business or financial break for which one has been waiting.

10 of Wands—Major career gains, for individual is operating at full capacity.

10 of Cups—Heavy emotional costs regarding someone else.

10 of Swords—Emotional or psychological bankruptcy. The edge of the abyss of despair.

STRENGTH.

Arcanum XI—The Enchantress
Astrology: Leo

(See note on reversal of cards VIII and XI on page 28.)

The sign of Leo, with which this card is associated, is ruled by the Sun. At the opening of the second act of the forever-running musical, *The Fantastiks*, the narrator informs us that "The story is not done until we have all been burned a bit and burnished by the Sun!" The Sun as a harsh and blinding symbol of truth is a fairly common literary device. The healing rays of the Sun can be destroying rays for those unprepared for such exposure.

In literature, Joseph Conrad's novel, *Heart of*

Darkness, well illustrates the principle, for the protagonist, Marlow, takes a journey to Africa that also proves to be a night journey. The probable effect of learning the truth about himself is suggested by a conversation he has with a steamer captain on the "dark continent." The captain tells him that a recent passenger of his had hanged himself on the road. When Marlow asks why, the captain replies that either the country or *the sun* was too much for him.

It takes all The Fool's moral strength to continue his night journey, but as is suggested by the woman closing the jaws of the lion, The Fool appears up to the challenge.

As a Master Number 11, the Fool must be prepared to undergo many trials and great hardship. But he can do so for he now possesses the inner strength, a name by which this card is also known.

DIVINATION:
Moral fortitude. Aggressive woman.
Reversed—Difficulty coping.

A ruler needs inner strength to govern himself and others and in the Minor Arcana, 11s are:

KINGS
King of Coins—Business type. Rigid outlook. Well organized. Conservative.
King of Wands—Fair, honest, and just. Understanding person—one to whom you can tell your troubles.
King of Cups—A man of keen sensibilities. Artistically inclined. A good lover but somewhat manipulative.
King of Swords—A blunt, hardnosed, forceful type. Usually an executive of some kind. Lawyer or doctor.

THE HANGED MAN.

Arcanum XII—The Hanged Man
Astrology: Water

In any type of analysis there is usually a period of progress followed by backsliding or resistance. This proves true for The Fool also and as The Hanged Man he has totally reversed himself and dangles in time and space. In T.S. Eliot's *The Wasteland*, the clairvoyant Madame Sosostris, during the course of a Tarot reading, says she cannot find The Hanged Man and that the consultant should fear death by water. Since the card of The Hanged Man is associated with the element of water, there is the suggestion of symbolical death—of drowning.

As a 12, The Fool must resolve his inner conflict before moving on. Twelve presents many psychological difficulties.

DIVINATION:

Reversal of values. Inertia. Sacrifice.

Reversed—A grim omen. The indication is that the individual is incapable of either a change in thinking or of taking positive action.

In one sense, the feminine principle could be understood as the reversal of the masculine principle, and so in the Minor Arcana 12 refers to:

QUEENS

Queen of Coins—Highly organized female. Often a business woman or executive.

Queen of Wands—Woman of keen insight and understanding.

Queen of Cups—Compassionate woman. Very warm and affectionate. Devoted wife and mother.

Queen of Swords—Strong-minded woman. Highly independent. Widow or single woman.

DEATH.

Arcanum XIII—The Reaper
Astrology: Scorpio

This card depicts The Grim Reaper mounted on horseback and carrying a banner. The banner is black and over it is a white emblem. The fact that The Reaper himself is garbed in black armor and rides a white charger, presents a contrasting image of black-on-white. This is not yet the imagery that will signal the end of The Fool's journey. Rather, this powerful imagery indicates that The Fool is under a compulsion to continue the night journey. This is further borne out by the number of the card, 13, for a night journey consists of three stages. This would mark the end of the first stage, which began in Arcanum X with The Wheel of Fortune, leaving Arcana XIV to XVII for the second stage and Arcana XVIII to XXI for the third and final stage.

As a 13, The Fool is subject to making changes in his modes of thought and action. These changes are of a transitory nature and do not reflect the basic psychological changes The Fool will undergo on his journey.

DIVINATION:

Change in the life. Reaping what one has sown. Transformation. Death.

Reversed—Inability to accept or make necessary changes.

According to Edgar Cayce, "thoughts are things," and no change in outer space can come about until there has been a change in inner space. And so in the Minor Arcana, the thirteenth card is indicative of *thoughts* and is symbolized by:

KNIGHTS

Knight of Coins—Thoughts about money or material affairs.
Knight of Wands—Thoughts about business or career.
Knight of Cups—Loving thoughts.
Knight of Swords—Unhappy or bitter thoughts.

TEMPERANCE.

Arcanum XIV—The Angel of Time
Astrology: Sagittarius

After the challenges of The Wheel of Fortune, Strength, The Hanged Man and The Reaper, the appearance of The Angel of Time at this point of The Fool's journey is a cool and refreshing sight indeed. The figure, clad in white with one foot in blue waters and the other on green earth, suggests that The Fool in Arcanum XIV is arriving at the proper balance of material and spiritual things. The fluid that the figure is pouring from one golden goblet into another suggests a fusion of ego and id impulses. This is further reinforced by the triangle on the angel's gown, which is a symbol of unity and completion.

In another sense this could be seen as the "time out" card, for The Fool has faced severe trials, but the worst is yet to come. At the outer gate of hell his guiding angel pays him a visit to reassure and comfort him.

As a 14, The Fool feels a sense of harmony and inner peace.

DIVINATION:

The end of a period of adjustment and the beginning of inner harmony and improved relations with others.

Reversed—Disenchantment with a change that has been made.

In the Minor Arcana the final Court Card may represent anybody or anything not accounted for by the rest of the pack. In particular, men and women under thirty-five, children, babies and pets are represented by:

PAGES

Page of Coins—A serious young person. Quiet or withdrawn. Good head for studies or business.
Page of Wands—Fair-minded and straightforward youth. Loyal and faithful friend.
Page of Cups—Warm and affectionate youngster.
Page of Swords—Independent and adventuresome youth. Willful and obstinate child.

Arcanum XV—The Devil
Astrology: Capricorn

In Arcanum XV The Fool has reached the nadir of his night journey. It is the ultimate meeting "in death's dream kingdom," that confrontation with his own shadow and the long dark night of the soul. What that shadow is will depend on the individual's genetic and psychological makeup. More than anything else, the lesson of this card is to rid oneself of *fear* for in the words of Franklin D. Roosevelt, "We have nothing to fear but fear itself." It is not unlike the scene in the film, *The Wizard of Oz,* when Dorothy and her companions stand in fear and trembling before the majestic and terrifying visage of "the great and terrible Oz," until thanks to her small dog, Toto, it is discovered that what they feared were screen images and stage illusions. What makes The Devil a frightening monster is essentially our own imaginings. If we fail to dispel the illusion we will suffer psychological paralysis, and as the miniature male and female figures on the card suggest, we will remain in bondage to The Devil within ourselves. But The Devil is purely a product of our psyche and the only reality he has is what we attribute to him.

As a 15, The Fool is under dark influences that need to be conquered before psychological and spiritual integration can take place.

DIVINATION:

Fear. Evil influences at work.
Reversed—Much the same, only slightly less so.

Arcanum XVI—The Lightning-Struck Tower
Astrology: Mars

People react to truth in various ways. For The Fool, truth comes in the form of a cosmic deity who has "loosed the fateful lightning of his terrible swift sword." The house of his psyche, symbolized by The Lightening-Struck Tower, is going up in flames and its inhabitants are being hurled headfirst to the ground. The Fool was a fool because he believed that a material edifice could wall him off from the ground of Being and ultimate reality. He was a fool to have built the tower in the first place. He was a fool to believe that brick and mortar could protect him from disaster. And he was a fool to have lived in it so long. As in the case of The Hanged Man, his world has been turned completely upsidedown, but this time, truth has come with a vengeance. It is the culmination of The Fool's night journey and at this point there is some question whether he will survive the impact of the cosmic lightning bolt. If he does, he can continue his journey. If not, it's the end of all.

As a 16, The Fool has to learn how to deal with happenings of a sudden and dramatic nature, and to adapt himself to drastic changes. In some ways, this is a critical juncture in the journey of The Fool. If The Fool does not adapt, his journey may have been fruitless.

DIVINATION:

Psychological crisis. Accident or disaster. The possibility of accident is greatly increased if The Tower appears in the same spread with the 3, 7, or 9 of Swords.

Reversed—Still a crisis, but less traumatic.

Arcanum XVII—The Star
Astrology: Aquarius

The middle stage of the night journey that began with Arcanum XIV and The Angel of Time is completed in Arcanum XVII and The Star. Following the fear and trembling of The Devil and the blinding illumination of The Lightning-Struck Tower, The Star is a spiritual oasis. The Angel of Time poured the fluid of life from one goblet to another. On this card, Hebe, the spirit of youth, is pouring the waters of the celestial and terrestial realms into the river of life. This is definitely a card of hope as after the destroying storm there appears the light of a star. For untold centuries, the star has served as a symbol of promise and hope renewed. The Star can be revered, or it can be a guiding beacon. In the film *Pinocchio*, the philosophical Jiminy Cricket tells Pinocchio that all he wishes will come true when he wishes on a star. And, much like the three wise men, The Fool might choose to follow this star as his guiding beacon.

In contrast to the earlier white-on-black imagery of the card of The Reaper, the white-on-black emanations of the radiant Star suggest that The Fool's journey will be successful. The future is beginning to look very good for The Fool. His journey appears to be taking a successful twist. He is about to gain a new awareness.

As a 17, The Fool entertains great hopes for the future.

DIVINATION:

Hope. New lease on life.
Reversed—Rainbow's end and death of a dream.

Arcanum XVIII—The Moon
Astrology: Pisces

With Arcanum XVIII the Fool starts the upward ascent of his night journey and the return to light. But to complete his journey he must pass through the country of The Moon. As the card suggests, there are all kinds of unseen dangers waiting in store for him. There is a certain excitement and glamour to the lunar landscape but the light of The Moon is illusory and if The Fool deceives himself and lingers there, thinking he has returned to the light of truth, his journey will be at an end. He will be likely to fall prey to the jackals of self-deception waiting to devour him, or to the crayfish of delusion who will pull him down into the murky deep.

As an 18, The Fool is susceptible to forces of illusion and deception.

DIVINATION:

Deception. Delay. Illusion.
Reversed—A difficult period but person beginning "to see the light."

Arcanum XIX—The Sun
Astrology: The Sun

After the night, day. After The Moon, The Sun. Clearly The Fool's journey has been a success. He has returned to the light, and it is the warm, direct light of The Sun and truth. He is unclothed now for he no longer has anything to hide from himself or the world. He rides a docile horse, suggesting that he is in harmony with his libido urges. He holds no reins. He is in control of himself. The Fool is smiling and his arms are outstretched to receive the full rays of The Sun.

Perhaps, most extraordinary of all, The Fool appears on this card as a young child. It is possible that The Fool's night journey was also a spiritual odyssey and that during its course he heeded the words of an earlier pilgrim on the Path of Light, who said, "Unless ye be converted and become as little children, ye shall not enter the kingdom of heaven."

As a 19, The Fool has undergone a profound psychological and spiritual rebirth.

DIVINATION:

Paradise found.
Reversed—Disappointment in love.

Arcanum XX—Day of Judgment
Astrology: Fire

Arcanum XX, Day of Judgment, further confirms the success of The Fool's night journey. The earthlings on the card are rising from the coffins of their dead selves. That there are three figures in the foreground—a man, woman and child—is significant; it suggests that the three stages of the night journey are now one. The trinity of figures further suggests that The Fool has achieved psychological wholeness for three is a number of completion and perfection.

But the central figure dominating the upper portion of the card is an angel sounding forth a trumpet call from on high, indicating that The Fool's rebirth is spiritual as well as psychological. Tradition has it that he is Michael, the leader of the Forces of Light in heaven, who routed the devil and the Forces of Darkness. Possibly he is the same guardian angel who first appeared to The Fool in Arcanum VI, The Lovers, as "Cupid," firing the arrow of inspiration, and later, in Arcanum XIV as The Angel of Time, who helped him conquer the darkness within himself.

As a 20, The Fool has fulfilled his destiny and is ready to return to the Path.

DIVINATION:

A milestone in one's life. Decision of the utmost importance is made and a major step taken.

Reversed—Opportunity has been missed.

Arcanum XXI—The World
Astrology: Saturn

Arcanum XXI, The World, is the final numbered card of the Major Arcana and marks The Fool's return to the world following the completion of his night journey and his rebirth as a soul on the path leading to cosmic consciousness. The laurel wreath indicates that the return has been a victorious one, and the dancing figure suggests great joy. Yes, that is the word for this card—*joy!*

The person dancing appears to be a woman but may be androgynous as suggested by the card's number, 21, which contains both a feminine and masculine root number. Again, this at least partly represents the duality of The Fool's nature. This is also suggested by the four astrological signs depicted—Taurus, Scorpio, Leo and Aquarius—the former two being feminine, the latter two, masculine. In the hands of The World figure are two wands, representing the lunar (feminine) and solar (masculine) powers. Everything, in short, indicates the fusion of opposites with the end result of unity and wholeness.

The Fool has now passed through every stage of the Tarot. The world to which he has returned is not the same one that he left. This is suggested by the division of the card: The zodiacal signs are *outside* the wreath, The World figure is *inside*. So The Fool lives and breathes and has his being in the world of outer space, but the "real world" for him has become the world of inner space and higher consciousness.

As a 21, The Fool has found fulfillment.

DIVINATION:

The cup runneth over.

Reversed—A karmic bill falls due. This will be an extremely emotional period but one necessary for inner growth.

THE FOOL .

The Unnumbered Card—The Fool
Astrology: Air

Because The Fool is unnumbered, he is both the first and the last card of the Major Arcana. When he appears at the end of the sequence, The Fool has completed his inner journey and is starting a new outer journey. He passes blithely through the world, the appearance of which has been transformed by his own inner transformation: Where once was discord, all is now harmony. But the world itself has not changed one whit; it is the soul which has evolved. Once The Fool succeeded in building harmony in inner space, harmony appeared also in outer space, as if by magic.

To the world he may still appear to be a fool but he is a wise fool indeed for he has successfully undertaken the journey into self. Possibly too, he has heeded the words of Saint Paul who said, "The unspiritual man does not receive the gifts of the Spirit of God, for they are folly to him. . . . If anyone among you thinks that he is wise, let him become a fool that he may become wise. For the wisdom of this world is folly with God."

The Fool is not worried about the abyss yawning below. His eyes are fixed on the eternal heavens. And he knows he has nothing to fear from outer space; he has conquered inner space.

At the end of the Tarot sequence, The Fool is no longer a cipher but a Master Number—22. As a 22, he will go out into the world and will help to transform it with the power of love.

DIVINATION:

At or near the beginning of a sequence, The Fool is a fool. When, however, he appears at or near the end of a sequence, he is a wise fool and has profited from his experiences.

Reversed—In the approximate center of a spread, action has been taken, but there is still confusion or conflict. At or near the end of a spread, the lesson has been puzzled over, but the consultant is not quite sure exactly what it means.

3

Destiny Times Nine: Setting Up the Chart

Now that we have had an introduction to the numbers and the Tarot, we need to see how they work together. Our first step is to set up an astro-numeric chart, because the Tarot spreads in this book are designed to be used with such a chart.

In order to erect the chart two pieces of information will be necessary: we will need the name and date of birth of the individual who is going to be read.

This table gives the number value of each letter in our alphabet and is used in calculating the name numbers. Note that K as the eleventh letter, and V as the twenty-second letter of the alphabet may be considered as Master Number letters and in a chart are written thus: $K = 11\frac{1}{2}$, $V = 22\frac{2}{4}$. This is to indicate that the potential is there and will be realized if the person succeeds in living at the top of his or her abilities.

1	2	3	4	5	6	7	8	9
A	B	C	D	E	F	G	H	I
J	K	L	M	N	O	P	Q	R
S	T	U	V	W	X	Y	Z	

K and V have the value of Master Numbers and are written respectively as $11\frac{1}{2}$ and $22\frac{2}{4}$.

As is the case with a horoscope, an astro-numeric chart is really an embarrassment of riches. There is a veritable army of numbers. Where does one start? Just as there are nine root numbers, there are nine numbers of special significance in a chart, which are known as the Keys. These are the numbers referred to as the Cornerstone, Roof and Secret Passion, and the three pairs of numbers for the Inner Self, Persona and Destiny. There are other numbers in a chart, but these etch in the basic profile.

We shall examine each of these individually and learn how the number is found and what it means. We shall then see how it applies in the chart of a specific individual.

Each number in a chart will manifest some of the characteristics attributed to it in the opening chapter. The following table may be used as a capsule guide for interpreting the nine Keys, but for greater depth the reader should refer to the opening chapter.

Number Guide to the Keys

1*—Originality, leadership, independence.
2 —Cooperation, association, sensitivity.
3 —Self-expression, creativity, conviviality.
4 —Work, stability, hangups.
5 —Adventure, involvement, higher consciousness.
6 —Responsibility, adjustment, home and family ties.
7 —Cosmic concern, introspection, inner conflicts.
8 —Material power, success, law.
9 —Universality, social reform, emotional intensity.
11—Messenger of Light.
22—The Master Builder.

*Any 1 derived from a compound number always has the Special Number 10 behind it. For example, 64 reduces first to 10 and then to 1. While the number is written in the chart as "1" the numerologist bears in mind that this individual has the potential of harnassing creative abilities and leadership qualities in humanitarian service.

Now we are ready to begin. The first thing to put on the chart is the month, day and year of birth for the person we are doing, and of course, the name. The question that arises at this point is, "Which name?" "Do I use the name that appears on my birth certificate?" "Do I use just my first and last name, or shall I include my six middle names?" "Do I use my maiden name, married name, my nickname, my alias, or my *nom de plume*?"

These questions are not frivolous. If a person's name is the nucleus of a chart, there has to be some agreement as to which name is the correct one to place on the chart. This is rather a large discussion topic and will be gone into in greater detail in Chapter 6, but for the time being, suffice it to say that you *use the name by which most people know you.* In other words, use the name you and most people think of as "you"—at least, at this point in time. If it includes middle names, fine, use them. If not, do not use them on the chart. Initials tend to be tricky. One rule of thumb might be that if you are as well known as W.C. Fields, by all means, use the initials in making up the chart; otherwise, do not use them. If there is any question about which name to use, you might set up additional charts for your different names and see which one seems to offer the best fit.

The essence of a chart is provided by the Name and Birth numbers so they would be the logical place to start in our discussion of the nine Keys:

EXPRESSION NUMBER—The "Expression" number is the term numerologists employ to describe the Name number—that is, the name by which you are known to most people. This is only common sense. The number your "known name" reduces to is obviously what you are expressing to most people with whom you come into contact on a day-to-day basis. After deciding which name to use, place it on the chart. Consulting the table at the beginning of this chapter, find the number value for each letter in the name. The correct way to do this is to start with the vowels—A, E, I, O, U and Y—and write the number value for each *above* them. Then write the value for the consonants *below* them. Next, figure the total of the vowel numbers and then the total of the consonant numbers, add them together and then reduce to a root number.

Let us say your name is Elmo Hoskins. You would write it thus:

```
5       6        6       9        26
E L M O     H O S K I N S
  3 4         8   1 11  5 1      33
                              ───────────
                              59 = 14 = 5
```

The vowel total comes to 26, the consonant total to 33, and when added together, the final total is 59, which reduces to 14 (5 + 9 = 14). This is then reduced once again to arrive at a root number. The result in this case is 5 (1 + 4 = 5). So the Expression number for Elmo Hoskins is 5. Note that the "K" in his last name is the Master Number 11 and so that was not reduced.

BIRTH NUMBER—A numerology chart is also known as an astro-numeric chart and as the term implies, what is important in addition to the name is the time of birth. The Birth number and the Expression number are looked at as "two of a kind" and are considered the numbers of Persona. In the ancient world the term was employed to describe a mask worn by an actor, and psychologically, the persona is a kind of mask that a person affects to describe the life role he or she is playing. In the chart, more than anything else, the numbers of Persona describe the *person* and the way he or she performs in everyday life.

To find the Birth number write down the day of birth—that is, the day of the month. If, for example, Elmo Hoskins was born on April 1—the Birth number would be "1." The same principle would hold true had he been born the 2nd, 3rd, 4th, 5th, 6th, 7th, 8th or 9th day of the month.

But should Mr. Hoskins have been born anywhere between the 10th and 31st of a given month, it would become necessary to reduce the number to a root. So Elmo has a Birth number of 1 because he was born on the 1st of April but he would also have a Birth number of 1 had he been born on the 10th $(1 + 0 = 1)$, the 19th $(1 + 9 = 10 = 1)$, or the 28th $(2 + 8 = 10 = 1)$. And the same holds true for the rest of the root numbers.

If, however, Elmo had been born on the 11th or 22nd day of a month, the number would not be reduced and would appear on the chart as $11\frac{1}{2}$ or $22\frac{2}{4}$.

The Birth and Expression numbers are the two central Keys of the chart and for Elmo Hoskins they are, respectively, 1 and 5. This is a relatively harmonious pairing, suggesting someone who is an original, an innovator, a leader (1), but who is also adventurous and who is actively involved in a number of things (5).

Now let us determine the other seven Keys and then we will look at the total configuration.

CORNERSTONE—This represents the foundation of the life and is found by looking at the number value of the first letter of the first name that the person habitually uses and is known by. For Elmo, it is another 5 (E = 5), and would reinforce his adventuresome nature as indicated by his Expression number. This is not only the way he appears to the world but this is where he *starts* and what he *builds* upon.

INNER SELF—The Cornerstone and Persona numbers are "out front." They are what the world sees and the world knows. But what is the individual like inside? What are his or her dreams? Hopes and fears? Secret desires? These all-important qualities are discovered by looking at the two numbers of Inner Self—the Psyche and Soul Urge.

The Psyche number is found by adding up the number value of each consonant in the name and then reducing to a root number. Should the result come to a Master Number—11 or 22—it is not reduced but written $11\frac{1}{2}$ or $22\frac{2}{4}$. Some numerologists employ the term, "quiet self" for this number, but Psyche seems to connote more. It summons up echoes of classical mythology and the maiden loved by Eros who later became united with him in spirit. As implied by the myth, this is one of the more erotic numbers in a chart and suggests the libido yearnings of an individual along with other inner strivings.

But while the Psyche drives are vague and undifferentiated, the Soul Urge is conscious, clear and overwhelming to the individual. This is easily one of the single most important numbers in a chart; it indicates what a person wants and desires more than anything else in the world. It is found by adding up the vowels and then reducing their value to a root number. Looking at Elmo's chart, we see that he has a Psyche number of 6 $(3 + 3 = 6)$ and a Soul Urge of 8 $(2 + 6 = 8)$.

As these tend to be rigid numbers, he is going to be much more conservative than we might have originally suspected, and his leadership and involvement are going to be harnassed in ways to benefit community and society. And with a 1 on the Persona he may remain single, but his Psyche number of 6 will create a strong desire for a mate.

DESTINY—An individual may or may not fully succeed in living up to the potential of the Persona numbers, or in finding a way to accomplish what his or her Inner Self numbers motivate him or her toward, but there is no denying Destiny. The numbers of Destiny—the Path and Goal—are derived from the date of birth. This, of course, is in tune with the natal chart of astrology, for a horoscope is a chart "of the hour," and is based entirely upon the date of birth. Therefore the individual's destiny is going to be pretty much the same, whether it is learned from an astrologer or a numerologist.

The numbers of Destiny are the dominant numbers in a chart for the simple reason that there is no escaping from them. The Path is the road one must take in life; the Goal is the destination that must be reached.

The Path is found by taking the month, day and year of birth and then reducing that number to a root.

We said that Elmo was born on April 1, and to complete the picture, let us say that the year was 1948. Thus, he was born on the first day of the fourth month of 1948. His Path can be found by the following procedure:

Month	4
Day	1
Year	1948
	1953

$$1953 = (1 + 9 + 5 + 3 = 18 = 9)$$

Elmo's life Path number suggests that he will do something on a global scale for 9 is the number of universality. It is a challenging Path, but Elmo's other numbers indicate that he will be able to measure up to it.

In finding the Path number, it is important to follow the system exactly as outlined above and add all numbers together *before* reducing to a root. Let's say, for example, that Elmo was born on April 1, 1952. The year 1952 reduces to 8 $(1 + 9 + 5 + 2 = 17 = 8)$ and if you add to that the month number 4, and the day number 1, the result is 13 $(8 + 4 + 1 = 13)$ which reduces to 4. It is true that no matter which method you employ you will get the same root but let's see what happens when you use the procedure explained above:

Month	4
Day	1
Year	1952
	1957

Now, when we reduce 1957, we get the Master Number 22 rather than 13, and so the correct life Path is not 4 but rather $^{22}/_4$, which makes all the difference.

The other number of Destiny is the Goal and that is found by adding the number of the birth month to the number of the birth day and reducing to a root. Elmo's Goal is a 5 (4 + 1 = 5), and with a 5 Cornerstone and a 5 Expression, he should experience little difficulty in achieving this Goal.

SECRET PASSION—This term gets its name from the fact that while the other Keys can be quickly discerned from glancing at a chart, the Secret Passion number is not readily apparent in that it has to do with the number most often repeated in the "chart name," which is the name by which the person is known to most people.

Keep in mind that most of the root numbers have three letters that answer to the same vibration. For example, "A" has a 1–vibration behind it as do "J" and "S." In the case of 9, there are only two letters under that powerful vibration—"I" and "R." All the other numbers have three alphabetical associations. Now turn back to page 49 and look at each individual number in the full name of Elmo Hoskins. We see that five numbers—3, 4, 8, $1\frac{1}{2}$ and 9—appear once. However, 1, 5 and 6 appear twice. Quite often, there will be only a single number that is repeated more than any other, which clearly is *the* Secret Passion, but there can be more than one Secret Passion. In Elmo's case, there are actually three, for we have seen that 1, 5 and 6 each appear twice. This would tend to neutralize the importance of the Secret Passion in Elmo's case. But all three numbers appear elsewhere in the chart, consequently each gets further reinforcement. In a chart, repetition is of the utmost importance. So Elmo definitely has a strong sense of his individuality (1), but is one who seeks involvement with others (5), and is a person who has a strong attachment and sense of responsibility toward home and community (6).

THE ROOF—This number exerts a pervasive influence. As its position on the chart suggests, it is the highest level toward which an individual can aspire, but even more symbolically, it is the covering influence of the house of personality. It is found by adding together the Expression and Path numbers and then reducing to a root number. For Elmo, the result would be as follows:

$$
\begin{array}{ll}
\text{Expression} & 5 \\
\text{Path} & \underline{9} \\
& 14 = 5
\end{array}
$$

Finding the Roof number by adding the reduced expression and Path numbers is actually a short-cut method and in most cases will be correct. But should you come up with a 2 or 4 Roof, it is best to go back and add the full compound Expression and Path numbers, because instead of a 2 or 4, the result might be a Master Number, 11 or 22. For example, a person with a 1 Expression and on a 1 Path would be more likely found under the challenging 11 Roof rather than the 2. But you would only find that out by adding the full compound Expression and Path numbers of the chart.

It is now clear that more than any other, 5 is "Elmo's number," for it is his Cornerstone, Expression, Goal, Secret Passion and Roof. It is also clear that wherever Elmo is to be found, he will be very much at the center of things and there will be very much variety and many changes in his life. His 5 Goal calls for constant change and he should have a minimum of trouble in making these changes and arriving at this Goal. Five and everything for which it stands is the foundation of his existence (Cornerstone), the role he plays in everyday life (Expression), something he has a strong taste for (Secret Passion), and that to which he aspires and which acts as a covering influence for him (Roof).

Throughout this book each explanation of a significant chart number will be followed by a "case history." That is, reference will be made to the chart of a specific individual. There are several ways that this may be done. One would be to use celebrities and historical figures. Another would be to invent somebody such as our friend, Elmo Hoskins, and stick with him. Neither of these methods is without merit, but the problem is that with each the dice are loaded. In the first instance, the numerologist is selecting somebody famous or infamous whose particular chart or number happens to apply in a given case. In the other, because the character did not exist in the first place, he will have no choice but to follow the destiny his creator has charted for him.

In order to avoid those two pitfalls, we will chart an individual whose personality, character and career will be sufficiently well known to a substantial portion of the readership. And what is more, we will stay with him throughout the book. Other charts will be referred to from time to time but his will be central. Either numerology works or it does not. If it works, there should be something resembling proof so that readers can judge for themselves whether the theories are applicable. And if it works, it should work most of the time for any individual who has ever lived. Numerology must stand or fall on this premise.

No self-respecting numerologist would claim one hundred percent accuracy on a personality profile chart for the simple reason that free will exists and the individual is always free to make his or her own decisions, no matter what their numbers are. But the testament of the centuries is that most people do indeed follow most of their numbers most of the time.

The individual whose chart we shall examine in some degree of depth is that of the world's first consulting detective—Mr. Sherlock Holmes.

Casebook—The Singular Affair of the Numbers of Mr. Sherlock Holmes

As was the case with Elmo Hoskins, we shall begin our investigation by finding the Expression and Birth numbers. First, the Expression:

```
    5       6               6       5       22
 S  H  E  R  L  O  C  K     H  O  L  M  E  S
 1  8     9  3     3  11    8  3  4     1    51
                                          ─────────
                                          73 = 10 = 1
```

The biographers of Mr. Holmes inform us that he was born on the feast of Twelfth Night, which is January 6. So the Expression number for Sherlock Holmes is 1 while the Birth number is 6.

Let us begin, however, with the Cornerstone for that is the building block of personality. The first letter of the name by which Mr. Holmes was known to most people was "S" which has a number value of 1 so it is apparent that he built his life upon independence and leadership.

In some ways the two numbers that make up the Persona (Birth and Expression) are the most representative of the individual for as the name suggests, they indicate the personality—that is, a characteristic way of acting and reacting in everyday life.

In order to have a unified personality, it is important that the Birth and Expression numbers are in harmony for otherwise there will be problems. For Sherlock Holmes there *were* problems because his Persona numbers are really fighting each other: 1 is active and dominant while 6 is retiring and passive. This conflict would, in fact, make for something of a split personality. A 6's deepest desire is for stability, home and marriage, while 1 craves independence and pursues an innovative and adventurous career.

This 1/6 division would help to account for the failure of any marriage Mr. Holmes might undertake, or for that matter, the failure to take a mate at all. Although he never completely solved the problem, he did make an interesting attempt to reconcile these opposing numbers of home and independence by making a rather cozy nest at his Baker Street digs and spending a good deal of time there. One would have to look long and hard to find another detective whose address is as famous as 221B Baker Street.

To move along to Sherlock's Inner Self numbers, we begin by adding up the consonants in his name to find the Psyche, and we get a total of 51 which reduces to 6 (5 + 1 = 6), while the vowels add up to the Master Number 22. Interestingly enough, Mr. Holmes has an 11 vowel count in both his first name and his last name, so that the Master Number 22 is itself the product of two Master Numbers. So Sherlock Holmes has a Psyche number of 6 and a Soul Urge number of 22/4. These numbers are fairly compatible with his Persona numbers since one of his Persona numbers is also 6, and 1 and 22 are both members of the executive club. But that repetition of 6 intensifies the vibration of the number and suggests that what Mr. Holmes is manifesting outwardly, he is also feeling inwardly. This would make for greater unity of personality than was evidenced originally by the 1/6 split on Persona.

A 6 on both Inner Self and Persona would be the mark of a highly responsible individual. As a double 6, he would love nothing better than to spend a convivial evening by the fireside. As readers of Dr. Watson's narratives know, Mr. Holmes was very much a pipe-and-slippers man and his customary uniform was his mouse-colored bathrobe. The double 6 also suggests that despite the loner aspect of his 1 Expression number, he was a man who probably had deep regrets about remaining single and childless.

It is clear that this is not only the chart of a born leader—with a 1 Cornerstone and Expression—but one also, because of that Soul Urge of the ultimate Master Number 22, who would think of himself as having a special destiny. Here then is a man able to exert leadership while maintaining a universalist outlook. No ordinary gumshoe, Sherlock Holmes might see himself as a knight in shining armor, in search of the grail, a man with a quest. Above all, he would see himself as an actor strutting the world, center stage. The 22 vibration is a heavy one, but with a Cornerstone and Expression of 1 combined with a double 6, the number of Responsibility, he has powerful equipment to carry out his self-appointed mission.

The Persona gives some idea of the type of transportation we will use; the Inner Self reveals what we shall seek on our journey; the Path of Destiny is the direction we must follow; and the Goal of Destiny is the destination we must reach. It is, in short, the Way. In order to find Sherlock Holmes' Path number we use the same system that was employed for Elmo Hoskins. The full date of birth for Mr. Holmes is January 6, 1854,[1] which is reduced as follows:

Month	1
Day	6
Year	1854
	1861 = 16 = 7

The Goal, we know, is found by adding the month and day and this also reduces to a 7 (1 + 6 = 7).

The chart of Sherlock Holmes is a heavy one indeed for he has a double 7 Destiny! The 7 Destiny is both enigmatic and lonely, but one rich with spiritual rewards. And it is possible that Mr. Holmes did follow his chart in this respect. Just when he "got the call" we can only surmise, but because his 7 Path is derived from the compound number 16, we are reminded of Arcanum XVI in the Tarot, The Lightning-Struck Tower. The implication is that "the message" is going to come suddenly and dramatically and could come as the result of an accident or close call of some kind. Quite possibly it came with what Dr. Watson was to mistakenly label, "The Final Problem," that near-fatal encounter with death when he confronted Professor Moriarty at the abyss of the Reichenbach Falls. Believed dead by Dr. Watson and the world, Holmes spent some three years wandering and meditating. As the good Dr. Watson tells us in "The Adventure of the Empty House," he did return to London and private practice, but he was never quite the same again. Always a private person, he apparently did not reveal even to Dr. Watson his innermost strivings. It may be that his Secret Passion is instructive, for 3 is a number of great spiritual significance in many religions and Holmes has 3 as his Secret Passion number. You will remember that the Secret Passion is the number repeated most often in the full name. While Elmo Hoskins had three Secret Passions, Mr. Holmes has only one. Three is repeated twice and no other number in his name is repeated more than once.

We know that Holmes spent long hours in his Baker Street rooms in meditation and it is possible that he was "solving cases" on planes of existence other than Earth. Three is also the number of self-expression and of music. As Dr. Watson knew only too well, the Great Detective had what amounted to a passion for scraping away on the violin.

The final Key for Mr. Holmes is the Roof, which in many ways is the driving force for the life. Adding Holmes' Expression and Path numbers together, we find that the result is 8 $(1 + 7 = 8)$.

As 8 is the central power number, this would make for strong drives on Mr. Holmes' part, for his deepest desires would be for power and success. Because 8 is also the number of law and is traditionally the card of Justice in the Tarot, the 8 Roof helps explain why Sherlock Holmes chose to become a detective. The fact that he became a criminal investigator rather than a criminal is explained by other numbers in his chart for an 8 can go either way and certainly he was fond of telling Dr. Watson that he would have made an excellent criminal.

Now with all 9 Keys of the chart before us, we are in a position to make some kind of assessment. First, let us examine the numbers:

Roof 8
Inner Self .... 6, $22/4$
Persona 6, 1
Destiny 7, 7
Secret Passion 3
Cornerstone 1

With a 1 Cornerstone and Expression he was equipped for leadership. But we look again at Mr. Holmes' chart and find that the name number total is 73, which reduces to 10 and then 1. So the invisible Special Number 10 is behind the 1 in the chart and has a cosmic potential that 1 itself does not possess. In the chart of Elmo Hoskins there is also a 1 on the Persona but because there is no 10 behind it, spiritual potential would not be there unless other factors in the chart so indicated, which in Elmo's case, they do not. But in Holmes' case, they do because in addition to the invisible 10, there is that Master Number 22 on the Soul Urge and the double 7 Destiny. What form it may have taken and when it may have occurred we cannot know until we go deeper into the chart.

To sum up the Keys: From the Roof we gain a sense of direction and soul knowledge; we build our lives on the Cornerstone; are further directed by our Secret Passion; stabilize our behavior pattern via our Persona; aspire and create within our Inner Selves; and finally, attain our Destiny by following the prescribed Path to our life destination, the Goal.

We have, so far, only scratched the surface of the chart of Sherlock Holmes, but the nine Keys have provided us with a remarkably compact profile. We have learned that he had a very strong will to power (Roof: 8); that he would succeed, but with his own methods and in his own way (Cornerstone and Expression: 1); that he would undertake considerable responsibility (Birth and Psyche: 6); and that his efforts would be global in scope (Soul Urge: $2\frac{2}{4}$). Most of this does not come as any great surprise to the readers of Watson's accounts, but what is most revealing and something of a surprise to at least some of the followers of the career of the Great Detective is that his ultimate concern would be with a Higher Law (Destiny: 7/7).

One mystery that Sherlock Holmes never solved is the paradox of his own personality. It is beginning to appear that his chart may provide some important clues to help unravel that mystery.

We are ready now to take up our first Tarot spread and then see its application in a consultation, but first a word about the handling of a Tarot deck. As stated earlier, the Tarot spreads in this book are designed to supplement and add a further dimension to one's astro-numeric chart. The chart should be erected first and read and interpreted before the spreads are laid.

Custom dictates that a Tarot deck be wrapped in a dark-colored piece of velvet or silk—preferably purple—and kept in a wooden box. This is said to protect it from harmful vibrations. It is not essential to do this and your deck will still work without it, but it makes sense to do everything possible to intensify the magick of the cards (this spelling of "magick" is not a typographical error but rather is used to distinguish the pure magick of the Tarot from the type of magic employed by practitioners of the "Now you see it; now you don't" school). Make no mistake about it, it is magick; no other explanation seems to suffice. Maintaining the maximum effectiveness of the deck is important; after all, if you bought a Rolls-Royce, you would protect your investment by keeping it in a safe garage.

One of the tenets of magick is to always follow the same ritual in a step-by-step fashion. It really is not much different from the ritual of starting a car or the ritual of baking a cake. There are certain steps to follow and there is an order to the procedure. Departure from the time-proven method generally results in less than maximum effectiveness whether it is a stalled car or a burnt cake.

Every Tarot reader eventually develops his or her own working method and one is not necessarily better than another. But for the person looking for guidelines, here is a method that has been used with excellent results:

> The reader—that is, the individual who will be spreading the cards and then reading them for someone else (or him- or herself)—takes the deck first and shuffles the cards with a clear understanding of which spread is going to be thrown and the manner in which it will be read. He or she then hands the cards to the consultant—the person for whom the reading is being done—and asks him or her to reverse three cards and to replace them in the pack, in reverse position. The consultant is then asked if he or she is left- or right-handed. If right-handed, the consultant should use the *left hand* to cut the deck into three piles and shuffle each pile separately. When the cards have been shuffled to the consultant's satisfaction, he or she again uses the left hand to put the deck back together in any order he or she chooses. (The left hand is used as it is traditionally the "unconscious hand" as opposed to the right hand which is the "calculating hand.") The reader then takes the deck and throws the spread according to instructions. Most spreads start with the top card of the deck, follow in sequence, and are laid in a right-to-left direction. Each spread determines the number of cards to be used.

> The same spread should not be repeated for the same person on the same day, although any number of different spreads can be done for the consultant during the course of a reading. Following the reading, the cards should all be returned to an upright position and then wrapped in a cloth and returned to their wooden box.

As the spreads in this book were designed specifically for use in supplementing an astro-numeric chart, they will differ from conventional Tarot spreads in that the emphasis will be more on the Life Plan or overall pattern of a particular individual rather than questions of immediate concern. If you are doing a Tarot reading for someone who has a question such as, "Would I be wise to marry?," or "What are my chances for getting this particular job?," you should use conventional spreads such as the Horseshoe or Celtic Cross. A work that contains a rich assortment of classic spreads is *The Tarot Shows the Path*,[2] written by one of the world's great teachers and practitioners of the Tarot, Rolla Nordic.

The Spread: Triangle of Destiny

This spread is based on the nine Keys of a chart which, taken together, offer a blueprint of destiny.

First, a significator card is selected to represent the consultant, and in this case, it is based on the consultant's Path number. This would preferably come from the Major Arcana, so if a person had a 7 Path, as does Mr. Holmes, he or she would choose the seventh card of the Major Arcana, which is the card of The Chariot. Or, if preferred, a card bearing the same number from the Minor Arcana can be used. The important thing is that the consultant should have some feeling of empathy with the card actually used. Once the significator card has been chosen, it is removed from the deck, placed face up on the table, and the Triangle is then built around it.

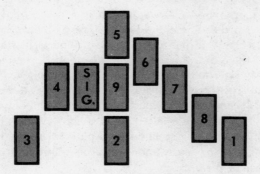

The cards are to be read as follows:

1—Cornerstone
2—Secret Passion
3—Persona (Birth Number)
4—Persona (Expression Number)
5—Roof
6—Inner Self (Psyche)
7—Inner Self (Soul Urge)
8—Destiny (Path)
9—Destiny (Goal)

Following the diagram, cards are spread clockwise. With the exception of the significator, which is placed face up on the table before the other cards are laid down, they are dealt face down. After all nine cards are in the Triangle, the reader starts with the #1 card and reads all of the cards, in order.

The consultant's astro-numeric chart should be referred to during the reading of each card so that a synthesis can be attempted.

The Tape:

The Consultant is a woman whose galvanic energies and real-life exploits make Auntie Mame pale by comparison. As this spread deals with the nine Keys of her chart, they are reproduced below, along with the spread:

Chart		Tarot
Cornerstone	6	Card 1—5 of Coins
Secret Passion	5, 9	Card 2—2 of Coins
Persona (Birth)	6	Card 3—9 of Coins
Persona (Expression)	8	Card 4—7 of Wands
Roof	4	Card 5—8 of Wands
Inner Self (Psyche)	5	Card 6—4 of Cups
Inner Self (Soul Urge)	3	Card 7—9 of Cups
Destiny (Path)	5	Card 8—The World
Destiny (Goal)	7	Card 9—4 of Wands

SK: Your Cornerstone is a 6, which is a number of responsibility, particularly in regard to home and family. The matching card of the Tarot is the 5 of Coins, which has to do with fulfillment in financial matters. Taken together, the indication is that you love nothing better than to go out and spend money on your home. In other words, money gives you a sense of fulfillment not for the mere acquisition of it, but as a means to beautify your surroundings and help the members of your family.

Consultant: That is certainly true. I am forever rearranging things around my home or finding something to put in a nook or cranny to set other things off. Being surrounded by beautiful things gives me a tremendous sense of pleasure.

SK: The Secret Passion is what turns you on and your chart shows that there are two things that interest you and they are represented by the numbers 5 and 9, which have to do with adventure, travel, involvement and enterprises of a global nature. This card, the 2 of Coins, shows a man with an ocean behind him and ships sailing off to the far-flung parts of the world. But the man himself has a coin in each hand, with the left hand lower than the right, suggesting that he is having a hard time balancing his finances so that he can do everything that he wants to do.

Consultant: Isn't that the truth! You could give me a million dollars tomorrow and I would have it spent before the sun went down.

SK: The Persona, in many ways, is "the person." It is, at least, the person the world sees and recognizes. Your Persona numbers are 6 and 8, and they have to do with taking responsibility around the home and of enjoying considerable position and influence in the community. The 9 of Coins indicates that there is always something unexpected coming up around your home that involves a cash outlay.

Consultant: Don't remind me!

SK: But the figure on the card is admiring a bird that is perched in his hand, and he is standing in a beautifully cultivated garden. So, however much something may cost you in the way of money, energy and time, the results are more than worth it as far as you are concerned. If you are anything like the figure on the card, you are a very happy person in your home surroundings.

Consultant: My home is my canvas.

SK: Your 8 Persona number has to do with high finance, but the 7 of Wands suggests a goodly number of changes in regard to career and business dealings. I think changes generally work out fairly well for you, as 7 is a number of victory.

Consultant: I really have no complaints on that score.

SK: The Roof is what motivates a person, and yours is a 4, the number of work. But since 4 is one of the missing numbers on your chart, there may be a tendency on your part to feel overwhelmed or oppressed by work. This card, the 8 of Wands, says the same thing, for it suggests an imbalance in the realm of work.

Consultant: (laughing) Well, I don't have to tell you that I never have been very good at details. I always have so much to do, I just can't ever seem to keep anything straight.

SK: Oh, I hadn't noticed. By the way, wasn't this reading originally set up for yesterday?

Consultant: You're asking me!

SK: Now we get to the "real you"—the Inner Self. Look at these cards, will you. Up to now, for the "outer you," there were nothing but Coins and Wands, which have to do with money and business. But now we come to the Inner Self and we come up with the two Cup cards, the 4 and 9, and as you well know, the suit of Cups has to do with the days of wine and roses.

Consultant: Does that mean I'm a closet alcoholic?

SK: No, what the cards indicate is that beneath that busy, enterprising exterior, you are a total romantic. The 4 of cups has to do with unexpected love affairs and 9 of Cups is the Wish Card, so basically you are something of a sentimentalist and a dreamer.

Consultant: Exposed at last! And after all these years.

SK: Actually, the Tarot is only agreeing with your chart numbers 3 and 5, the numbers of adventure and romance. Now for the cards of Destiny. First the Path. We said that you have a 5 Path, which indicates one who leads a storybook life. The card here is The World, and that sums it up exactly, for here is a dancing woman clothed—at least, partially—in royal purple, holding the wands of power, enveloped by the laurel wreath of victory and skipping merrily through life.

Consultant: That card is forever coming up for me.

SK: You may not want to face this, but it looks as though you are doing something right. And now we are ready for the final card, which is the Goal of your life. In your case, we observed that you have a 7 Goal, which is the number of cosmic affairs. This could be a bit of a problem for your Path is on one plane, your Goal on another. The Goal card is the 4 of Wands. Ordinarily, this card has to do with a financial windfall, but in this case I think that the windfall has to be considered a spiritual windfall.

This card is the 4 of Wands. Four is the number of work, and the suit of Wands has to do with work. So I think the Tarot is trying to tell you something.

Consultant: That the spiritual windfall will not just be dumped in my lap, and that I will have to go out and work for it?

SK: Right! But I think you will make it. You see, there are two Destiny cards here, The World and the 4 of Wands. Looked at numerically, the number of the World, 21, reduces to a 3, and when added to the Goal card (4 of Wands) it produces a 7, the number of spiritual rewards and your ultimate number of Destiny.

---

[1]William S. Baring-Gould, *Sherlock Holmes of Baker Street—A Life of the World's First Consulting Detective*, Bramhall House, New York, 1962, 294.

[2]Rolla Nordic, *The Tarot Shows the Path*, Esoteric Pulbications, Phoenix, Arizona, 1960. Available directly from the author: 121 West 72nd Street, New York, N.Y. 10023.

4

A Question of Karma:
The Challenge—Karmic Lessons

The drawing up of an astro-numeric chart is based upon the assumption that there is purpose in the universe. Recalling to mind the magickal principle of, "As above, so below," it would follow that there is also purpose in the individual life. And it is possible that the individual purpose is in some way a reflection of the cosmic purpose.

As we saw in the preceding chapter, one way of ascertaining that purpose is to learn our Destiny numbers so that we will understand the Path we need to take and the Goal we must reach.

Concerning the saga of The Fool, we saw that his story started with a journey. But there were obstacles along the path that he took. There were the physical dangers of his youth and later, the inner terrors of the nighttime of life.

And so it is on any life path—there are both physical and psychological obstacles to overcome. Until we succeed in surmounting them, we will be unable to move on to a higher stage of development.

A most important limitation is what is known in numerology as the Challenge. The Challenge is not so much an obstacle as it is a lesson that needs to be learned, or better, a limitation to be overcome. More than likely, it is a lesson that we failed to learn in a previous life. Looked at one way, the doctrine of reincarnation is a way for the cosmic forces to give us time to correct our mistakes. If we are unsuccessful in one life, we do not fail, but instead have another opportunity to matriculate in the Life School of Continuing Education. We continue until the lesson has been learned and then move on to the next stage of development. Ultimately we complete our tasks, accomplish our mission and attain perfection. But that usually takes a while.

Looked at from this standpoint, the Challenge is a most instructive device that helps us prepare for Commencement Day. It will admittedly be an area of limitation, but once we understand the nature of our individual Challenges, we are in a position to do something about them for we can at least look upon the face of our adversary.

With regard to numerology, how do the Challenge numbers apply? Look at a number and see how it alters as a Challenge. Take the power number 8, for example, a Destiny number—Path or Goal—would suggest that what was required of us would be to scale the human heights, take top-level responsibility and excercise power wisely. To become a recluse or take a back seat, would, with an 8 Path, be a serious failing.

But on the Challenge side of the chart, the 8 would have quite a different meaning for it would indicate that somewhere along the line we had suffered from an overdose of power and an over-concern with material things, and that the lesson for this life would be not the taking, but rather, the relinquishing of power and the pursuit of spiritual or humanitarian concerns.

In a chart, there are usually *three* important life Challenges (in some instances there are none or the same one is repeated). As they are taken from the birth time, begin by setting down the root digits for the month, day and year of birth. In this case, the Master Numbers 11 and 22 are reduced to a root number.

The root numbers for Sherlock Holmes' birth date are:

Month (January)......1
Day 6
Year ....9 $(1 + 8 + 5 + 4 = 18 = 9)$

To find the *First Challenge*, take the month and day and subtract the lesser from the greater. Mr. Holmes' first Challenge is a 5 $(6 - 1 = 5)$.

The *Second Challenge* is found by taking the day and year digits and subtracting the lesser from the greater. The Second Challenge for Sherlock Holmes is a 3 $(9 - 6 = 3)$.

To find the *Final Challenge*, take the first two Challenge numbers and subtract the lesser from the greater. For Mr. Holmes it is a 2 $(5 - 3 = 2)$.

The Challenges tend to run concurrently with the cycles (to be taken up in Chapter 8), so the first one is from birth to approximately age 28; the second from age 28 to 56, and the third and final one from 56 on. The first two are considered Minor Challenges; the final one serves as a Major Challenge and while it is most powerful in the later years, it is actually experienced as a force throughout one's life.

In relation to the attributes associated with the numbers, a Challenge usually means one of two things: Either the person is overdoing something or underdoing it. A careful study of the entire chart should provide the necessary clues. Guidelines for interpretation are suggested by the following table:

Table of Challenges

1

a) Learn to assert your individuality. Don't be afraid to speak up for your opinions.

b) Understand that the world does not revolve around you, your needs and your desires.

2

a) Learn humility and the value of cooperation. Associate with others.

b) Be less sensitive. Learn to stand on your own two feet.

3

a) Find ways of expressing yourself through the arts. Socialize more and meet people.

b) Handsome is as handsome does. Don't try to trade always on your charm; stop talking and start doing.

4

a) In the Classroom of Life, take notes, and do your homework. In short, get to WORK.

b) You have a head for details, to the exclusion of everything else. You are hung up on trivia and need to take a broader view of things.

5

a) Learn to accept change. Become more involved.

b) Put those suitcases away, try the rocking chair on for size and become less of an activist. Alcohol and drugs should be avoided.

7

a) The will to believe is not enough; you must go out and *seek* Spirit.

b) There is a world out there; come out of your shell and relate to it.

8

a) Authority figures are not all manipulating capitalists. Money can be fun.

b) In gaining the world, have you lost your soul?

9

There are no direct 9 Challenges but if an individual has this number as a Karmic Lesson, it would be in the same category as a Major Challenge. As it is the number of human understanding this would be a considerable hurdle to overcome.

0

a) The mark of an evolved soul. There are no particular Challenges to overcome, and the individual can choose what he or she needs to learn.

b) There is no particular Challenge but everything *can* be a Challenge if you let it.

Casebook—The Five Challenge vs. The Seven Percent Solution

We shall now look a little more closely at the Challenges of Sherlock Holmes and the manner in which he dealt with them. They were:

Challenge	*Age*
5	1–28
3	28–56
2	56 on

The First Challenge Sherlock Holmes had to face was a 5. This would be a rather difficult one for a young person as 5 is the number of the senses. An individual under such a Challenge—particularly an earth sign and Sherlock Holmes had his Sun in Capricorn, one of the three earth signs—would have an intense desire to experience everything in the realm of sensual gratification. Holmes' keenly developed senses were to prove a powerful instrument indeed in the hunting down of criminals. But on the negative side, he began to explore the pleasures of the flesh at an early age.

One way that Holmes attempted to combat the problem was to become totally involved in his work, and he succeeded to a large extent. Another way was to sublimate his libidinous urges with music, which proved to be not only an esthetic experience but a sensual one as well, and here again he succeeded to a large extent.

But he did not succeed entirely and his solution was of the seven percent variety—namely, cocaine. We do not know exactly when Sherlock Holmes became a drug addict, but facing a 5 Challenge from birth to his late twenties, he probably started experimenting fairly early. This drug problem would help to account for the prolonged presence of Dr. Watson, for the two didn't really seem to have much in common, and on cases, Watson was worse than useless. But as a medical man he was able to provide Holmes with a regular fix and offer him professional assistance when he was strung out. But poor Watson! There must have been times when he felt absolutely helpless, such as after the closing of "The Sign of the Four Case," when the sympathetic doctor asked what Holmes got out of the business.

Holmes' reply spoke volumes. He said that there was always the cocaine bottle.

Watson, that kindhearted soul, did his best to wean Holmes off drugs but did not have much success until Holmes had passed his twenty-eighth birthday, and incidentally, the 5 Challenge.

Holmes' Second Minor Challenge was a 3. Looking at his chart, we see that 3 was also his Secret Passion. Essentially, 3 is the number of self-expression and the detective was extraordinarily versatile in a number of areas. His passion for music we have already mentioned, but he was also very creative in his work and expressed himself in a variety of hobbies and outlets. In addition to his scientific writings and monographs on esoteric aspects of crime detection, he was an accomplished prizefighter, swimmer, mountain climber, and displayed considerable finesse with swords and pistols.

But 3 is also a number of conviviality and there Holmes seems to have fallen down completely. This challenge was the one starting at age 28 and lasting until 56, and in Watson's accounts at least, there doesn't seem to be anyone besides Watson whom Holmes is involved with in a social way.

It appears then that Mr. Holmes would have to get a mixed grade in this department: At self-expression his accomplishments were many and varied; as a social butterfly, he was a caterpillar.

The Final and Major Challenge—the one that actually lasts throughout the life—was for Sherlock Holmes a 2. He was certainly not a leaning vine so the Challenge to him quite obviously was to learn the lesson of cooperation. This is similar to the 3 Challenge that he faced during the middle period of his life in that the lesson was to get out and cultivate relationships with other people.

Here again, Holmes does not seem to have succeeded very well. It is true that as a private detective he did cooperate with Inspector Lestrade and other officers at Scotland Yard, but always on his own terms. It cannot really be said that he ever worked with them at all; he merely informed them where the loot or the body was when the fun was over. Association is perhaps the prime meaning of the 2 Challenge, and the only person he ever really worked with at all was Dr. Watson. And Holmes didn't tell Watson any more than he had to tell him. The good doctor was forced to muddle through in his own singularly bumbling fashion.

For Holmes, the major force of the 2 Challenge began at age 56 and by that time he was living the life of a hermit on the Sussex Downs. The only creatures he was associating with on a regular basis were bees.

Admittedly, with Sherlock Holmes' numbers, cooperation would have taken some doing. With a Cornerstone of 1 and another 1 on the Persona, he would be compulsive about his independence. To say nothing of that double 7 Destiny! Seven being the number of introspection, Mr. Holmes would in all matters seek out his own counsel rather than that of others.

So with regard to his Challenges, Sherlock Holmes does not seem to have come off too well, but as we can see, there were mitigating factors. And in a way, it is reassuring for it does indicate that the Great Detective was human after all!

Karmic Lessons

A Karmic Lesson may be seen as a different order of Challenge. To borrow a metaphor from academe, the Challenges are curricular units such as science and math that are requisites for graduation, but owing to our weakness in these areas, we are going to have to grind away in order to pass them. Karmic Lessons, on the other hand, are courses that we have failed which must be made up.

Karma could be stated as the Law of Compensation and summed up with the Biblical injunction, "As ye sow, so shall ye surely reap." If you do something that constitutes an injury to someone else, at some future time an injury will be done to you, so that you may fully learn the implications of your actions as they reflect on others. Conversely, should you fail to do something that needs to be done, you will be placed in a life situation where you will have to do it or pay the price.

There are several ways in which karma operates, and they might be termed Instant Karma, Delayed Karma and Life Karma. The Katzenjammer Kids would be an example of Instant Karma for the crimes of Hans and Fritz were usually paid in full by the final panel of the comic strip where they were generally on the receiving end of a vigorous paddling over the knees of the Captain and the Inspector.

Instant Karma may be painful, but the outcome of Delayed Karma may be considerably more costly both in physical and in psychological terms. Watergate could be seen as an example of Delayed Karma. Few men who reach the office of President of the United States enter with an appellation such as "Tricky Dicky," and for Nixon the karmic sword of justice descended slowly but inexorably.

Most costly of all, however, is the Life Karma. This is well illustrated by the "life readings" of Edgar Cayce in which he used his clairvoyance to point out that suffering from a problem or affliction was often karmic in origin having been the result of a sin of commission or omission in a previous life. A striking case in point was the life reading for a college professor who had been born blind and was informed that in an earlier life in Persia he had the grisly task of putting out the eyes of enemy tribesmen with a red-hot iron.[1] His sin was not so much committing the action, but rather, doing so with relish. In short, he was totally unable to identify with the victim or understand what it was to be deprived of one's sight. Being born blind in his present life gave him the opportunity to learn the lesson. His chart would most likely show a karma in 9, the number of human compassion.

In a chart, the Karmic Lessons are indicated by the missing numbers in one's name. In an average name of fourteen letters, there are generally two or more Karmic Lessons. In order to find the missing numbers, you must look at the full name—that is, the one that appears on the birth certificate. Karma dates from birth and is revealed by the name you were given at that time. In the following chart, the number of the Karmic Lesson corresponds to the missing number in the name. If, for example, you had no 1s, that is, no As, Js, or Ss in your name, you would have to learn the lesson of that number and should refer to it in the Table of Karmic Lessons.

Table of Karmic Lessons

1

Past—In a past life, this person failed to be an individual. There was a lack of independence and a fear of leadership. More than anything else, there was a failure to build an integrated sense of self, a desire to deny the "I" or "me" and to exist parasitically as only a part of something or someone else.

Present—In this life the person will not be able to disappear into the wordwork but rather, life will place him or her in situations where he or she will have to go it alone, assume leadership and above all, develop the courage to be oneself.

2

Past—The number 2 card of the Major Arcana of the Tarot is instructive here for The High Priestess is a woman who has shut herself away from the company of others. A Karmic 2 has done this on another plane of existence by failing to cooperate or experience empathy with others. More than likely, the individual was insensitive to the feelings and needs of those in the immediate circle and lacked diplomacy.

Present—This time around, the Karmic 2 will be forced to associate each day with people who will not be easy to get along with, and he or she will succeed only by being a paragon of patience, tact and diplomacy. Essentially, this lesson is learned by accepting others as they are, and by developing forgiveness, understanding and love.

3

Past—Essentially, 3 is the number of creativity and self-expression. With 3 as a Karmic Lesson, the indication is that in a past life the individual was like the servant of the nobleman who had a talent and buried it in the ground rather than developing it. For the Karmic 3 this parable hits very close to home for the person finds that the "buried talent" in that other life has been taken from him or her in the present one.

Present—Words will not come easily for the Karmic 3 and creative energies of any kind will be difficult to harness and channel. There will be a deathly fear of mixing with others, of getting up and giving a speech, of taking part in a play, but life will have a way of forcing him or her "on stage" until the lesson is learned.

4

Past—In another incarnation the tendency was always to take the easy way out. This person chose to live by wits rather than work. Details were glossed over and often skipped entirely. Little care was given to the physical body so that health was left largely to chance.

Present—This lesson is learned by the sweat of the brow. Neither health nor anything else of a physical nature can be overlooked in this life. Physical fitness will be attained only by constant care, proper diet and regular exercise. All personal business matters will have to be placed on a firm foundation or they will self-destruct.

5

Past—Five is the number of the physical senses and as most people do not shut themselves off from physical experiences, it is unusual to find it as a Karmic Lesson. It seems to appear only when there was an earlier abuse of personal freedom and a failure to become involved in the world of people and things.

Present—In this existence the individual will find that a retreat into the ivory tower is not a viable option. Attempts to hide are useless, change will carry this person to the center of life and action. This is the "suitcase karma" and much movement of a turbulent nature can be expected until the individual learns to cope with all life situations. Above all, it is the lesson of learning to live with change.

6

Past—This is perhaps the most common Karmic Lesson found in the charts of people in western society. It is indicative of a failure in another life to meet one's responsibilities toward another or others. Essentially, it is a karma in marriage. Often the entity neglected or misused the partner, children or others in the immediate family. Unable to adjust to a marital situation, he or she often walked out and abdicated responsibility.

Present—In the present life the individual is unable to find a suitable mate and feels desperately lonely; or what is more likely, he or she will find a mate, but there are real problems in the marriage that must be faced. In order to pay this karmic bill, the individual must find a way to make the current marriage work by adjusting and by being extremely patient and understanding. Invariably, the Karmic 6 is tempted to seek a separation or divorce, but to do so sets the karma in motion and can only lead to disaster. For the individual with this lesson, the quickest way to pay off the karma is to remain with the first partner for if the Karmic 6 walks off, things will only get worse. Either he or she will experience loneliness and misery or, worse yet, make a second, third or fourth marriage with progressively greater problems.

7

Past—Seven is the number of Spirit and an individual with a 7 missing in the name is one who failed to comprehend the unity of the universe and the ways of the spirit. This person would only accept as the truth what could be ascertained with the lower five senses.

Present—Fate will have a way of forcing this person into situations that will point up the fallacy of a purely materialistic approach to life. He or she will find the self undergoing trauma after trauma until the still small voice of the God within is heard and the individual realizes that the Higher Truth is indeed "the substance of things hoped for, the evidence of things not seen."

8

Past—Eight is the central number of power (the others being 7 and 9) and is associated with material things. Thus, a karma in 8 often indicates a disregard or misuse of power or the law. Primarily this lesson has to do with money, which is the central medium of power in our society. In another incarnation the person may have failed to exercise prudence in saving and spending.

Present—This time around, power, position and wealth will not be easily obtainable and responsibilities of a material nature will forever press upon the individual. And whether born in unfavorable financial circumstances or otherwise, money will be an ever-present concern. The eighth card of the Major Arcana is Justice (see note on page 28) associated with balance, and this is exactly what the individual will have to learn: to keep the things of this world in proper balance, and that most definitely includes the checkbook.

9

Past—This is rarely to be found as a Karmic Lesson for 9 is the number of humanity. The ninth card of the Major Arcana is The Hermit, whose sense of caution prevents him from entering into the mainstream of humanity and thus he walls himself off from the world of people.

Present—In this incarnation the entity will hunger after human companionship, but will find it difficult to form relationships until he or she attains an understanding heart and fully realizes that "Any man's death diminishes me, because I am involved in Mankind."

Casebook—A Study in Seven

Examining the chart of Sherlock Holmes for the Karmic Lessons, we find only one missing number, and that, incredibly, a 7! We are reminded immediately that the number 7 does play a rather strong role in Mr. Holmes' chart, for he has a double 7 Destiny: A 7 Path and a 7 Goal. Later we shall discover that in addition to his Karmic 7 and his 7/7 Destiny, he also has an opening Pinnacle number of 7 and a Rational Self number of 7. His chart is, in effect, a study in sevens.

In the Tarot, Arcanum VII is The Chariot, a card of triumph and victory and in many ways, reflects Holmes' life. Seven is the number of introspection and Sherlock Holmes was a very meditative man. Seven is the number of rationality, of mental analysis, and few men have employed the art of deduction more brilliantly than Holmes. Seven is the number of solitude and much of the time Holmes lived within himself. Seven is the number of melancholy and Holmes, we know, suffered severely from this. When music failed to relieve his states of acute depression, he resorted to hard drugs. Seven is the number of scientific research and Holmes' Baker Street lodgings often resembled nothing so much as a scientific laboratory. But his major contribution in this area was to place the business of detection on a scientific basis. Seven is the number of investigation, and as a crime investigator, he was without peer.

But Sherlock Holmes would be most responsive to the 7 vibrations if and when he switched his investigations from the realm of matter to that of the spirit, for above all else, 7 is the number of spirit and religion. If we take into account that the "B" in the address, "221B," has a number value of 2, then Holmes' cozy flat at 221B Baker Street seems to have been the appropriate place to learn the 7 Lesson, for the address adds up to a 7 $(2 + 2 + 1 + 2 = 7)$, and thus his physical home would itself prove to be the instrument for finding his way back to his spiritual home.

Instinct vs. Reason

Two other related numbers are informative in revealing how an individual will act during periods of stress. They are the numbers of the Instinctive Self and the Rational Self.

The Instinctive Self number indicates how an individual will react in a crisis situation. To find this number, start with 9 and subtract your total number of Karmic Lessons from it. So if you had four missing numbers, you would have four Karmic Lessons, and you would subtract 4 from 9, leaving a result of 5.

The Rational Self number suggests the way an individual would approach a problem in ordinary everyday life with time to think matters over, as opposed to a crisis situation in which one would have to act instinctively. To find this number, add up the numbers of the first name only and reduce to a root number. Then, take the Birth number—that is the *day* of birth—which has also been reduced to a root number, and add them together. If the result is a compound number, reduce to a root.

The numbers in the Instinctive Self Table apply to the result when the number of Karmic Lessons has been subtracted from 9. If, for example, you have three Karmic Lessons, the number 6 is the one that would apply (9 − 3 = 6). A person should have no more than six Karmic Lessons so we begin with the number 3.

Table of the Instinctive Self

3 (Six Karmic Lessons)

It would be unusual to find a person carrying this heavy a load of Karmic Lessons. Such people would be almost totally unorganized, and much of the time would be at odds with themselves and the world.

4 (Five Karmic Lessons)

This would be a Molehill type, for he or she would be a stickler for details of the most inconsequential kind. The litany of life would be, "Of all sad words of tongue or pen, the saddest are these—it might have been," for he or she would be forever riding off in sixteen directions at once and getting nowhere.

5 (Four Karmic Lessons)

A restless individual and a scatterbrain. He or she would live for pleasure—particularly the fleshly variety, but often would be unable to enjoy anything because of a bad case of nerves.

6 (Three Karmic Lessons)

A highly responsible individual and one whose first concern would be for family and friends. The home would be the castle.

7 (Two Karmic Lessons)

This person would require solitude. Opiates—in the form of religion, philosophy or the real thing—would form the central part of this person's life.

8 (One Karmic Lesson)

This person would be "Captain Cool," and could always be counted upon to remain a pillar of strength. Would have considerable respect for authority and anything representing the power structure.

9 (No Karmic Lessons)

A rather blasé individual. Many things do entice, but few can hold. Much of the time, life for this person is a bloody bore.

The numbers in the following table represent the result of the first name number and day of birth added together and reduced to a root number.

Table of Rational Self

1

"I am in control of my fate; I am the captain of my soul," would be this individual's credo.

2

This would be a "turner" and a "leaner": He or she would always be turning to others for help, and often leaning on them.

3

Such a person would be highly creative in meeting life situations. Often, he or she would depend on a smile for protection.

4

"Don't bother me, can't you see I've got *work* to do!," is the way this person escapes.

5

Change is the operative word for this individual. He or she will change jobs, careers, and mates as often as he or she changes underwear.

6

Very keen on meeting responsibilities. Would often solve problems by calling the family together and holding a "council of peace."

7

This person always goes to the self for answers. A highly meditative individual. Finds solace in drugs.

8

"Papa and mama know best," is this individual's response. Would always approach things from a material or legalistic viewpoint.

9

This person would be something of a knight errant and would have a kind heart.

How did the Sherlock Holmes of a crisis differ from the everyday Sherlock Holmes? We have learned that in order to find the Instinctive Self we subtract the number of Karmic Lessons from the number 9. As he has only one Karmic Lesson, Holmes' Instinctive Self would be an 8 $(9 - 1 = 8)$. We see that he would be "Captain Cool" in a crisis, the one others look to as a tower of strength. In her seminal work on numerology, Florence Campbell says the number 8 type will handle emergency situations with a cold and calculating mind and manner. She also says the number 8 type will have the solution to the problem at hand and will set all those hanging about to work on that solution.

Hmmmmm. Wonder if Florence Campbell had our friend, Sherlock Holmes in mind?

It was said that the Rational Self number was found by adding together the reduced digits of the first name and birth numbers. The number value of "Sherlock" reduces to another 1, which gives him a Rational Self number of 7 $(1 + 6 = 7)$. This is the person given over to meditation and/or drugs, and we know that Sherlock Holmes arrived at many of his deductions in his study at 221B Baker Street. Solitary and silent, he would piece things together over a pipeful of shag tobacco—although a difficult case would be a "three-pipe problem." And of course, when things were really taxing, there was always the seven percent solution, but that was usually an escape from boredom.

There are several strong numbers at play in the chart of Sherlock Holmes, but the one that appears to predominate is 7, for in addition to being his double Destiny number, it is also his Karmic Lesson number and his Rational Self number. Seven is the number of science and investigation, and Sherlock Holmes was to employ the methods of science in making his investigations with Dr. Watson in nighttime London. But 7 is also the number of cosmic concern and one would like to believe that the mundane investigations that he carried out were but a prelude to a full-scale investigation of the one great mystery.

Failure to cope successfully with Karmic Lessons or life Challenges may often affect one's health. Also, some of our afflictions are karmic in origin due to "overspending" in the time before. Here, as in other areas of life, self-knowledge is an invaluable aid in recognizing and dealing with our strengths and limitations. Health problems that have a karmic basis can often be alleviated by "settling our debts."

The Spread: Wheel of Health

This spread deals with the parts of the body associated with the numbers 1–9, which are as follows:

    1—Head
    2—Kidneys, stomach
    3—Throat, lungs
    4—Circulatory system
    5—Genitalia
    6—Heart, back
    7—Breast, solar plexus, glands
    8—Nervous system
    9—Overall physical and mental health

Cards are laid out in the manner of a directional compass:

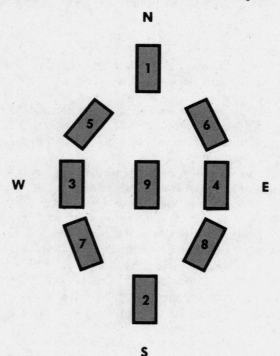

After laying out nine cards as indicated by the diagram, repeat the process twice more until there are three cards down in each pile, twenty-seven in all.

Beginning with the #1–North pile, the three cards are turned over and interpreted intuitively. By and large, negative cards such as the suit of Swords, The Devil, The Moon or The Lightning-Struck Tower would indicate accident or affliction while positive cards would suggest few or minor problems in a particular area of the body.

If a card from either the Major or Minor Arcana has the same number as its pile, it would be significant. For example, should the 7 of Swords appear in the #7–SW pile, it would suggest that the person was on the verge of a nervous breakdown, while the seventh card of the Major Arcana, The Chariot, would indicate that the problem had been overcome.

The three cards in the center are indicator cards for the overall state of one's physical and mental health at the time of the reading. If problem cards appear in a pile corresponding to a part of the body where there has previously been no problem, a trend would be indicated, but as is the case with most Tarot spreads, *a trend only, not a certainty*. Essentially, the consultant is being warned to guard his or her health in that region of the body and to take whatever measures may be dictated so as to offset the trend.

The Tape:

> 1—6 of Cups, The Star, Page of Wands
> 2—Ace of Cups (reversed), 10 of Coins, 9 of Coins
> 3—Page of Swords, King of Swords, 5 of Swords
> 4—Page of Cups, 6 of Swords, 5 of Wands
> 5—Knight of Wands, 8 of Coins, 9 of Cups
> 6—Queen of Coins, 4 of Wands, Day of Judgment
> 7—6 of Wands, 10 of Swords, 8 of Cups
> 8—Queen of Cups, 4 of Swords, Knight of Swords
> 9—The Lightning-Struck Tower, The Angel of Time, The World

The consultant is a widow with a teen-aged son and a married daughter in her twenties.

SK: This spread is pretty much a general picture of your health as it is now but it also gets into afflictions or illnesses past or future. The cards in the #1 slot have to do with the head. They will tell us quite literally where your head is at. As two of the cards are the Page of Wands and the 6 of Cups, the Tarot seems to be saying that you have recently had to face an emotional decision concerning one of your children. Is that true?

Consultant: That would be my son. I think I mentioned to you that he is retarded and this fall he is starting in a new school and I am rather concerned about it.

SK: This is certainly understandable. The center card here is The Star, which suggests that you are basically optimistic about his progress. Taking all three cards into consideration, the implication is that excessive concern about your son could affect your own health. The Court Cards, as they are known, are "the people" cards and if any of them appear in a health spread, they are in some vital way connected with the person's physical and psychological well-being. Because The Star is so affirmative, I would say that, in general, your mental or emotional health is pretty good, but if you do get occasional headaches, they probably are rooted in worry about your son.

Consultant: I have had some rather severe headaches but somehow I never connected them with my son.

SK: As I said before, I don't think this is a serious health problem for you because you are basically very positive, but I think it is important to keep in mind that worry over your son's mental health can affect your own mental health.

The #2 cards have to do with the kidneys and stomach and here you have the Ace of Cups reversed, and the 10 and 9 of Coins. Do you have digestive problems?

Consultant: Not serious, but on occasion I do.

SK: Since you are a Virgo, that sort of goes with the territory for I think you know that each sign of the zodiac is said to govern a particular area of the body and although a person may enjoy perfect health throughout life, it is the "zodiac sign area" that is the plane of vulnerability. The potential for affliction is always there and stress particularly can bring about problems in that area. One example of this would be Nixon. In the early part of his presidency he liked to boast that he was never sick, but after Watergate flooded the Oval Office he began to suffer knee problems. Needless to say, this area is governed by his sign, which is Capricorn.

But as far as you are concerned, these "stomach cards" appear to be saying much the same thing as the "head cards." For the reversed Ace of Cups seems to deal with an emotional relationship that is in some way upside down. I see the 9 and 10 of coins as "emotional money." The 9 is expenditure, but the 10 is receiving. The 10 of Coins I call The Wall Street Card. As it is the center card, it seems to be echoing the good news of The Star, in the first slot, and the conviction that things are going to work out as far as your son is concerned. Therefore, your health—at least, in that area of the body—is going to be okay too.

Consultant: I certainly hope that is true about my son, although I realize, of course, that there are limits to what can be achieved.

SK: The next area has to do with the throat and lungs. I know you are a heavy smoker so this could be a problem area.

Consultant: Is that what the cards say?

SK: Pretty much. But what the Tarot is suggesting is that any problems that become manifest would be caused more by people than tobacco. Cigarettes could be a contributing factor but there are two people here—the Page and King of Swords—who could be the root of any problems in this area. You have a daughter who is married to an older man?

Consultant: Yes, that's right.

SK: That's what the cards tell me: The Page of Swords is your daughter and the King of Swords is her husband. But as the King is the center card, he seems to be the real problem.

Consultant: I am not overly happy with the way their marriage is going.

SK: Well, along with the King and Page of Swords is the 5 of Swords. And the 5 of Swords says, "Yes, there are problems, but don't worry, matters are in control of the Spirit Guides."

Consultant: I hope that's right because I don't feel there is anything much I can do to help them resolve their problems.

SK: I am afraid that is why they appear in your health spread. For if you felt there was something you could do you would probably do it. And whether you succeeeded or failed, it would be less important—from the standpoint of your health, at least—than the fact that you were able to take positive action.

Consultant: My daughter's marriage is similar to the problem of my son in that I have done everything I can do and now have to wait upon events.

SK: The next area taken up by the spread is the circulatory system and this is also, potentially at least, a matter of concern. The center card here is a warning card, the 6 of Swords. I see the 6 of Swords as related to the 6 of Cups that turned up before. There was an emotional decision to make concerning a loved one, namely your son, and in this case, the 6 of Swords is next to the Page of Cups, which I see again as your son.

But so far, at least, for each slot, you always manage to get a "saving card" and in this case it is the 5 of Wands. In the Tarot 5 is the number of spiritual fulfillment and I think this card may provide the key to the whole spread and why your health is, on the whole, fairly good. You are a creative artist—and a very fine one—and your answer to stress is to do some beautiful things with water color and oils.

Consultant: When I go to my studio, the outside world ceases to exist for me.

SK: From a health standpoint, that's a very sensible way to handle it.

The next set of cards deals with the genitalia, and this appears to be yet another potential problem for here the center card is the 8 of Coins, which I again see as emotional money, and there is some kind of imbalance somewhere that would seem to reiterate what was said earlier about your son and daughter. The 9 of Cups is known as The Wish Card, which suggests that you wanted the children very much but then your disappointment may have been all the greater in view of what happened.

Consultant: Who is this man on horseback?

SK: Actually, that is not a man, it is a card of thought—in this case, thoughts about what you do creatively. It is similar to that card in the last slot, the 5 of Wands, and once again the Tarot is saying that work is your savior.

Consultant: It does help me to retain my sanity.

SK: The heart and back are our next areas for study, and they appear to be areas that are problem-free. The Day of Judgment suggests that you are about to take an important step. I imagine it is related to your work, for the center card is the 4 of Wands. There is apparently a woman involved, namely the Queen of Coins, who is very much a business type. Are you in the process of getting up a show?

Consultant: No, but what I am thinking about is changing galleries and I am dealing with a woman on that.

SK: Well, that looks good then, for the 4 of Wands says that it will prove financially rewarding. In any case, I don't think you need worry about having a heart attack.

Consultant: That seems to be about the only thing I don't have to worry about.

SK: You needn't worry about your heart, but you shouldn't worry about the other things because worry will only make things worse.

Consultant: The Tarot has said that repeatedly, hasn't it?

SK: I'm afraid it has. So this is more than a word to the wise. Although, in the realm of emotions, I don't know how many of us can remain wise for very long.

Now the next region of the body we are going to take up is the solar plexus, which is also under the governship of Virgo. We will probably get much the same reading as we did with the slot dealing with the digestive system.

Consultant: You mean you are going to give me some more bad news?

SK: Actually none of the news has been totally bad. Most of it, in fact, has been on a cautionary note, and you have always managed to come up with a positive card in each slot that acts as a counterweight to any negative influence. Yes, the Tarot is coming in on cue for we have here the 6 of Wands, 8 of Cups and the center card is the 10 of Swords.

Consultant: That doesn't look very good at all!

SK: Well, we didn't expect it to. There is a difference here though. We saw before that this area of vulnerability related to your Sun sign was intensified by concern over your children. Here, the combination of the 8 of Cups and 10 of Swords indicates a feeling of loneliness following the death of your husband.

Consultant: It was a blow I haven't really gotten over.

SK: But once again, what saves you is work. And the 6 of Wands is a very specific card, for it deals with the arts. The implication here is that after you lost your husband, you became married to your work.

Consultant: That's quite true. Before my husband's death, I was more or less of a Sunday painter, but now, as you know, I do it full time.

SK: The nervous system is what we are going to look at next. The cards here are the Queen of Cups, Knight of Swords, and the 4 of Swords in the center. Well, nerves are a problem for most people, so don't worry, you have plenty of company. In your case, any problems you have with nerves seem to be rooted in the past for these appear to be mainly memory cards. The Knight of Swords suggests unhappy thoughts about the loss of your husband, and since the Queen of Cups is usually a happily married woman, that card, too, is commenting on the loss. The center card—the 4 of Swords—seems very specific in this case for it shows a man who appears to be lying on a coffin, namely your late husband.

Now, we are going to look at the indicator cards, and it is possible they will offer some fresh insights. They do, in fact, for they are The Lightning-Struck Tower, The Angel of Time and The World. I would interpret these in order of appearance: The Tower card suggests that you're still picking up the pieces of your past in regard to your husband and children. The current family problems, in fact, have given you considerable anxiety, and it is this, more than anything else, that is tied in with any health problems you now have or may come down with in the future.

But the all-important center card is The Angel of Time, which in the Tarot is the card that follows the card of Death, but it is a card of regeneration and happiness.

And then, the last card in this spread is also the last numbered card in the Major Arcana—it is the card of The World and this dancing woman seems to be the very embodiment of unity and joy.

Consultant: Those last three cards were most interesting. What the Tarot really seems to be saying is that when I manage to change my feelings and thoughts, my health will be affected for the better.

SK: Exactly, that is a very astute analysis.

Consultant: The Tarot then has a strong psychosomatic orientation?

SK: And I suspect, for good reasons. I read that 75 percent of all people who go to doctors for treatment for this, that, or the other, are suffering from psychosomatic ailments. But I suspect that is a conservative estimate. It is probably closer to 90 percent.

Consultant: You mean, that it's all in their minds?

SK: Not that, exactly. Of course, a lot of people go to doctors with imaginary complaints. But I think that the overwhelming majority of the people who habitually seek medical help have afflictions, diseases, illnesses or whatever that are only too real. The point is that they were brought about by their own thinking.

You know, I'm reminded of Edgar Cayce and the very accurate health "readings" that he did for people. As you know, I'm sure, Cayce had no medical knowledge himself, and everything he learned about a patient was through clairvoyance, which interestingly enough means "clear seeing." And over and over again, he would tell the person that he or she brought on the affliction through his or her own thoughts and actions.

And of all the words that Cayce uttered in his productive lifetime, perhaps the ones that offer the most profound insight into living a healthier—and therefore, happier—life, are these three words: "Thoughts are things!"

Consultant: Thank you so much. I am definitely going to remember that.

SK: I am sure you will for the final card in your health spread is The World. I think the Tarot is saying that if you succeed in changing your thoughts you will gain the world.

---

[1]Gina Cerminara, *Many Mansions*, New American Library, 1967, p. 47.

5

What's in a Name?: The Rose

"What's in a name?" asked Shakespeare, "That which we call a rose, by any other name would smell as sweet."

Most intelligent men and women would agree. And it is just possible that Shakespeare and most intelligent men and women would be wrong.

Speaking of roses smelling as sweet by another name, consider Cary Grant. Would he have smelt as sweet to his adoring fans for close to half a century as "Archibald Leach"? That is the name with which he started, but it seems doubtful that "Archibald Leach" would have had the staying power of "Cary Grant."

Names are the every essence of numerology, and they provide, in effect, an index of the personality. That they do is beyond dispute and can be easily demonstrated. Why they do is a large question and cannot be easily answered. But as stated earlier, if the universe has purpose, and the individual life shares in that purpose, there must be some way of learning what it is.

Perhaps the astrologer Marc Edmund Jones hit paydirt when he made the statement, "Man is not what he is because he was born when he was, but he was born when he was because he was, potentially, what he is."[1] Looked at from this approach, a name is a counterpart to the horoscope: Both offer a means for reading the cosmic plan of an individual life. In one instance, the cosmic light sheds its rays in the language of planets, and in the other, the language of numbers.

For many who have been exposed to the scientific tenets of our society, this concept eludes easy capture. "But a name is purely the expression of parental whim," someone will reply, "so numerology is obviously ridiculous!"

First of all, something is obviously ridiculous only if it can be demonstrated to be false. Quite to the contrary, numerology over the centuries has proved to be astonishingly accurate. And it is no deep dark mystery; anyone who has taken the time to make the acquaintance of the basic principles of numerology can demonstrate it anywhere, any place, at any time.

And, in fact, one can have a certain amount of fun doing it. Next time you are gathered socially and the conversation has attained a new level of mediocrity, you might liven things up a bit by dropping The Numerology Bomb: Simply point out that each person vibrates to certain numbers and that this is determined by both the time of birth and the name.

At this point heads will begin to turn and people will be studying you with an uncertain air. They will be wondering if you are making sport of them or if they should give some thought to calling in the little men with white jackets. After some verbal give and take, you commence to set up your opponents by making the flat statement, "According to the laws of numerology, your name is the key to your character, personality and destiny."

At this point, the more condescending will give you a look usually reserved for those suffering from extreme fatuity and say something to this effect: "How can an intelligent person like you believe in this sort of rot?" The less refined types will be somewhat more caustic in their approach and will offer a blatant version of the horse laugh.

After you have been unmercifully assailed for some moments, you must then pretend to overplay your hand and say that you can make a basic character assessment of a person you do not know and have never met, based on an analysis of *the first name alone*. All that the skeptic needs to do is to provide you with the first name of a person known to him or her but not to you. Or, it could be the first name of a celebrity or historical personage, famous or infamous.

You will, of course, be challenged on this "reckless" proposal, and so when someone swallows your bait—possibly being foolish enough to place a small wager on the enterprise—you then proceed to deliver the goods, which to the uninitiated will seem absolute sorcery.

To the numerologist, however, it merely represents the following of certain basic principles. The major points of analysis of the first name are the "three bricks": Cornerstone, Keystone and Capstone. These are considered along with the Opening Vowel and what is known as the Core. As always, the numbers of the name will have the attributes associated with them, but each letter has a special meaning of its own, as does the Opening Vowel. In fact, the Opening Vowel is so important that you could almost base your analysis on that alone and win your bet. Before going any further we need to know more about the vowels and also the letters of the alphabet.

Two tables follow, and once again, the Tarodic and astrological associations have been included for added insight into the letters:

Table of Opening Vowels

A

Number—1   Sign—Aries
Tarot—The Magician   Planet—The Sun

A person with a first vowel of "A," such as Barbara, will be, in some way, a pioneer, an innovator, an original. This will be an assertive individual, highly creative, with a keen mind, but may be somewhat dogmatic. This is a person who will have a way with words and will communicate naturally and easily.

E

Number—5   Sign—Leo
Tarot—The Hierophant   Planet—Mercury

The People with "E" as a starting vowel, such as Ted, like to experience life fully and directly. Change is their life style and variety is their middle name. This might be called "the physical E," for its numeric value is the number of the five senses.

Freedom is the important thing. For this reason, marriage is not always successful. Due to the association with The Hierophant, there is often a heady mix of the spiritual and sensual.

I

Number—9   Sign—Sagittarius
Tarot—The Hermit   Planet—Uranus, Mars

Intense emotion is the hallmark of the "I" person. He or she tends to have a broad, humanitarian outlook, but can also be extremely selfish. As 9 is the apex of the power numbers, essentially what the "I" person wants is power—power over people. But power, like electricity, can be used for good or ill. However, this individual usually will have the universal outlook and desire power in order to build utopias.

The people with a leading "I" for an Opening Vowel, such as Michael, are extemely intense, but like The Hermit, they may go into seclusion and hoard their resources, or they may let their light be a beacon to others.

O

Number—6   Sign—Virgo
Tarot—The Lovers   Planet—Venus

Virgo, the sixth sign of the zodiac, is a sign of service, while 6 is a number of responsibility. Both of these traits are reflected in the person with an Opening Vowel of "O." As the letter "O" is enclosed, this person tends to be somewhat reticent and self-effacing. In Arcanum VI of the Major Arcana, a man is about to receive inspiration from his guardian angel in making a decision. And while "the leading O" does not carry a bow and arrow, he does like to give advice.

This person spends much time in the home, likes fine things and strives to keep everything harmonious.

Above all, "O" is a teacher in the broadest sense of the word, and in this regard, Socrates may be seen as the prime example.

U

Number—3   Sign—Gemini
Tarot—The Empress   Planet—Jupiter

"Sweet *Sue*" might be said to typify "U" people. For the most part, they are easygoing, charming, affable. The Empress is associated with Venus, ruler of love, beauty and harmony, and so there is usually a touch of class about "U's." They tend to be good raconteurs and sparkling conversationalists. But there is another side to their nature, and they can be quite secretive and use conversation as a form of concealment. They have strange and vivid dreams.

The number 3 and The Empress both represent creativity and this is the touchstone of a "U." *J*ulius Caesar, who, in addition to being a warrior and ruler, was a writer as well would be an example.

Y

Number—7   Sign—Libra
Tarot—The Chariot   Planet—Mercury, Negative Moon

Numerologists are not in accord over using Y as a vowel. Some will employ it in this capacity, but only under certain specific conditions. In a name such as C*y*, you either count it as the opening vowel or there is none. If it makes sense to use it as an opening vowel at all, it is reasonable to be consistent about it.

In Arcanum VII of the Tarot, The Charioteer has his hands full reconciling opposing forces. This is further reinforced by the association with Libra, the sign of the balance. What "Y" people, such as M*y*ron, have to balance is suggested by the planetary influences of Mercury (mentality) and the Negative Moon (emotional turmoil). There tends to be a division between the mind and the emotions; this is further complicated by the fact that the emotions are waging a little war of their own.

These individuals tend to represent the secrecy of 7 and are highly introspective. Often moody, they are usually able to keep secrets for they do not like to divulge any more information than is necessary. They are often brainy types who can think a problem through and get to the bottom of things.

Table of Letters

A —1 (The Magician): Forceful and direct.

B —2 (The High Priestess): A prisoner of the emotions.

C —3 (The Empress): Radiates Joy and Creativity.

D —4 (The Emperor): Efficient and practical, but sometimes overly conservative.

E —5 (The Hierophant): Both sensual and spiritual.

F —6 (The Lovers): Self-doubts, uncertainty.

G —7 (The Chariot): Life presents many challenges to this introspective individual.

H —8 (Justice, see note on page 28): Attempt to balance between material and spiritual.

I —9 (The Hermit): The light of inspiration is there but on occasion it may be concealed.

J —1 (Wheel of Fortune, The Magician): Inclined to leadership, but tends to go around in circles.

K —1½ (Strength, see note on page 28; The High Priestess): Uses talents to aid the community or nation.

L —3 (The Hanged Man, The Empress): Often associated with sacrifice or reversals.

M —4 (The Reaper, The Emperor): Efficient with regard to bringing about physical change.

N —5 (The Angel of Time, The Hierophant): Outgoing.

O —6 (The Devil, The Lovers): Brooding and secretive.

P —7 (The Lightning-Struck Tower, The Chariot): Introspective but strongly power-oriented.

Q —8 (The Star, Justice, see note on page 28): A powerful vibration that can be either inspiring or destructive.

R —9 (The Moon, The Hermit): Great understanding and desire for world betterment.

S —1 (The Sun, The Wheel of Fortune, The Magician): The will is all-powerful.

T —2 (Day of Judgment, The High Priestess): Highly spiritual.

U —3 (The World, The Empress): Self-contained.

V —2¾ (The Fool, The Emperor): The mark of the Master.

W —5 (The Hierophant): Well-meaning but
unorganized.

X —6 (The Lovers): Heavy burdens must be borne.

Y —7 (The Chariot): As the shape of the letter
suggests, there is a parting of the ways—the right-
hand path leads to God, the left-hand path to
more material pursuits.

Z —8 (Justice, see note on page 28): Understanding
and love of all Life.

As mentioned previously, the points of analysis for using the Tables are
known as the Three Bricks—Cornerstone, Keystone and Capstone—along
with the Opening Vowel and Core. They are found as follows:

CORNERSTONE—This has been taken up elsewhere; it is the first letter
of the first name by which the person is known.

OPENING VOWEL—Consult the Table. This often provides the key clue
to the personality.

KEYSTONE—This will apply only when a name has an odd number of
letters, in which case it will be the middle letter. For example, the name,
"Oscar" has five letters, so the Keystone would be "C."

CAPSTONE—As the Cornerstone is the first letter of the first name, the
Capstone is the last.

CORE—This is the sum of all the letters in the first name added together
and then reduced to a root digit.

Casebook—Rasputin and the Numbers of God, Flesh and the Devil

We have everything we need to know for our high-wire stunt. Let us now
put it to the test. You are at a dinner party, have made your offer, and
someone has been foolish enough to take you up on it. The challengers
huddle in a corner of the room, come back smiling, and tell you they have
chosen an historical figure whose first name is "Gregory." What they do not
tell you is that the last name is "Rasputin," but as we shall see, the first name
of "Gregory" will be quite sufficient for the task at hand. One note here. We
use Gregory rather than Grigori because we are working in English. To get a
true reading we would have to use the Cyrillic alphabet. When working in
English, we use the Anglicized version of the name. Your fellow party-goers
must give you that version.

Re-examining the quintet of methods we have employed, we see a
distinct pattern emerging. There are but two numbers—7 and 5—the 7
appearing three times, the 5 twice. The very fact that there are three 7s
suggests the Holy Trinity and someone who is highly religious. But the
brace of physical 5s indicates a strong pull toward fleshly gratification. The
repetition of both 7 and 5 suggests a division between the spiritual and the

sensual. In fact, the split between the sensual and spiritual is really built into both numbers to begin with, so the 7/5 emphasis only intensifies this conflict. And as both numbers are associated with drugs, we get a picture of a man who will be influenced by negative forces or harmful addictions.

The spiritual-sensual division is further reinforced by the "parting of the ways Y" as the Capstone. We point all this out in our analysis, concluding with the deduction that this was a man who was probably a spiritual leader of some sort, but one who privately—or not so privately—was very much prone to drugs and other pleasures of the flesh.

The five-point analysis we have employed is not some kind of trick—although it may appear so to the uninformed—but merely a means of extracting the meat of a chart. In much the manner that an astrologer can hit upon the essentials of an astrological chart by knowing the sign and house positions of the Sun, Moon and Ascendant, the numerologist can make an extrapolation, using key letters in a name.

This is not to imply that everyone in the world who is known as "Gregory" is going to be a tippler and a woman chaser. What a name indicates is *potential*. In Rasputin's case, his first name pinpointed the basic conflict of his life between the physical and the spiritual. How each individual handles this conflict will depend on other factors in the chart, the genetic makeup and particularly the way in which that individual exercises free will: What is most profound about our lives are not the challenges we must face, but rather our manner of meeting them.

Whether charts are astrological or numeric, they tend to be all of a piece. From the moment of his birth, people knew that Gregory Rasputin was to be no ordinary individual for in the words of his daughter, Maria, "On the night of January 23, 1871, a great meteor burned its flaming path across the sable skies of western Siberia. A 'shooting star' of such magnitude had always been taken by the God-fearing *muzhiks* as an omen of some momentous event. And although they were not aware of it, a momentous event had indeed occurred. The arcing path of the meteor turned downward over the little village of Pokrovskoye; but before it could come to earth, the last of its substance was burned away; and at that very moment; a seven-pound boy was delivered by Anna Egorovna, the wife of Efim Akovlevich Rasputin."[2]

Note that Rasputin was a *seven*-pound baby born on a "5 day" (2 + 3 = 5); the numbers of God and man appeared at the beginning.

There was a further division in Rasputin's Persona numbers for his Birth number was a 5 (January 23), while his Expression number was a 6 (see chart). If anything would make for a split personality it would be these two numbers on the Persona, for 5 is the number of adventure and romance; 6 is the number of home and responsibility. This was re-echoed in his numbers of Destiny for he had a 5 Path opposing a 6 Goal. His Inner Self was equally torn between a stay-at-home 6 and a global 9. He was unquestionably a man of sorrows and divisions.

But from the standpoint of numerology, what is significant is that the first name alone provided an accurate insight into the chart as a whole. Later, when we looked at the full name and birth data, we gained additional details about Rasputin's life, but the basic structure provided by the first name alone remained unaltered: He was condemned to walk the face of the earth forever torn between the ways of the flesh and the Way of the spirit.

```
        5    6              1     3    9          24 = 6
     G  R  E  G  O  R  Y    R  A  S  P  U  T  I  N
     7  9     7     9  7    9  1  7     2     5    63 = 9
                                                  87 = 15 = 6
```

1½ Roof   9/6 Inner Self   5/6 Persona   6/5 Destiny

Casebook—The Detective and the Doctor

You have completed your feat of unravelling the complex mystery that was Rasputin, but some of your adversaries remain unconvinced. They intone the cries of the superstitious: "Fluke." "Lucky guess." Or to those totally prejudiced, the most descriptive epithet of all—"coincidence."

But you are spoiling for fresh conquests and proceed to go yourself one better. "This time," you say, "give me the first name of not one, but *two* people, past or present, who were in some way associated, and in addition to describing the character of each, I will tell you whether or not the relationship was one where the parties were more or less equal, or if not, who was Number One and who was Number Two."

Again, your enemies caucus and this time give you the names of "John and Sherlock." Having a penchant for the deductive, it does not escape you totally that "John and Sherlock" could of course refer to the doctor–detective team of Dr. John Watson and Mr. Sherlock Holmes. But they may very well have some other pair in mind, for there are of course other Johns in the world, and even possibly, other Sherlocks. And in any case, why resort to guesswork when you have something approaching scientific accuracy at your disposal.

You take the two names—"John and Sherlock"—and proceed to match them for each of the five points of first-name analysis. Starting with the Cornerstone you note that "Sherlock" has a Cornerstone of 1 (S = 1), the sign of leadership. But don't jump to conclusions just yet, for in examining "John" you see that this also is a 1 Cornerstone (J = 1).

At this point the score is tied 1—1. But you do make a mental note of the fact that while the Cornerstone numbers are the same, they are of a different quality for you bring to mind that the "S" represents an all-powerful will, while the "J" may be "inclined to leadership, but tends to go around in circles." So both letters have a number value of 1, but the "S," associated as it is with the Sun, is stronger than the disorganized "J."

Moving over to the Opening Vowel, you see that "Sherlock" has the forceful fiery "E," the letter of experience and action, whereas "John" has the reticent "O," the counsellor rather than the general. This would give "Sherlock" another edge over "John."

Neither name has a Keystone so we go to the Capstone and discover that "John" ends on a vibrant note of 5 (N = 5), but nevertheless has to check to power, for "Sherlock" exits with the Master Number 11 (K = 11). And, according to our Table, "N" may be "outgoing," but "K uses talents to aid community or nation."

It is when we arrive at the Core number, however, that it clearly becomes no contest: For "Sherlock" it is the executive 1 (46 = 10 = 1), while "John" is the subservient 2 (20 = 2). Your analysis then would be that "John" may have possessed some leadership ability (J = 1), but unlike the stong-willed and Sun-driven power of "S" (Cornerstone of "Sherlock"), his "J" Cornerstone would make for erratic or indecisive leadership. Along with his wordy "O," the 1 would probably pertain more to literature than leadership. Quite clearly, "John" is the junior member of this partnership for "Sherlock" has both a Cornerstone and Core number of 1 and a Master Number 11 (two more 1s!) for a Capstone.

It was stated before that charts tend to be all of a piece and should we wish to test this hypothesis with the two gentlemen in question, we note that the full-name number for Sherlock Holmes is 73, which reduces to the Special Number 10, and once again to a 1, whereas the total for "John Watson" is 40, which reduces to 4. In addition, Watson has a Soul Urge of 4 as opposed to Holmes' Master Number, 22. Holmes is clearly in command all the way.

One small puzzle that this investigation has helped to clear up is why Holmes and Watson were associated in the first place. The answer lies in the Expression number: Holmes has a 1 as opposed to Watson's 4. When we recall that the numbers 1 and 4 are of the same family—the House of the Sun—it is clear that there would be an attraction, but since 4 is the negative Sun, the individual bearing that number would play a subordinate role in any kind of 1/4 relationship. To the forceful 1, the humble 4 has a kind of homey-old-shoe comfort about it, and Watson seems to have filled the bill nicely as he had 4s to spare.

Casebook—Shakespeare by Another Name?

In closing this chapter of *What's in a Name?*, it seems only fitting that we return to the originator of that question, for a forceful counter-argument is offered by the Immortal Bard himself in his own name. As he is one of the very few people in the history of the world to be known by a single name, we shall use that for our analysis:

```
     1    5        5   1    5      17
  S  H  A  K  E  S  P  E  A  R  E
  1  8    11     1  7        9      37
                                    ——
                                    54 = 9
```

The first item that catches our eye is that Cornerstone of 1—the number of leadership and literature.

Then the Opening Vowel is the "Executive A-1," indicating originality, creativity, a person who "will have a way with words."

Also of note is the Secret Passion, that is, the number most often repeated in the name, which is again, 1. The Keystone is also a 1, as is the Psyche number in the Inner Self department of the chart. The chart is also rich in 5s—there are three of them, including the Capstone—and the Expression is a 9. Here then is a man who will be a leader in literature; it will be the literature of experience and it will appeal to all of humanity. And since Shakespeare was born on April 23, his final Destiny number, his Goal, is also 9 (4 + 5 = 9), the number of what would have been called the "Universal Man" in Shakespeare's time.

With a starting number of 1 and an ending number of 9, the message is complete: A new sun will arise in the world of letters, and somehow, this individual's life and career will encompass the whole spectrum of human experience.

The Spread: You and Your Name

For this spread, use the name that appears on your chart, that is, *the name by which you are known.* Keep the chart on the table in front of you as a reference when laying the cards. On the chart, of course, the number value of each letter of your name will have been worked out.

After the cards have been cut and shuffled, start from the top, count down to the number value of the first letter of your first name and place that card on the table. As you are simulating your name with the cards, you will eventually have two or more horizontal rows. After the first card has been laid, count down to the number value of the second letter of your first name and place that card to the right of the first card (this spread goes from left to right) and continue this process until you have accounted for all the letters in your first name. If your name were "Zeke," for example, this is how it would work: You would begin by counting down eight cards (Z = 8) and place the eighth card as the beginning card of the top horizontal row. You would then count down five cards (E = 5) and place that card to the right of the first card you laid on the table. Then, the eleventh card after that (K = 11), and then the fifth card from that point (E = 5). The top horizontal row has been completed and represents your first name.

Using the same method for the rest of your name, continue counting from where you left off in the deck and lay another row under the first until you have placed a card corresponding to the number value of each letter of that name. Keep going until you have a row of cards for each letter of the first, middle and last name. Should you go through the entire deck, merely start over in order to conclude your name. For example, if your last name is "Blossom," and on reaching the final "O" the third card is the last one in the deck, you then count three more from the top (O = 6), and four more for the last letter (M = 4) so as to complete your name.

Read this spread by starting with the top row corresponding to your first name, and then your other names in order.

This is essentially a depiction of your life as revealed by your name.

Your first name will deal with key incidents, people and events in your past; your last name more with the present and future. Any middle names will relate particularly to psychological and emotional concerns.

The key card in this spread will be the one corresponding to your Expression number. If, for example, your Expression is a 5, then the fifth card that you turn up—regardless of which name it appears in—will be of particular significance.

The Tape:

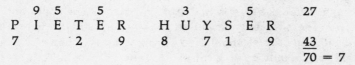

```
     9  5    5         3         5        27
     P  I  E  T  E  R     H  U  Y  S  E  R
     7        2  9        8  7  1     9    43
                                          ──────
                                          70 = 7
```

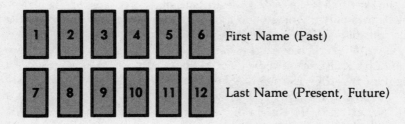

1	2	3	4	5	6	First Name (Past)
7	8	9	10	11	12	Last Name (Present, Future)

1—10 of Cups
2—4 of Swords
3—Knight of Swords
4—Knight of Coins
5—King of Cups
6—The Reaper

7—The Lightning-Struck Tower
8—The Sun
9—Queen of Cups
10—The Star
11—7 of Coins
12—King of Coins

The consultant is a youth in his early twenties, who at the time of the reading was planning to quit his job as a bartender and go to Europe where he hoped to find work.

SK: The cards in the top row represent your first name and should provide us with key incidents and people in your past. The bottom row is your last name and should tell us where your head and feet are now and where they will be in the near future.

But before we get into that I want to turn over the first and seventh cards as you have both a Cornerstone and Expression number of 7. The first card is the 10 of Cups; the seventh is The Lightning-Struck Tower. "Seven" people are usually into either religion or drugs and these cards suggest both: Ten cups is a lot of drink, and those people falling out of the Tower look like they have just heard the call from on high. Have you ever thought of going into the church?

Consultant: Not lately. But I have thought very seriously about it. As far as alcohol is concerned, I have done a lot more than think about it (chuckling). It is not hard to come by when you work as a bartender, but it is hard to get off once the stuff grabs you.

SK: Might say that it comes with the territory. Now starting with the first letter of your name, we go back and look at the 10 of Cups a little differently. There's a man and woman with their arms outstretched and two children dancing. It looks like you had a pretty happy early childhood.

Consultant: The early part was just great. I was a very happy youngster.

SK: Yes, but I don't think that lasted very long for this next card, the 4 of Swords, shows a man lying on a coffin. He appears to be in a church for there is a stained glass window depicting a Biblical scene, and the young man has his hands clasped in an attitude of prayer. As the stained glass panel shows only a woman and a child, the man on the coffin could have been your father. Did he die when you were very young?

Consultant: He might just as well have; he didn't stick around very long.

SK: That also seems to be indicated by the following card, which is the Knight of Swords. The man waving the sword can't seem to get away fast enough.

The next card, the Knight of Coins, shows another man on horseback. But he is holding a coin instead of a sword and I get the impression that he is just a little kid who has to go out and do a man's work and find some more of those coins to help keep the home together.

Consultant: That is certainly true. The funny thing is that this kid is on horseback because I've always been a horse freak.

SK: Well, that seems to be showing up. For of the four cards we've turned over, half of them are horses.

The King of Cups is next and I see that as your "adopted father." He is into the arts, happily married and very warm and affectionate. Do you know who he is?

Consultant: Sure do. That was my music teacher in high school; he was sort of a father-figure to me.

SK: Well, there you are on horseback again, this time as The Reaper. This card is also known as Death, and it seems an appropriate place for the card as it comes in the slot for the last letter of your first name, and so would mark the death of childhood.

Consultant: There seems to be an archbishop or somebody on this card and that could mean death to my thoughts of going into the church.

SK: Right, but don't be too sure. Of the four figures on this card besides The Reaper, the churchman is the only one able to stand on his feet and take a direction of his own choosing.

Consultant: I hadn't looked at it that way. You may be right.

SK: We said before that this card of The Lightning-Struck Tower is particularly important because it represents both your starting point in life (Cornerstone) and the way others see you and the way you see yourself (Expression). We interpreted it before in a religious sense, but now that we are looking at the cards in sequence, it pretty much seems to represent where you are now, for quitting a job and going off to Europe for the first time is more than a little like getting hit by lightning.

But it looks like it's going to work out, for here you are on a horse again, but this time The Sun has come up, and it looks like you're really wallowing in your new-found freedom.

Consultant: I like that card!

SK: It's just about my favorite. For when you can see daylight *and* the Sun, the problems don't seem to be problems any more.

Looks like you're going to have much to be happy about for you seem to have run into a very lovely older woman—a woman who is very open-hearted and generous. She is the Queen of Cups and she is a good person to have in your future.

Consultant: I think I know who she is. It could be a friend of a friend who I'm supposed to meet in Europe.

SK: Is she involved with the arts in any way?

Consultant: Very much so. She's a woman who is supposed to help me make contacts in that area.

SK: I think she is going to be more than just a sparkplug for you as she is a very romantic woman and she is right next to the Sun. The next card we turn over is The Star so it appears that she knows some biggies in the theatre and can do something for you there. Any woman who is right smack in the middle of the solar system and causes the Sun and stars to shine must be very special indeed, and I think she is going to transform the world for you, or at least, the way you look at it.

Consultant: Now, I am beginning to feel much better about running off to Europe.

SK: The next card is the 7 of Coins. somehow, I see this as an American in Paris. Is Paris where you're going to be the whole time abroad?

Consultant: Well, that's where I am starting out. But the kind of work I am interested in doing may take me to another country.

SK: That's what this card suggests. This man is looking at these coins rather wistfully and it looks like he is getting ready to take a trip somewhere so that he can find more of them.

Consultant: It might be Italy because I am thinking of studying art in Rome.

SK: If you do, that should work out rather well for the final card in your last name is the King of Coins. And while the card before showed a young man gazing longingly at a money bush, this somewhat older man is sitting on a throne in what appears to be an Italian garden. He has a large coin in one hand and a sceptre in the other and he appears relaxed and successful. The message here seems to be that after that trip to Rome, you will not only achieve material success, but you will be, in effect, a kingpin in your field.

But on second thought, I am not at all sure that art is all you are going to study in Rome, as that is for many people the spiritual capital of the world. Now, if we go back to the preceding card—the 7 of Coins—you will notice that those seven coins are all inscribed with a star and that card is next to the card of The Star. There is more than a suggestion here of things of the spirit. And let's not forget that 7 is a very important number in your chart and it is also the number of faith and ultimate concerns. That 7 of Coins may be a "money card," but under the influence of the number 7, it is something more. And then too, there is spiritual money as well as money money.

Wait a second, let's go back to that final card, the King of Coins, and look at it again. You know, there are many kinds of royalty, and it is just possible that this man is a prince of the church, or at least, a priest who is at the top of his profession in the minds and hearts of his parishioners.

Who knows, it might even be a pontiff, for the Dutch spelling of your name, "Pieter," doesn't totally disguise the fact that it is "Peter," and wasn't it Simon Peter who received from Jesus "the keys to the kingdom of heaven"?

----

[1]Marc Edmund Jones, *How to Learn Astrology*, Doubleday & Co., Garden City, N.Y., 1971, VI.

[2]Maria Rasputin and Pattie Barham, *Rasputin—The Man Behind the Myth*, Prentice Hall, Inc., Englewood Cliffs, N.J., 1977, p. 10.

6

To Change or Not to Change: Mechanics of Name Alteration

Before we can talk about name-changing, we first have to reach some agreement as to what a name is. Earlier, we asked the question, "What's in a name?" Now we have to ask the question, "What *is* a name?" You may be thinking at this point, "Purely elementary, my dear Watson," but actually this is one of the more controversial aspects of numerology.

There is one group of numerologists who maintain that your name is the name that appears on the birth certificate. That name, after all, is the name that your parents selected for you. They would argue that this is the name with which your identity was formed and is your true name unless you undergo a transformation of consciousness that leads to a name change. But oftentimes, that birth certificate name will contain two or more middle names that the person may never use or be known by. Sometimes, first or middle names are dropped or added shortly after birth by the parents or guardians, or later on, by friends or by the individual. Sometimes, first or middle names become converted to initials that the person habitually uses. And then too, most people are known by different names, or at least, different variations of their given name, at different stages of life.

The school of numerologists who maintain that the birth certificate name is the one to use in a chart take the position that that is the legal name, and therefore, the "official" name.

But because a name exists somewhere on a yellowing document, why should that be considered an individual's real name if it is never used? When we talk about people being under the numerical vibrations of their name, what do we actually mean? Are not vibrations reinforced by thoughts and sounds? So it stands to reason that a birth name that is never thought about, let alone used, would produce substantially weaker vibrations than one that is strongly in the minds and on the tongues of a number of people on a day-to-day basis. It is not so much the way a person signs checks, or the way a name appears in a yearbook, but rather, it is the name he or she and most of the people in their life actually use and associate with that individual. In sum, *it is the name by which an individual is known.*

People do have the capacity to change and the name by which a person is currently known indicates where he or she is in life. If you are doing a chart for someone else and there is any question about this, erect a chart for both names, and see which is the more accurate. In fact, if you wish to go into greater depth, set up a chart based on the birth certificate name and one on the name by which the person is now known. The first chart will essentially represent the past; the second, the present. It would actually behoove you to set up two or more charts as a matter of course for then your analysis would be based upon greater depth and understanding.

So, yes, we do use the birth certificate name in our chart-making but only as a starting point. In other words, the birth certificate name reveals the original plan; the name by which the person is currently known indicates how the plan has been altered by that person, by others and by the various forces. There are also other occasions when the birth certificate name will be used and these will be taken up in due course.

Blueprint of Destiny

The ancient Greeks believed that "character is fate." The numerologist believes much the same but goes a step further by stating that your character is revealed by your name, and that your name is, in effect, a "blueprint of destiny." But unlike cattle, we are not physically branded. Names can be changed. And by changing our name, do we not change our destiny?

Before we can even attempt to deal with that overpowering question, it should be stated at the outset that there are two distinct schools of thought on this matter among numerologists: The first says that you can change nothing; the other that you can change everything.

They are both right. And they are both wrong.

Let us first examine their arguments and try to decide if one school may be closer to being more right and less wrong. The "You Can Change Nothing School" starts with the premise that the name given to you at birth contains the basic program for your life as determined by the cosmic forces and that you can no more alter that program than you can alter your horoscope.

On the other hand, the "Everything People" feel that since your name is *you*, when you change your name, you become another "you."

The defenses of the "Nothing School" are more easily assailed for the simple and obvious fact is that people *do* change their names. Many do it by marriage. Some do it in a court of law. Most do it easily and naturally by shedding first or middle names, acquiring a title or changing the spelling of their name. For a large number of people, the name is changed for them by other people who give them nicknames or in some way modify the original name. Once this happens, the person has, in effect, a new name and is under somewhat different vibrations than before. Numerology is based on the Law of Vibration, and any change in a name will have to affect the vibrations a person is under. It seems the better part of idiocy to say that this law works sometimes—say, at birth—but not at others. A law is a law because it always works in the same way. When it ceases to do this, it ceases to be a law.

The "Everything School" is more difficult to deal with because it appears to be on the side of the vibrating angels. Each letter of your name does vibrate to a certain number and the cumulative effect of these letters has a great deal to do with your personality, character and destiny. So, if you are unhappy with your Casper Milquetoast personality and unfulfilled destiny, it is nice to feel that you can drive in to a used name dealer and simply trade in your Model-T-of-a-name for a sparkling Stutz Blackhawk VI and zoom off rejuvenated down life's highway.

The basic problem with the "Everything School" is the idea that something such as character can be created anew by merely changing the label. If you have a box of cornflakes, you can place them in a jar marked "Caviar," but they are still going to look and taste like cornflakes. Perhaps what is most superficial in this philosophy is the implied assumption that the universe is without purpose and that the name given to a person at birth has no program, karmic lessons, guidelines—in short, no cosmic plan. It is simply a set of clothes that can be cast off and an entire new wardrobe chosen.

Both of these extremist schools of thought appear to be equally inconclusive. It may be, however, that there exists a middle way.

Let us begin with the assumption that our original name—that is, the name we were given at birth—along with our date of birth, provides the basic cosmic plan for our lives. Let us assume further that it is we ourselves on another plane of existence who have chosen that name along with our corresponding time of birth, not entirely unlike the way someone might program a computer. But since we are humans, much will depend on how we exercise our free will. And being human, we have the choice of forging ahead on our path and reaching our goal in record time with banners flying, or a choice of arriving late after a series of mis-steps, or even a choice of being sidetracked indefinitely.

Take an individual with an 8 Path. This individual must, by the dictates of that path, take authority and power, but there are any number of ways he or she can do that. In much the manner of university students, we plan a course of study in our freshman year, but by the time we have become seniors, that original program may have undergone many alterations, or even been scrapped entirely. In order to fulfill our revised program it becomes necessary to acquire different equipment in the way of books, lab materials, musical instruments and courses.

In the University of Life our name is one of our basic frames of reference. Thus, if a chart indicates that a client might benefit from a name change, the optimum time to do it would be *after* he or she had embarked on a new direction in life and wanted a name that would be in keeping with it. In this sense, the name would be part of the new direction and would help a person who has chosen a different undertaking or career. The important thing here is that in order for name-changing to be effective, it is necessary to do one's homework. Choosing a name with powerful vibrations is dandy, but no miracles are going to drop in your lap simply because you decided to change your name to "Napoleon Gump." (The real Napoleon is one of those individuals who would have been better off leaving his name alone, but that is another story we shall get to shortly.) If you lack the mental equipment, inner resources and drive of a Napoleon, few empires will come your way. So if you would be Lord Admiral of the Ocean Seas, begin by learning what ships and the sea are about and only then, worry about the name. It is as St. Mark wrote: "For the earth bringeth forth fruit of herself; first the blade, then the ear, after that the full corn in the ear."[1]

Who Should Change?

Before any change is contemplated, the entire chart should be taken into consideration. Keep in mind that making a name change of any degree will affect not only one of your Persona numbers, but possibly both numbers of the Inner Self as well. In fact, making a change of so much as a single letter could create an entirely new configuration of Inner Self and Persona numbers.

The first thing to look at in a chart are the two numbers of Persona. Ideally, they should be similar or compatible. If the present Persona numbers are compatible, one should be hesitant to make a change, and if they are similar, any change that altered this natural harmony could be a serious error. You should remember that it is the Birth and Name number that comprise the Persona, and if they are the same, it is the sign of wholeness and integration, for even though they might not represent the ideal "you," they are all of a piece.

If, however, the Birth and Name numbers are incompatible, that is the time to consider making a change. In addition to blending with your Birth number, any name change should also be convivial with your Destiny and Inner Self numbers. Yes, it is true that you will be getting new Inner Self numbers, but will you be getting a new inner self? Where you live at the deepest levels of your being is not going to change at the drop of a number. If, for example, you have conservative Inner Self numbers of 6 and 8, and you effect a name change that replaces those with a "tennis bum 3" and a "party person 5," it simply is not going to work. Those 6 and 8 vibrations have been stamped on your subconscious and like Banquo's ghost, they will come back to haunt you.

The Path should get special consideration. If an individual has a 2, 4 or 6 Path, it would be most unwise to select an Expression number that would better befit Daddy Warbucks, who is, of course, a 1.

If your first name will be affected by the change, other factors to consider are the Cornerstone, Keystone and Capstone. There is also the Core to take into consideration, and most importantly, the Opening Vowel. Once you have ascertained that your new name number will be a good friend to your other Persona number—that is, of course, your Birth number—and at least on speaking terms with your Inner Self and Destiny numbers, you would be wise to set up a chart with the proposed name and match it in every way with the original chart to make sure that more will be gained than lost through making the change. Quite frankly, in many cases there will be more lost than gained, so make sure. Also, if you are making a change, it is best not to rely on initials as most people are not known by them, and they don't really seem to work in numerology.

In making your calculations, you must never lose sight of the Destiny numbers. *These numbers are on your birth path, they cannot be changed.* And in making any change in the chart, you should ask the question, "Will this help or hinder following my Path and attaining my Goal?" If there is any question at all, make no change until you have thought it through or received expert advice on the matter.

Once you have decided upon a change of name, you may or may not wish to go through the courts. What is much more "official" as far as you are concerned is that you fix that name in your thoughts, along with the characteristics of that name—qualities you have already started to develop within yourself.

After you have psychologically and spiritually accepted the change, set up a chart with that name and keep it in a prominent place where it will serve as a daily reminder of the inner and outer changes you are helping to initiate with the altered vibrations.

The next step is to become known by that name to the people in your community. Contact your bank and people you do business with, informing them of the change. More than anything, however, let the people you see regularly—your friends, neighbors, business associates—know you by your new name. Whatever you do, don't keep it a secret! Within a few months, there will be a discernible personality alteration, a change in the way you feel and act, a change in the way you are treated and a general change in your fortunes as the new vibrations take effect and manifest the traits of the individual you have *worked* to become. And do not be too surprised if you find, along with your increased powers, that opportunities also will be increased five-fold, ten-fold or a thousand-fold, for changes that start in inner space are invariably reflected in outer space.

Casebook—Napoleon Drops a Vowel and an Empire

In numerology, the addition or deletion of so much as a single letter in the name can make all the difference. The classic case is Napoleon, who in his opening years of power had continued to use his original signature, "Napoleon Buonaparte." As he grew in power, he decided to slim down his name, if not his waistline, by simply dropping the first vowel of his last name and so signed himself, "Napoleon Bonaparte."

To the superficial observer, a minor change at best. To the numerologist, however, an ominous sign, for the alteration contained the seeds of his ultimate fall from power. His original Expression number was a 7, one of the top numbers of power, and in the Major Arcana of the Tarot, 7 is the card of The Chariot. The Charioteer may be seen as the God of the Sun, and was a good card for Napoleon to identify with, inasmuch as he was a native of Leo, the one sign ruled by the Sun. In the Tarot, 7 is also a number of victory. But in making the change, Napoleon's Expression number became a 4, and while in the Tarot it is the card of The Emperor, in numerology, it can be the number of the born loser!

In calculating the Expression, while the total numeric value of a name is reduced to a root number, the compound number behind it must be kept in mind for it is part of the "hidden machinery" of the number that appears on the chart. The number from which Napoleon's 4 was derived was 13, the number of Death and endings.

Considering that Napoleon was the #1 man in Europe at the time and one who, for close to a score of years, had always been the #1 man on the battlefield, it seems a bit odd that Waterloo, the scene of his downfall, has an Expression number of 1 (37 = 10 = 1). Only one problem. It was not Napoleon's number. On the day of Waterloo, it belonged to his adversary, the Duke of Wellington, Sir Arthur Wellsley (64 = 10 = 1).

Casebook—Of Cabbages and Kings

Film stars Clark Gable and Carole Lombard had much in common, but of particular importance to their careers was a certain vowel. Their case might be classified as "the trade of an e for an e." For it seems that their original names were "Clarke Gable" and "Carol Lombard." Mr. Gable, in effect, made a gift to Miss Lombard of his Capstone vowel. It was from this point on that both began to rise to stardom. As a result of this exchange, something else that the couple shared was the number 9: It became for both, their Core. In Gable's case, 9 also became his Expression number, while Lombard's new Name number moved up into the Alpine heights of the Master Number 11, as did Gable's Capstone.

The "Y" and Wherefore of Mr. Carter

As was stated earlier, you may or may not decide to change your name, but sometimes the matter is out of your hands as others will do it for you. That is to say, if enough people call you by a name or know you by a name, that name has become your name and *is* your name whatever your name might have been before.

Theoretically, numerology does not accept the use of nicknames as they are not considered very official. But what about a president who officially requested that he be referred to by his nickname? James Earl Carter used the name "Jimmy" while in office and it became the name by which he was known to people around the globe. By going from "James" to "Jimmy," Mr. Carter retained his Cornerstone of 1 (J = 1)—the number of presidents and leading detectives—but his Capstone changed from an "S," which is also a 1, to a "Y," which is 7, the number of hallelujah, hosanna, and "Gimme that old time religion." And as all the world knows, Jimmy Carter is a "born again" Christian. Numerology would suggest that his spiritual rebirth occurred when he became "Jimmy" instead of "James." And whatever he gained spiritually by the name change, he lost nothing materially, for his Expression number moved from a 5, the number of politicians, to 9, the number of presidents.

General Dwight Eisenhower was another president who was known by his nickname. The shift from "Dwight" to "Ike" transported him from a 3 Expression to the upper echelon of the Master Number 11. One suspects that somehow Eisenhower's campaign would not have had the same impact had his supporters been adorned with buttons reading, "I like Dwight."

Casebook—Can Huck Finn Live Life as Goody Two-Shoes?

Mark Twain might be taken as a case in point of someone who *by design* changed his name and in so doing altered his destiny. This is, of course, the pseudonym of Sam Clemens. (I use this rather than Samuel Longhorne Clemens because I assume that is the name he was known by.) Let's begin with the original chart which looked like this:

9		Roof
3	11½	Inner Self
3	5	Persona
5	22¾	Destiny
	Sam Clemens	

After working as an editor and journalist for several years, Sam decided to take the Mississippi boatman's call of "Mark Twain" as his pen name. Mark Twain literally means, "Two fathoms—safe water." A rather whimsical way to change a name perhaps, but let's see what happens when "Sam Clemens" becomes "Mark Twain":

6		Roof
9	11½	Inner Self
3	11½	Persona
5	22¼	Destiny

Mark Twain

The first thing that leaps out at us is the Expression number, which escalates from a 5 to the Master Number 11. Eleven had been—and in fact remained—his Soul Urge number. In effect, he took on a Persona that was in keeping with his deepest desires.

We know that the Destiny numbers always remain the same and that the all-important Birth Path of Sam Clemens/Mark Twain was the Master Number 22. And as the Roof number on the birth chart was 9, the top number of power, it is clear that this is an individual who has a power chart to begin with and thus should be able to handle the added voltage of the high-frequency 11.

Essentially, both charts tell the same story: This is a man who was creative and had a way with words (3 on Persona), someone who inwardly aspired to higher things and top-level accomplishments as a "messenger of light" (11 on Inner Self) and in a life of much travel and change would in some fashion become the "master builder" (5 and 22 on the Goal-Path of Destiny). The chart of "Mark Twain" intensifies and raises the original power vibrations. There is little question that this gave him a considerable boost in his chosen career.

But on the level of human happiness, whether more was gained than lost is a moot point. Eleven is a rather taut and somewhat dizzying vibration. To have not one, but two 11s in the chart along with the ultimate Master Number, 22, may be a bit much for a mortal to bear. Also, 11 is a tricky vibration as in addition to being the Messenger of Light, it can be the number of martyrdom and of shouldering tremendous burdens. It often brings grief in its wake. And we know that this was all too true for Mr. Twain, whose personal life moved from crisis to crisis, who died an embittered man.

So we can see that this is something of a mixed chart. It might well be that had the young Sam Clemens turned up in the office of a numerologist during the mid-nineteenth century, the advice he might have received would have been, "Sam, I don't know about this 'Mark Twain' chart; it's awfully intense. Take my advice and stay 'Sam Clemens.' You may not sell as many books but you'll be happier in the long run."

Casebook—Scotland Yard Loses Its Man

For a final example in this chapter of name-changing, let us approach the question from another angle and see how a life might have been led if the name had *not* been changed. Certain Sherlockian scholars, who claim to have consulted the archives, declare that the intended name for Sherlock Holmes had originally been "Sherinford," but that the parents, or one of them, decided *before* he was born to change this to "Sherlock." As "Sherinford Holmes," would our old friend have had substantially the same character and destiny or not? Let's look at the name and see:

```
    5   9       6            6     5     31
 S  H  E  R  I  N  F  O  R  D    H  O  L  M  E  S
 1  8     9     5  6     9  4    8     3  4     1    58
                                                    ──
                                                    89 = 17 = 8
```

		Roof		
6		Roof	8	
4	4	Inner Self	6	22/4
6	8	Persona	6	1
7	7	Destiny	7	7
Sherinford Holmes			Sherlock Holmes	

We see that the number 8 would exert a powerful influence over him as it would be both his Core (6 + 2 = 8) and Expression (8 + 9 = 17 = 8) numbers. Eight is the number of law and was important in the chart of "Sherlock Holmes" as the Roof number, but having an 8 as both a Core and an Expression number would give it a somewhat different emphasis.

Notice that the 1s have virtually disappeared and been replaced by 8s. What does that mean? Since 8 is the number of law, there is no reason to feel that Holmes would have followed a different career; what might be different is the way he would go about it. Because 1 is the number of the lone wolf, and 8 the number of The Establishment, the chances are that instead of working with Scotland Yard, he would have been working *in* Scotland Yard.

And horror of horrors, we know that 8s attract 4s and there are now two of them on Holmes' Inner Self. One 4 is bad enough, but two would have given him the soul of a file clerk. Those 8s, along with his Capricorn Sun, would have made him an ambitious file clerk indeed. With his native talents, there is little question he would have made a very efficient inspector or chief file clerk, but it is unlikely that Dr. Watson would have found much to write about.

The Spread: The Sherlock Holmes "Missing Clue"

The individual responsible for revealing this most fascinating spread—who due to his high position in British public life, prefers to remain anonymous—claims to be a Baker Street Irregular. The appellation coined by Holmes and first revealed to Watson while assisting on "The Sign of the Four Case," refers to a group of street urchins whose services Holmes would commandeer from time to time. It has come to refer to a formal society of devotees of Holmesian literature. He had occasion to exchange correspondence with Dr. Watson shortly before his passing. He makes the astonishing claim (and here he has permitted us to quote him directly) that, "According to John Watson, Holmes took more than passing interest in the workings of the Tarot and found it a distinct aid in cases that failed to lend themselves of a fortuitous solution. . . .He (Holmes) went so far as to inspire the spreading of the cards that you will find forthwith."

He further states that Holmes stored his deck in a Persian slipper that was always kept in a wooden box of Egyptian origin. If this is true, it would clear up the mystery of "the other Persian slipper," for as Watson has mentioned on more than one occasion, Holmes had a predilection for keeping his shag pipe tobacco in a Persian slipper that resided on his mantelpiece by the fireside; the logical inference being of course that the "Tarot slipper" was the mate to the one housing the Great Detective's tobacco.

The English writer's remarks about Holmes and his relationship with the Tarot may well be apocryphal although the letter does bear the ring of truth. But that need not deter us here. What is important is that the spread is an extremely effective one in deciding whether or not to take a particular course of action and what the consequences are likely to be. Combining as it does the arts of logic and detection, it is only appropriate that it be dedicated to the man who consciously or unconsciously inspired it.

The spread contains seven cards, which is also appropriate considering the significance of that number in Holmes' chart. What is most interesting, however, is that only six of the cards appear on the table; the seventh one remains in the deck as the "missing clue," and is found through deduction.

After shuffling, the cards are laid in the following manner:

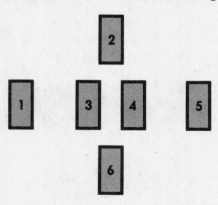

Card 1—The Tale: This is essentially "the plot" of the consultant's question or problem.

Card 2—The Client: That which is most strongly impressed on the consultant's mind at the time of the question.

Card 3—The Moriarty Factor: Obstacle or adversary.

Card 4—The Baker Street Card: This represents a powerful counter influence to Card 3 and indicates benevolent forces at work on the problem. If this card is negative, it would serve as a warning against taking a particular course of action. At best, there will be delays and/or obstacles to overcome.

Card 5—Deductions: Summing up of the issues involved.

Card 6—Solution: A tentative answer.

Card 7—The Missing Clue: An indicator for making a decision or taking a course of action. The entire spread should be re-examined in light of this indicator card.

METHOD FOR FINDING THE 'MISSING CLUE'—When the six cards on the table have been turned over and read, add up the numbers that appear on their faces and get a total. All numbered cards of the Major and Minor Arcana count their own values. The values of the Court Cards are: kings—11, queens—12, knights—13 and pages—14. If The Fool appears as one of the six table cards, there will be two Hidden Clue cards, one derived from counting The Fool as zero, the other as 22.

For this spread the Tarot pack is imagined in the following sequence: First, the four suits of the Minor Arcana in the order of Coins, Wands, Cups and Swords, and then the twenty-two cards of the Major Arcana starting with The Magician and ending with The Fool. Keep in mind that there are fourteen cards in each suit of the Minor Arcana, and once the total of the first six cards has been added together, the following guideline will help in locating the card:

Number Total	Suit
1–14	Coins
15–28	Wands
28–42	Cups
43–56	Swords

If the total is between 57 and 78, the card will be in the Major Arcana. If the total is over 78, start again with the Minor Arcana.

Let's say that the six-card total comes to 48. This places the indicator card in the suit of Swords (43—56), and thinking of the numerical sequence, 48 thus becomes the 6 of Swords (43—Ace, 44—2 of Swords, 45—3 of Swords, 46—4 of Swords, 47—5 Swords, 48—6 of Swords), and the consultant would then be advised that while the other cards described the problem, and explained what course of action to take (or avoid), the key factor supplied by the Missing Clue was a warning that the consultant's mental health was in jeopardy and was more important than any decision that had to be made. The solution would be that the individual learn to relax and let nature take its course.

After the Missing Clue card has been arrived at through deduction, it should be physically located in the pack because the cards immediately in front and behind will suggest surrounding influences.

If you are giving a reading for someone and have done several other spreads on the same question without getting definite answers, this is the spread to use. It is a good ending spread for a reading because if the time is ripe for an answer or a decision, the solution will be given in the form of the "missing clue."

The Tape:

The consultant is a married woman who finds fulfillment in a professional career. She has recently left her teaching position and is contemplating a career change. She is concerned about whether or not it was a wise choice.

The spread follows:

> Card 1—The Tale: The Enchantress (See note on page 28.)
> Card 2—The Client: The Reaper
> Card 3—The Moriarty Factor: 10 of Coins
> Card 4—The Baker Street Card: The Devil
> Card 5—Deductions: King of Swords
> Card 6—Solution: 6 of Cups
> Card 7—The Missing Clue: The Wheel of Fortune

(11 + 13 + 10 + 15 + 11 + 6 = 66. 66 − 56 = 10 in Major Arcana: The Wheel of Fortune.)

SK: Judging from other readings we have done on this question, the card of Strength sums up the situation as much as any card could. I gather that you have put up with an extremely trying situation for some time, and that without another job in the offing, the pressure was all for another season in hell until something else turned up. It took courage and strength to stick it out as long as you have, and perhaps even more fortitude to tell your boss what he could do with the job.

Consultant: That lady on the card is wrestling with a lion and that is exactly what I feel I have been doing for the past several years.

SK: The card of The Client has to be one of the more important cards in this spread, for it is really what is uppermost on your mind right now. And The Reaper seems apt indeed as death has come to your present career. On this card I look at the two heads that are on the ground and I see that these people are smiling. In this sense, death can be a very positive thing for the death of an unhappy or unfulfilling situation often leads to the birth of something more rewarding.

Consultant: Having been trained in mathematics and science, I don't know if I accept the Tarot. But I must admit that these cards do have a way of reflecting feelings. If anyone knows how it feels to struggle with a lion and then find oneself in pieces all over the ground, it is me. These two cards say it exactly.

SK: For The Moriarty Factor, you have the 10 of Coins, which I call The Wall Street Card.

Consultant: Is that good or bad?

SK: Ordinarily it would be good, but as The Moriarty Factor represents an obstacle, this seems to be saying that when one is not working, money can indeed be an obstacle.

Consultant: My husband and I have talked about that aspect of it many times, particularly now that we have all of our children in college.

SK: Yes, I can see you have. That's really the meaning of The Devil, which is The Baker Street Card. The Moriarty Factor and The Baker Street cards are both in the center. One is the major obstacle and the other is the major influence, and both are really the center of your life right now: Money, or at least the money you have been accustomed to receiving, is a problem at present, and there is some fear, or worry at least, of how you and your husband are going to cope until the right kind of job opportunity comes along for you.

But the King of Swords comes up in the Deductions slot, and I interpret that to mean an employer of some kind will be coming into your future.

Consultant: I certainly hope so!

SK: That appears to be the case for the Solution card is the 6 of Cups and that has to do with a decision. The fact that it is a Cups card, rather than a Coins or Wands card, indicates that it may not be exactly the kind of position you want, or the salary may be less than you had hoped for, because it is going to be a decision about which you are going to have strong emotions.

Consultant: But those last two cards do mean, at least, that something will be coming along.

SK: There seems little question but that there will be something, but it may not come for a while and it may not be exactly what you want.

Consultant I am just wondering if it is something I will want to take, or something I will feel I *have* to take.

SK: Judging from the cards so far, we don't really know, but the Missing Clue card should give us that information, or at least provide a strong hint.

Consultant: Let's find it then. How do you know where to look for it?

SK: By the numbers on the cards that have come up. We add these six cards up, and the total will tell us what the indicator card is. So Strength is 11 (see note on page 28), The Reaper—13, 10 of Coins—10, The Devil—15, King of Swords—11, and 6 of Cups—6. That comes to a total of 66 and that means the Missing Clue card is The Wheel of Fortune, which looks pretty good.

Consultant: Does that mean I am going to win at roulette?

SK: That is possible, but since everything else in this spread has been talking about your job future, it is probably doing the same. Let me just find the card in the pack so that we can see what the surrounding influences are. Here it is, between The Moon and the 2 of Swords.

Consultant: Those cards don't look too good.

SK: As the saying goes, "There is some good news and there is some bad news."

Consultant: Let me have the good news first.

SK: Well, the good news is, as the card indicated before, something is going to come your way and it is going to mark the beginning of a happy trend.

Consultant: But?

SK: It's not going to happen right away. That's what the 2 of Swords and The Moon are saying. But if you can just hang in there, things will eventually take a turn for the better. I really don't have any worries on that score for the first card that we turned over really said it all about you—it was The Enchantress, which is also the card of Strength.

7

A Time to Weep and a Time to Laugh: Personal Years, Months and Days

After meeting someone for the first time, we walk away with two sets of "facts." The first has to do with what the person has told us in *words* and the second, usually more accurate, is what we have perceived or intuited about that person. The message that is received through the senses is sometimes at odds with what the individual tells us. The person may be speaking "love," but we may be receiving "hate." It is difficult to say exactly how we get this information, but the slang expression we use is "vibes." If someone has had a job interview and a friend asks how it went, the reply might be, "Not so hot. I didn't get very good vibes from Mr. Jones."

This terminology may be more precise than we realize; behind it is the realization that we are all, in effect, human radio stations that can "send" and "receive" thoughts and feelings that reach us through invisible waves that might be termed vibrations, or "vibes."

In addition to affecting each other through the emitting of vibrations, we also affect and are affected by invisible forces in the cosmos. One example of this would be the Tarot. Once we accept the premise that unseen—possibly cosmic—forces are at work in a Tarot reading and the valid answers are not just "coincidence," then the question comes to mind, "How do the cards work?" One answer is that they operate through thought and feeling vibrations that are picked up by an unseen "receiving station." This, in turn, gives off other vibrations, causing the cards to arrange themselves in a coherent and relevant pattern.

The Moon is one "sending center" with which we are all familiar. It affects not only the tides of the sea but also the tides of the psyche. This explains why many police stations put on extra officers on the night of a full moon. The time of a full moon, incidentally, coincides with the time when the Sun and Moon are 180 degrees apart in the heavens. This is an aspect known to astrologers as an opposition, causing disharmony through powerful negative vibrations. In a famous experiment, Dr. Frank Brown, of Northwestern University, discovered that oysters taken to Illinois from their habitat on Long Island, opened and closed in synchronization with the tides on Long Island. It was believed at first that the oysters had some kind of built-in "cosmic clocks," but further research revealed that the oysters were actually reacting to vibrations from the Moon.[1]

We know we are also affected by vibrations from the planets. Astrology has as its basis the influence of planetary vibrations that occur when two or more planets form aspects to each other. For example, when Mars is square to Saturn (90 degrees apart), that aspect is considered hostile or negative as opposed to a trine (120 degrees apart), which is considered harmonious. Astrologers have been claiming this for centuries, but until John Nelson came along, there was precious little in the way of scientific support for this theory. As a scientist employed by RCA to investigate the causes of atmospheric disturbances, Nelson discovered that electrical storms were most severe when certain planets were square or in opposition to each other, and that atmospheric conditions were most harmonious when these planets were in trine aspect, exactly what astrologers had been saying for hundreds of years.[2]

Many scientists have difficulty in accepting the tenets of astrology and numerology. In a way this is surprising, in view of the fact that many of the discoveries in science over the last hundred years have borne out that we live in a vibrating universe. What is molecular theory but the idea that there are invisible forces that act and react in accordance with vibrations given off and received. Virtually everything in modern science attests to the fact that we live in an electro-magnetic universe where all kinds of invisible forces undulate in rays or waves. Actually, the seed was planted by Isaac Newton. The gist of his theory of gravitation is that everything in the universe exerts a force on everything else. And in present-day terminology, that force could be described by the word "vibrations."

While much of astrology has been validated by the work of science—or, at least, individual scientists—this has not been true of numerology. And some of the very same people who swear by astrology are skeptical about numerology. One obvious reason for this is that it is difficult to find a "handle" for numerology. Astrology, at least, is tangible for one can, with great exactitude, calculate the comings and goings of the planets, and accept philosophically that they are subject to the energies released by planetary configuration.

But numbers? How can numbers vibrate? A planet is there, one can see it; but where are numbers? And if numbers exist anywhere besides the mind or a blackboard, how can they possibly give off energy in the form of vibrations?

These are not easy questions to answer. But let us say for the sake of argument that numbers are but symbols for celestial forces that we can neither see nor understand. The same thing might be said of planets. Or of Tarot cards. But while the forces are an enigma, the symbols are not.

The student of numbers realizes that each digit stands as a symbol for a type of influence or energy, and that once an individual chart has been drawn up showing the numerical configuration for a life span, predictions about this person can be made with considerable precision. And invariably, an astro-numeric chart will say substantially the same thing about an individual that the horoscope does. Is it not possible that numbers and planets alike are both the symbolic language of the gods? The message is the same; it differs only in form of expression. I like to think of numbers as parables, and for those who have eyes to see, the truths of the outer and inner universe are unfolded in them.

The 9 Cycle

Our years are numbered as are our months and days. In much the manner that an astrologer can advise a client of current influences due to planetary transits, a numerologist can do the same by examining the radical, or natal, chart and from that, compute the "personal time" periods. Nine is the operative number in personal time for that marks the duration of our ongoing cycles of days, months and years. If we are under the influence of a "1 Personal Year," we know that those vibrations will create opportunities and positive energies both within and without us, and thus, a "1 Year" will be a time to initiate new projects. Not only will our creative juices be flowing to the fullest, but somehow others will respond affirmatively to what we do at this time. Conversely, a "9 Personal Year" will be the time to complete things. A "9 Year" is a time of endings, but not a year to start anything new. To a lesser degree, the number on the ascendant for our Personal Months and Personal Days will also play a role in describing the influences that will be at work at a given time.

Personal Years

To calculate your Personal Year, it is necessary to know the number of the Universal Year. Simply take the calendar year for whichever time period you are interested in and reduce it to a root digit. So the year 1895, for example, would be a 5 Universal Year ($1 + 8 + 9 + 5 = 23 = 5$). In order to find your Personal Year, after you have determined the Universal Year, combine your month of birth to your day of birth, reduce it to a root if necessary, add it to the Universal Year and then reduce again to a root digit (unless it is a Master Number).

An easy way to remember this is to realize that you are actually using the number that appears on your chart as the Goal of Destiny. That number tells you what your life goal is. The reason it is used to determine the Personal Year is that it provides an indicator for a particular year as to what is required or may be expected of that year to help you reach your ultimate Goal.

It is important to understand that we are always operating under two sets of forces—the Universal and the Personal. So if it is a 5 Universal Year, it will be a time of change affecting everyone to some extent. The Personal Year you are in at that time will offer insight as to how you will be affected by the 5 Universal Year. If, at the time of a 5 Universal Year, you are in a 7 Personal Year, you will be motivated to make changes regarding your philosophical or religious beliefs; while in an 8 Personal Year, you would be more prone to make material changes. The year 1867 would have to be an important one for humanitarian endeavors as it was a 22 Universal Year ($1 + 8 + 6 + 7 = 22$). And in the England of Sherlock Holmes, it was virtually completing the process of turning Britain into a democracy as Parliament passed the Reform Act of 1867. It also would have been a very special year for the young Sherlock; not only was he under the 22-vibrations of the Universal Year, but he himself was in an 11 Personal Year ($22 + 7 = 29 = 11$).

A Personal Year begins with the calendar year in January, but comes into full force with the inception of the 1 Personal Month. As in astrology, there is a "cusp period." This occurs during the final quarter of the year, so that after October 1, an individual is under two sets of yearly Personal vibrations, one rising, the other falling. For example, while in a 4 Personal Year, there will be a lot of work to do and details that require attention. But sometime during October, November or December of that 4 Year, the rising influence of the 5 Personal Year (which "officially" starts in the coming January) will offer opportunities for relaxation, travel, or changes in lifestyle.

Figure out the Personal Year you are now in and consult the following table in order to know what to expect and what type of plans to make:

Table of Personal Years

1 Personal Year
For anything important that you wish to undertake, this is
the year to do it. In the Tarot, it is the number of The Magician,
and like him, you will have everything in the world at your

fingertips. If you have been planning to write a book, pick up your pen and start now! There is no better time for a creative venture than a 1 Year. It is, in fact, the very best year in a nine-year cycle to start virtually anything.

It is also an excellent year to get married and if the couple is compatible it will usually be a lasting marriage. As far as career is concerned, there is no better time to launch a new business enterprise. However, in a 1 Year you have to do it alone, without partners or agents. It is most emphatically a year for action as the rise or fall of one's fortunes for the other eight years of the cycle depend largely on what is done or not done during this all-important year.

KEY: INITIATE

2 Personal Year

A year of consolidation. You may have to take a back seat this year so be ready to do it gracefully. A time when family members and associates will be important to you. Emotions will be high and what will be needed more than anything else will be patience and understanding. Remember, they also serve who only stand and wait.

KEY: SMILE

3 Personal Year

A good year for just about anything, but more specifically, a good year for dealing with people. Renew old acquaintances and cultivate new ones. An excellent time for acting, singing, or any other form of self-expression. A good time for social activities and romance, but if single it is best not to tie yourself down with one partner. In all, it should be a rather pleasant year. The only real stumbling block for the year will be a tendency on your part to over-dramatize things, so guard your thinking. Outwardly, there should be few, if any problems; inwardly, there could be trouble if you allow yourself to become agitated over trifles or imaginary slights.

KEY: ENJOY

4 Personal Year

"Sufficient unto the day is the evil thereof," might be the way to describe this year. It is a year for tending to details and completing the task at hand. Be prepared to make sacrifices this year. It is definitely not a time to make important changes as they have a way of not working out in a 4 Year. However, a change that you do not personally initiate or that comes along in the natural flow of events can be quite solid as 4 is the number of a firm foundation. A marriage undertaken in a 4 Year can prove to be long-lasting so long as the initiative for it comes from another. In any case, the early months of a 4 Year marriage are going to be rocky as there will be all kinds of chores that will need attending to.

Another exception to breaking routine is when the year is actually a $2\frac{2}{4}$ Year. While all the general aspects of the 4 Year will apply, departures from routine can be made so long as what is done transcends the self and builds for the larger community. Tensions will be on the increase so give some positive thought to health by watching your diet; this would be the year to start (and continue) biking, swimming or any activity that develops the cardio-vascular system. It can be a decent enough year if you learn to roll with the punches and do what needs to be done.

KEY: STICK CLOSE TO YOUR DESK

5 Personal Year

A time of high adventure and excitement. Above all, a 5 Year is one of change. This is the time to take the Grand Tour or go big-game hunting. It is definitely a time to seek out the new and unusual and escape from routine. A cautionary note: 5 Years promote "change reactions," so don't make an important change of any sort unless you are prepared to make a number of other changes. Also, the vibrations are somewhat deceptive, and changes, particularly of the romantic variety, do not always endure. This would be the year to start a new romance, but wait for the more stable marital vibrations of the following 6 Year to take the vows.

KEY: EXPLORE

6 Personal Year

Responsibilities are the keynote for this year. Family matters will be important in a 6 Year, and adjustments will have to be made. A good year for buying or selling a home and the very best time for getting married. Much will be required of you this year, and it will be a very up or a very down year as far as your mate and family are concerned. The manner in which you meet the challenges and respond to the demands that will be put upon you is crucial to the success of a 6 Year.

KEY: BE ACCEPTING

7 Personal Year

This is the "desert island" year. It is a time when you will need more time for yourself—particularly, your Higher Self. Meditate. Read about religion and metaphysics. Get into yoga. A bad year for investments or business changes. A good year for long trips or extended vacations to out-of-the-way places where there will be plenty of time to read and think. Can be a year of growth if you look to spiritual matters. It is also a year to expect the unexpected.

KEY: WATCH AND PRAY

8 Personal Year

This is a harvest year and depending on how you have sown, so shall you surely reap. In general, it is a strong year for anything to do with power and wealth. It is one of the best times for founding business partnerships or for expanding or speculating. In regard to material things, virtually anything you want to do will be possible. One important difference between this and a 7 Year is that in a 7 Year material gains sometimes occur, but only when they are not sought. Conversely, in an 8 Year, there definitely will be material gains, but only if you get out and push to make them happen. On the debit side, this can be a time when karmic bills fall due and this would often take the form of loss of one kind or another. But in general, it is a year of power.

KEY: ATTACK!

9 Personal Year

This is a year of endings. This year begin nothing that you wish to last. Anything started in a 9 Year is doomed to an early death and is not likely to live out the year. This is a time for stocktaking, for tying up loose ends, and for putting things on the shelf. A good year for looking ahead and planning for ventures to be launched in the coming 1 Year. A year to think and plan, but not to act. Anything initiated in a 9 Year in the way of a friendship, romance, marriage, job or home, will more than likely be a thing of the past before the year is out. Often a time of sorrows, this year will in one way or another entail some pain or sacrifice on your part. One way to get through the year is to take a lesson from the ninth card of the Major Arcana, The Hermit, and seek "the wilderness of your soul" bearing aloft the lamp of wisdom. In a way, a 9 Year is like a spring rain which cleanses and gives the world a newly-washed look and prepares the earth for the fullness of high summer.

KEY: TAKE INVENTORY

Some years will be 10, 11 or 22 Years instead of 1, 2 or 4. Much, however, will depend on how the individual responds to the vibrations of that particular Personal Year.

10 Personal Year

As a 1 Year will invariably be a 10 Year also, the main difference will depend on the manner of expression the individual chooses. Initiation is the keynote for both, but the person whose thoughts and acts are outward and upward-looking and directed in the interests of the universe writ large will be living in a 10 Year.

KEY: BE THE GOOD SHEPHERD

11 Personal Year
This is primarily an "inner year." It is not a good one for starting material things or seeking self-advancement. It is, however, an excellent time for listening to the voices within and from afar. If those celestial voices are heeded, this year can mark the raising of consciousness.

KEY: LISTEN

22 Personal Year
This year belongs not to you, but to humanity. It is the year to harness your energies in the interest of others and build to bring them to fruition.

KEY: BE THE MASTER BUILDER

Personal Months

While the major Personal vibrations for any given time period are those of the Personal Year, the vibrations of the months and days are a contributing factor and need to be taken into consideration.

To find the Personal Month, take the number of your Personal Year and add it to the calendar month, reducing it to a root digit, with the exception of the Master Numbers. Let us say that you are now in a 4 Personal Year, and the month is June. As June is the sixth month, simply add that to the 4 and the result is 10 or 1. And while a 4 Personal Year is not a good time for starting new things, the 1 Month is, and so would be the best, if not the only time, in that year to get something started that needs to be started. The meaning of the Personal Months and Personal Days is, on a lesser scale, much the same as the Personal Years, so after making your calculations, consult the Table of Personal Years and read "month" or "day" for "year."

Personal Days

Ordinarily, there is no need to place too much stress on the Personal Day. For example, the time for romance is when you feel romantic, and the time for the beach is when the sun is shining. But for those special occasions when you're planning to ask the boss for a raise or throw a party, it would be well to have as much going for you as possible. You would be well advised to select a 1 or 8 Personal Day for approaching your employer, while a 3 or 5 Personal Day would be more appropriate for a party. The more positive vibrations you have working for you, the better your chances for success. When you start a new career, if you could arrange to do it on a 1 Day of a 1 Month in a 1 Year, your chances for success would be that much better. In fact, under a 1-1-1 vibration, it would be hard to miss. On the other hand, to take a major step on a 9 Day of a 9 Month in a 9 Year would be an invitation to disaster. An action taken under a 9-9-9 vibration would be guaranteed not to last more than five minutes.

To find the Personal Day, add your Personal Month number to the calendar day. If this is the sixteenth day of the month, which for you is a 5 Personal Month, then it is a 3 Personal Day $(5 + 16 = 21 = 3)$.

Let us carry this one step further and say that this is a 6 Personal Year for you. We know then that it will be a year of responsibilities and adjustments. Generally speaking, the month, and to a lesser extent the day, that has the same Personal vibrations as the year, will be the most important. A 5 Month of a 5 Year would be the very best time to take a vacation during that year; whereas in a 6 Year, a 6 Month would not be a particularly good time because the challenges and responsibilities of the year would all be intensified during that 6 Month.

By learning the when and how of our Personal vibrations, we are, in effect, charting the tides of our life. As Shakespeare stated it:

> There is a tide in the affairs of men,
> Which, taken at the flood, leads on to fortune;
> Omitted, all the voyage of their life
> Is bound in shallows and in miseries.

The Spread: Pictures of the Future

This spread is based on one's Personal vibrations and before doing it, the consultant should calculate when his or her next nine-month cycle will begin with a 1 Personal Month, and the Personal Year that will be in effect during that nine-month cycle. If the coming 1 Personal Month is a long time off, or if consultant has recently had a 1 Personal Month, the spread can apply retroactively and in that case, would cover past, present and future.

Lay the cards from right to left, forming a pyramid, as shown by the diagram. Card 1 represents the consultant's future (or recent past) 1 Personal Month. Card 2 is the 2 Personal Month and so on for the nine-month sequence.

The final three cards pertain to the Personal year. Cards 10 and 11 respectively represent the physical and spiritual aspects of the year. The peak card of the pyramid will describe the overtone of the year.

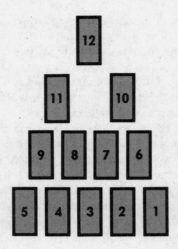

The Tape:

        1—4 of Coins
        2—8 of Swords
        3—The Lightning-Struck Tower
        4—4 of Swords
        5—The Fool
        6—3 of Wands
        7—9 of Coins
        8—6 of Coins
        9—10 of Cups
      10—Ace of Wands
      11—Queen of Coins
      12—2 of Cups

The consultant was in a 4 Personal Year at the time of the reading. Ordinarily, this spread starts with the nearest 1 Personal Month in the future. In this consultant's case it was decided to go back to her most recent 1 Personal Month, which was in June, just two months before the time of the reading.

SK: A 1 Personal Month is usually a good one for business affairs and with the 4 of Coins here, it looks like it was a pretty fair month for you financially.

Consultant: It was. As you know, my husband and I run a shop and June is really the beginning of our season.

SK: But with the 8 of Swords, I don't like the looks of July at all. Since this was a 2 Personal Month for you, I think it had more to do with emotions than finances. Did you have a misunderstanding with your husband at this time?

Consultant: That is putting it mildly. We lived in the same house and worked in the same shop but we simply stopped speaking.

SK: The card I am turning over now is the one for this month and I am afraid it is not a very happy one; it is The Lightning-Struck Tower. So it appears that you and your husband have decided to go your separate ways?

Consultant: We have talked about divorce before but this time—just last week, in fact—we decided to go ahead with it.

SK: I can see that for we are getting into the future now and the card for the next month is the 4 of Swords and that looks like a divorce.

Consultant: We talked in terms of getting the papers drawn up then.

SK: The next card, for the month of October, seems to confirm the separation for it is The Fool and The Fool always travels alone. But although he travels alone, there is real conflict in his mind about it. That duality, in fact, is what makes him The Fool, for he can't decide which course of action to take—whether to go this way or that way—and if he's not careful, he is going to fall right off that cliff.

Consultant: That describes exactly how I feel at this moment.

SK: The 3 of Wands comes up for November. And like the cards for September and October, there is a solitary figure. In this case, he is holding on to a staff for support and seems to be wondering what his next move should be. Since this will be a 6 Personal Month for you, it is going to be a family month in some way, and this could indicate a reconciliation.

Consultant: That looks very doubtful at the moment.

SK: But you have children and you have been married almost twenty years, so between now and November, feelings could change. Let's see what December looks like. It is the 9 of Coins and once again there is a lone person here, but unlike the dead man, the one about to fall off a cliff or the one leaning on his staff unable to move at all, this individual is standing upright, is smiling and seems to be at peace with himself. He's probably had a financial loss but he doesn't seem overly concerned about it. I think he has figured out what he has to do, knows that there are risks, but has decided to take them.

Consultant: Does that mean things will become final in December?

SK: It looks that way, as much as these things are ever final. But let's see what January and February look like. The January card is the 6 of Coins so it looks like you and your husband are going to come to some kind of decision about the business that month.

Consultant: Well, we have already talked about that and around the first of the year is probably when the papers will be signed.

SK: You're turning your share of the business over to your husband, are you?

Consultant: Yes, in return for a cash sum. He is also going to let me have the house so I can use that to set up a business of my own.

SK: The card for February is the 10 of Cups, which is not exactly a stranger to you. It came up for you all the time last year when you were taking classes.

Consultant: How well I remember!

SK: So it looks then as if February is going to be a somewhat heavy period for you emotionally. But this may be the last time it will come up for a while, as it is in a 9 Month, and 9 usually marks an ending of some sort.

Consultant: My life seems to be a series of endings.

SK: But endings are usually followed by beginnings so there is at least the possibility for a fresh start. In the Horoscope Spread I did for you the card in the twelfth house—which I consider the karmic house—was The Reaper. And that suggests that the main lesson that you need to learn in this life is to cope with change.

Consultant: After two husbands, twelve children and three businesses I think I am getting there.

SK: I think you are too. Now, the top three cards on the pyramid are indicator cards for the year. This one has to do with a *physical* aspect of the year. It is the Ace of Wands, which indicates that you are going to be embarking on a new business path. Aces are very powerful cards; it should work out quite well.

Consultant: I have had some good feelings about it.

SK: It not only looks good physically, but also *spiritually*, for this card is the Queen of Coins. The Queen of Coins is a fine business woman; she is well organized and knows how to handle money.

Consultant: So physically, I am going to start a business, and spiritually, I am going to feel up to running it?

SK: That's it, exactly. There's one card left and that's really the key to your year. Shall we turn it over?

Consultant: Does that mean I am going to be in my cups this year?

SK: Frankly, I am not sure what this card means as an indicator card for the year in your spread. Cups have to do with love and marriage and in this spread, most of the cards were Coins, Wands and Swords.

But whatever this means, it has to be good for I call this the Heart's Desire card. One way or another, this year is going to be exactly what you desire. As I look at the card I see two people—a man and a woman—and they are drinking to each other's health.

Consultant: But are they saying "Hello," or "Good-bye"?

SK: I think that's up to you. You know, I look back now to that card for the ninth month—the 10 of Cups. That's sort of a bittersweet card. There's a lot of emotion being expended. But also I think, a lot of affection.

It is one of those enigmatic cards for it means one thing, but it depicts something else. And what it depicts is a man and woman embracing and a very joyous family scene. But in a family—particularly, a large family such as yours—psyches can get rather frayed. So what the card seems to be suggesting is the question, "Is it worth it?"

And I can't tell you that. The Tarot can't tell you that. The only one who can tell you that is you.

[1]John Anthony West & Jan Gerhard Toonder, *The Case for Astrology*, Penguin, Baltimore, Maryland, 1973, pp. 179-180.

[2]Lyall Watson, *Supernature*, Anchor Press/Doubleday, Garden City, New York, 1973, p.38.

8

The Tides of Time:
Cycles and Pinnacles

Our numbers of Inner Self, Persona and Destiny tell us much about the way we are equipped for life's journey and where and how we need to go. Something else that is of profound significance in shaping our lives are the Cycles and Pinnacles for they are the major influences we will encounter on different phases of the journey. There are three life Cycles and four Pinnacles and they have much to tell us about where we will be physically and psychologically at a given point in time.

The Cycles and Pinnacles operate together so that from birth to the time of one's maturity, the individual is under the influence of both the opening Cycle and first Pinnacle. As they are of different lengths of duration, this person will remain under one set of influences, for example, the opening Pinnacle, while encountering somewhat different conditions and opportunities when entering the second Cycle.

Cycles

The Cycles could be thought of as the terrain over which we need to travel. It might be hilly or smooth; there could be lush valleys or stony flatland. Two people could have a 4 Path, which calls for hard work, but one could be working as a chimney sweep while the other wines and dines visiting potentates. In each case, the Cycle would provide an important clue as to the manner of work.

The opening cycle is a most important one for it lasts approximately twenty-eight years—the molding period of childhood, adolescence and early adulthood. The official time the first Cycle ends and the second begins is at the time of the 1 Personal year nearest to the individual's twenty-eighth birthday.

The second Cycle is also of considerable importance. It also lasts for around twenty-eight years and covers the period of time when most people choose their career and place in life.

The third cycle begins at around age fifty-six and so might be considered the Major Arcana Cycle as there are exactly fifty-six cards in the Minor Arcana and that period is now ended. If we think of the Minor Arcana as dealing with *material* things and the Major Arcana with *psychological* and *spiritual* matters, it will be more of an "inner space" period of our lives. In any event, much will depend on the foundation that was laid during the first Cycle and the structure that was built in the second Cycle. And while the first two Cycles are each twenty-eight years in duration, the third is in force for the remainder of our lives. Thus, that final Cycle is of particular importance because that is the one we will have to live with in the evening of our lives.

The Cycles run concurrently with the life Challenges. And if the Cycle is likened to the terrain, the Challenge represents the swamp holes, roadblocks or yawning pits we need to avoid or learn to surmount. If, for example, a person was in an 8 Cycle facing a 1 Challenge, he or she would have the opportunity to achieve wealth or power, or both, but must take care not to be too self-assertive or overly dominating in the process.

There is a direct connection between the life Cycles and our overall destiny; the three Cycles are calculated from the numbers of our month, day and year of birth. These, are, of course, the same numbers used in calculating the Path and Goal of Destiny.

The first Cycle is the *month* of birth, the second is the *day* of birth and the final one is the *year* of birth. In each case, the numbers are reduced to a root with the exception of the Master Numbers 11 and 22. So someone born on May 26, 1956, would have an opening 5 Cycle (May = 5), a middle Cycle of 8 (2 + 6 = 8) and a closing Cycle of 3 (1 + 9 + 5 + 6 = 21 = 3).

Pinnacles

As the Pinnacles are four in number, they may be considered the seasons of life. But spring may not be the beginning season. It may come at the middle, or end, or not at all. One person may have two or more winters of discontent while another enjoys an eternal summer. But as in life, a particular season is not necessarily "better" or "worse" than another; much depends on how we respond to inner and outer conditions. For some, winter is bitter and sharp; for others, it is a time to get out the ice skates or curl up with a good book by the fireside. The trick is to live in accord with the demands of the season. And by understanding our Pinnacles we can become men and women for all seasons.

Of the four Pinnacles, the second and third ones are of special significance for that is the sowing time for what one will reap in later life. These two Pinnacles last nine years each, while the first and fourth are of considerably longer duration.

A nine-year cycle is the basic unit of vibration and since there are four Pinnacles, the number 9 is multiplied by 4, which gives the figure, 36. The Path number of Destiny is subtracted from 36 to determine the duration of the opening Pinnacle.

To rejoin our old friend, Sherlock Holmes, whom we left a couple of chapters back, we note that he had a 7 Path, which would make him twenty-nine years of age at the time he ended his first Pinnacle and started his second ($36 - 7 = 29$). As the second and third Pinnacles are nine years each, he would begin his third Pinnacle at thirty-eight and his fourth and final one at age forty-seven, and as the case with the closing Cycle, the final Pinnacle remains in force for the remainder of one's life.

Now that we know the duration of each Pinnacle we are ready to discover what the seasons are. To find the *first Pinnacle* of life, take the month and day of birth, reduce each, add them together and reduce again, if necessary, except in the case of Master Numbers. As Mr. Holmes was born January 6, 1854, his opening Pinnacle would be 7 ($1 + 6 = 7$), which would last until he reached the age of twenty-nine.

The *second Pinnacle* is found by adding the reduced day and year of birth together. This gives Mr. Holmes a 6 ($6 + 9 = 15 = 6$).

The *third Pinnacle* is obtained by adding the first two Pinnacle numbers together. This would put Holmes in a 4 season at age thirty-eight ($7 + 6 = 13 = 4$).

The *fourth Pinnacle* is the reduced month and year of birth added together. So for his closing Pinnacle, Holmes has a 1 ($1 + 9 = 10 = 1$), although we keep in mind that the Special Number 10 is behind it.

Running concurrently with his 7-6-4-1 Pinnacles were his life Cycles of 1-6-9 (January 6, 1854). The first cycle ends at approximately age twenty-eight, but for Sherlock Holmes, it was in the year 1884 at age thirty, for that was his first 1 Personal Year nearest his twenty-eighth birthday (month and day of birth added together plus Universal Year for $1884 = 7 + 3 = 10 = 1$).

The numbers of the Cycles and Pinnacles have much the same meaning as they do in other areas of the chart, but following is a Table to aid in interpretation. To keep matters to manageable length, the word "cycle" will be used to refer to both cycles and pinnacles as they operate in much the same manner although the Pinnacle is actually the more important of the two. As the name suggests, it is the summit that can be reached during a given time cycle. For example, if a person is in a 7 Pinnacle, much could be attained in the realm of hidden things—particularly the raising of consciousness. Also, "Morning" will refer to the opening Cycle or Pinnacle, "Noon" to the middle Cycle or the second or third Pinnacle and "Evening" to the ending Cycle or Pinnacle.

Table of Cycles and Pinnacles

1

Morning—The child will usually be a loner, but will get a good education and develop his or her mental powers to their highest capacity.

Noon—This is an excellent place for the 1 cycle as the person will be in a position to exercise command of their creative powers.

Evening—This is often the "Eureka period" of later life when the mature man or woman gets the call or blossoms forth in the world of letters.

2

Morning—The child will be quite emotional and will crave constant attention from parents. However, the child will be both responsive and obedient.

Noon—Patience and cooperation are the key qualities manifested during a middle 2 cycle. Under this vibration a person will often seek a diplomatic or theatrical career.

Evening—There is a strong drive to be with other people during this cycle. The individual will sell the lonely house in the country and move to town. Husbands and wives who have separated will often come back together during this period.

3

Morning—This is the youngster with the million-dollar smile. Studies and friends will come easily and this child will be adored by everybody.

Noon—A very good spot for a 3 cycle as the individual is generally happily married, highly self-expressive and forever entertaining a house full of friends.

Evening—An active social period. Partnerships—both business and marital—become rejuvenated during this period. There is often an awakening or renewed interest in the joys of music and the arts.

4

Morning—The individual will be saddled with family responsibilities early in life. Parents may have problems making ends meet and the child will suffer some restrictions. The child will, however, be forever striving and will be considered a grind at school.

Noon—During a middle cycle the individual will have a positive passion for work. He or she will be extremely responsible in seeing the job through; details will be this individual's particular forte.

Evening—With a 4 closing cycle, the individual has to be pushed into retirement. If there is a rocking chair in the house, it will not see much use during this period. Could be a difficult time financially.

5

Morning—There will be an interesting childhood with considerable variety of experiences and friends, and much personal freedom. This is, however, a heady vibration and there can be a total lack of inhibition in tasting of the forbidden fruits.

Noon—Much excitement, involvement, travel and change. Pleasures of the flesh will predominate, and negatively, this could lead to a string of broken romances.

Evening—Can be a good closing cycle for under this vibration, the individual will take delight in living life to the fullest.

6

Morning—Home affairs will occupy much time during childhood although there will probably be a number of adjustments to make. More than likely there will be an early marriage.

Noon—Responsibility is the keynote during a middle cycle. This person will take on many burdens with regard to home and community matters. Marriages undertaken during this cycle are usually happy ones.

Evening—Often this indicates an early retirement, allowing this individual to spend more time with family members. This is the time when people pack up and run off to "that little place in the woods" they have always dreamed about.

7

Morning—Very difficult as an opening cycle for the youngster will often be introverted and have few, if any, friends. He or she may be a good student but more often will be a dreamy youngster who hears the beat of a different drummer.

Noon—As a middle cycle, this may be either an intensely spiritual period or an intensely lonely one, sometimes both. Not a good time for marriage as the person will essentially be a loner.

Evening—Positively, this is a period of the riches of spiritual knowledge and wisdom. Negatively, the person will pass that cup and hit the bottle.

8

Morning—As an 8 cycle can be all the way up or all the way down, the child will either be born with a silver spoon in his or her mouth, or experience a childhood where the wolf is never far from the door. In one way or another this youngster will be concerned with money, either through an excess or a lack.

Noon—The middle period is generally a strong place for an 8 cycle as it is the best possible indication for position and financial success.

Evening—If the life has been lived constructively, the individual should have absolutely no financial worries with an 8 closing cycle. But the number is both karmic and extreme: Either the individual will be at the top of the tree or will land in a ditch.

9

Morning—A highly intense and emotional childhood. Often the youngster will have unusual opportunities for travel and will meet a great variety of people. Nine is rather hectic for an opening cycle, but the childhood will be anything but dull. It is a childhood marked by endings as many people enter and leave the person's life.

Noon—A time of much freedom and large-scale projects. Under this vibration, the individual bids old habits and traditions adieu and lives the life of a free soul. Not, however, the best time for marriage.

Evening—Much will depend on the surrounding numbers in the chart and the way the life has been lived. As an "evening star," 9 is either the time when the individual hears the music of the spheres and sees the world bathed in brilliant, radiant colors, or it is a time of abject misery, melancholy and loss. Affirmatively, an individual who has never said "Boo" to a goose will step out of his or her shell and take an active role on the world stage.

As few young people attain the high vibrations of the Master Numbers in early youth, only the Noon and Evening cycles will be described.

11

Noon—With an 11 middle cycle, the individual will often have a mission that will involve the larger community. It is a time of public acclaim and success of the first order.

Evening—This vibration ensures that the person will continue to create and accomplish and that his or her works will reach the multitudes.

22

Noon—For the individual who can live up to this Olympian vibration, the way to the Universe is open.

Evening—Wisdom and action are often combined under this vibration and the result can be a most beneficial one for humanity as this is the mark of both the philosopher and the doer of shining deeds.

Casebook—The Sign of the Six

Freudian psychology tells us that the early years of childhood are the time when the personality is formed. The early influences and environment will offer a significant clue to the eventual character.

The numerologist does not disagree with this but feels that at best it is only part of the picture. Looked at from the angle of heredity, the eugenicist would claim that the character is written into the genes. This may offer a stepping stone on the road to truth, but it is possible that the pat formulas of both environment and heredity are equally superficial. There is, in fact, a cosmic plan that can be determined from the numbers a person is under at any given stage of his or her life.

With the chart of Sherlock Holmes before us, let us see if we can trace the pattern of his life from his Cycles and Pinnacles. We see that for approximately the first thirty years of his life, he was under a 1 Cycle facing a 7 Pinnacle. The combination of these two numbers flash an instant message: Here is a loner. We realize further that this is going to be an individual who will not be afraid to be an individual and will develop the mind to the fullest.

Any time a Cycle or Pinnacle bears the same number as one of the 9 Keys of the chart, the period will be one of particular significance. The highest manifestation of this will be if a Cycle or Pinnacle number coincides with a number of the Persona, Inner Self or Destiny. The individual would feel very much at home under those vibrations for in some way, it would touch the roots of that person's being. And we see that Holmes' 1 Cycle matched his Expression and Cornerstone numbers, and his 7 Pinnacle squared with both his numbers of Destiny!

In any chart, a number can be understood only in relation to other numbers, and the total configuration must be taken into account before one can arrive at a valid judgment. Ordinarily, an opening 1/7 cycle would be rather ominous; it depicts someone who will be isolated from society and probably an individual who will be brooding and melancholy. In the case of Sherlock Holmes, the difficulties would be somewhat alleviated in view of the fact that his 1 Cycle would enable him to develop the individuality that his Cornerstone and Expression numbers demanded, and his 7 Pinnacle would help prepare him for the Path (7) that would lead him to the Goal (7).

These would still be tricky years, but here at least would be a person who would have the necessary equipment to carry the burden.

As 1 and 7 are highly mental numbers, young Sherlock could have become simply a human adding machine. But sweet are the ways of adversity and what "saves" young Sherlock from turning into a bookish robot is his opening 5 Challenge! Under this Challenge, a person is strongly drawn to sensual gratification of all kinds. While this made life no easier for him—particularly in view of his weakness for narcotics—it may provide the key to his genius as a master sleuth; he used not only his brilliant reasoning powers, but all his senses in getting to the bottom of a mystery.

The Responsible Years

Now that we have been afforded some glimpse, at least, of the introspective youth of Sherlock Holmes, an enigma presents itself: What is puzzling is the sudden switch in lifestyle at about age thirty when as a consulting detective, he becomes, in effect, a modern-day knight errant, an avenging angel over the forces of evil and darkness. As a crusader against crime, he was to give so fully of himself, his energies and his time, that it might be said that during his thirties and forties he had virtually no life of his own, but rather devoted himself to the problems of his clients.

It is difficult to say how an environmentalist might deal with this complexity of human nature, but a numerologist would explain the change in lifestyle by "the sign of the 6." For, you see, in his twenty-ninth year, Holmes entered a 6 Pinnacle, which mandates the undertaking of responsibilities. During this period the inner demands would motivate him to share the concerns and problems of his London community. And this was further reinforced the following year, at age thirty, when he also entered a 6 Cycle. This double 6 vibration would have to prove irresistible for anyone, but for Holmes it was particularly forceful in that he had 6 as a number on both his Persona and Inner Self. So the taking on of responsibilities was something that was part of his personality, and something that he himself deeply wanted to do.

Looking at the other half of his Persona and Inner Self numbers, it can be seen that the cumulative effect would be quite positive; there was the energetic and pioneering 1 for an Expression, and the "Humanity, I am here to save you" Soul Urge of 22. Here then is an individual who is highly responsible and who has a strong inner drive to serve his community, but who will do it alone and in his own way. The Master Number, 22, suggests that the community could be the entire world.

The Spread: The Book of Life

The spread deals with the three life Cycles so these should be charted before the reading.

First a significator is chosen in accordance with the consultant's age and astrological sign. A Page is used for a man or woman under forty, a King for a man over forty, and a Queen for a woman over forty. Each astrological sign is associated with a suit of the Minor Arcana as follows:

Fire—Wands
Earth—Swords
Air—Coins
Water—Cups
Fire Signs: Aries, Leo, Sagittarius
Earth Signs: Taurus, Virgo, Capricorn
Air Signs: Gemini, Libra, Aquarius
Water Signs: Cancer, Scorpio, Pisces

So, if a forty-three-year-old woman wished to choose a significator, and her Sun sign was Pisces, she would select the Queen of Cups.

After the significator has been selected, it is placed face-up on top of the table.

This spread consists of three horizontal rows of seven cards each. The bottom row is the opening life Cycle that ends around age twenty-eight, the middle row is the second Cycle lasting from around twenty-eight to fifty-six, and the top row is the final Cycle after age fifty-six.

The age of the consultant will determine which part of the spread is Past, which is Present and which is Future. Even if the consultant is over fifty-six, at least a portion of the top row will deal with the future.

The middle cards, those indicated by an asterisk in the diagram, represent the dominant influence in each Cycle.

When the cards have been cut, shuffled and laid out in the manner of the diagram, begin by turning over the center card of each row—cards 4, 11 and 18. When these center cards have been read and interpreted in relation to the actual Cycles in the individual's chart, the cards are then read from right to left, starting with the bottom row.

Significator

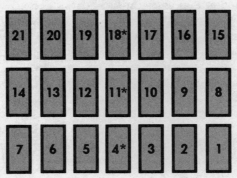

The Tape:

1—The Fool	8—The Lovers	15—Knight of Cups
2—7 of Coins	9—2 of Swords	16—Knight of Swords
3—5 of Swords	10—5 of Wands	17—The Moon
4—**The High Priestess**	11—**Justice** (see note on page 28)	18—**The Magician**
5—5 of Coins	12—King of Wands	19—6 of Swords
6—8 of Coins	13—The Reaper	20—The Hanged Man
7—Ace of Coins	14—6 of Cups	21—The Empress

Consultant's Chart:

Secret Passion 1
Persona (Birth) 2
Persona (Expression) 1
Roof 2
Inner Self (Psyche) 9
Inner Self (Soul Urge) 1
Destiny (Path) 1
Destiny (Goal) 3
Cornerstone 1

The consultant is a highly creative and energetic woman in her thirties who at the time of the reading was a teacher and housewife.

SK: We have done many readings before, but this is the first time we have tied the Tarot into your numeric chart, and in this case, it will be the life Cycles—the first extending to about age twenty-eight, the second to around age fifty-six and the final one lasting for the remainder of your life. Now, we have talked about your opening 1 Cycle and noted that you were a very creative, self-assertive child with a highly independent nature.

Consultant: I was hell on wheels!

SK: But looking at the center card of your 1 Cycle, I see it is The High Priestess who is not a 1 but a 2. And this suggests that maybe you were not quite so independent as you appeared. With all the 1s in your chart, you would cherish your independence, but The High Priestess here indicates that for a good part of your childhood and beyond, you were fighting a kind of seesaw battle between being all of yourself and being part of someone else.

Consultant: That war within me is still going on.

SK: That is strongly indicated in your chart, for you have a triumverate of 1s on your Inner Self, Persona and Destiny, but the other half of your Persona is a 2. In addition, 2 is your Roof number. That is bound to make for conflicts, which are indicated by The High Priestess as the central card of your opening Cycle and Justice (see note on page 28) as the key card of your present Cycle.

Consultant: You said that Justice is really *my* card as it goes with my sign, which is Libra.

SK: Yes, that is the card associated with Libra. But the card that is perhaps more "you" than any other is The Magician.

Consultant: I certainly respond most strongly to that card. I have to be The Magician just to get through the day.

SK: I know that card keeps coming up for you and almost always it has been very positive. This really isn't surprising considering that The Magician is a Number One and your chart is a veritable symphony of 1s: You have a 1 Cornerstone; a 1 Expression; a 1 Opening Vowel; a 1 Path; and, most importantly, a 1 Soul Urge. But 2 is the other half of your Persona and that is where the balancing act comes in. Everything in your chart shouts of this not-so-delicate balance between independence and dependence. The key card of your first Cycle is The High Priestess who has to balance between so many things, particularly, in your case, the need to assert one's individuality versus the need for a mate. And as Justice is the key card in your present Cycle, the Libra battle continues to wax hot and heavy.

Consultant: When you did my horoscope, didn't you tell me that as a Libra, I wouldn't be happy without a mate?

SK: Yes, but there again, the problem was thrown into bold relief at the outset by your Ascendant, which is Sagittarius. That is known as "the bachelor sign" for what a Sagittarian cherishes above all is independence.

Consultant: There are times when I envy people who want only one thing—career, marriage, or whatever—and then devote all their energy to achieving that one thing.

SK: Now, let's look at your Cycle from the beginning. The first card and the one that sets the tone for the Cycle and the life is The Fool.

Consultant: That is the story of my life, all right.

SK: In your case, The Fool is a fool because there is conflict within over which direction to take. This road? Or both? Or neither? But for you, the solution seems to be not simply an either/or choice, for everything in both your astrological and numeric charts suggests that you must learn to ride two horses simultaneously and still retain your balance.

Consultant: It's my sanity that I am worried about.

SK: Looking at the childhood years, the 7 of Coins suggests that you did not want for material things and as there are four Coin cards in this Cycle, money, along with material things, apparently has always played a rather special role in your life.

Consultant: I can't deny that. My parents were pretty well off; they liked to live well; and I acquired a "champagne taste" very early.

SK: In the 5 of Swords, I see someone trying to play boys' games but sometimes feeling left out. Were you something of a "tom boy"?

Consultant: Oh, was I ever!

SK: I think it is significant that this card is flanked by the key card of your 1 Cycle—The High Priestess. Duality is the name of the game with this card, and here she is being torn between individual pursuits and associations with others.

Consultant: That's it, exactly!

SK: It is also interesting that while this was a 1 Cycle, the key card was a 2.

Consultant: I guess that's the Libra thing again.

SK: I would say so. Now, on the other side of The High Priestess is the 5 of Coins. Here is an individual walking on crutches, with a woman leading him. Could this be your mother? Possibly there was a time when you were in college and felt overly dependent upon her for some reason?

Consultant: That would be right after I got out of college. I lived at home for a couple of years. By that time we were not seeing eye to eye at all. But I didn't have a steady job then and I couldn't just pick up and leave. It was a rough period for I felt absolutely stifled.

SK: But apparently you did something about it, for the next card, the 8 of Coins, shows someone hammering out his own destiny. But as this card is an 8—the same number as Justice and the balance—money matters were still not just the way you might have liked.

Consultant: Yes, there were several jobs there that didn't pan out, with gaps in between.

SK: But the first Cycle seems to have had a happy ending for here is the Ace of Coins and the beginning of a new and important business undertaking.

Consultant: That's correct for I started at the school where I am now just before I turned twenty-eight.

SK: Looking at the Cycle as a whole, it is interesting to see the sequence: It begins with a traveling card, The Fool; followed by the 7 of Coins, which in divination means a trip; and after that is the 5 of Swords, which looks like more travels and adventures. But then the picture changes and we find three Coin cards in a row.

Consultant: I guess I became somewhat more materialistic.

SK: I think it was more that you became *realistic,* for as a true native of Libra, you are not hung up on money for its own sake, but rather for the entree it provides to the good things of life. And as you grew older, your attitude toward it changed.

Consultant: In what way?

SK: The 7 and 8 of Coins tell the story here. For the 8 of Coins, which comes near the end of the Cycle, gives you the ability to understand what it is to go out and make money on your own. This is very different from the 7 of Coins, which suggests you just stood around and dreamed you could pick money off the trees.

Consultant: I guess I am much more security-conscious than I ever was before.

SK: As someone once said, "Revolutionaries at twenty; conservatives at thirty." But I think it would be very wrong to conclude that you started out as a romantic and ended up as a materialist. No way! That is the meaning of the two main cards—The High Priestess and The Fool—for the basic conflict is between security and adventure. And since I see you as the Eternal Romantic, you will never lose your desire for adventure. But you want the security so that you will have the leisure to travel, to search, to experience Life.

Consultant: You are absolutely right. If I were to find myself in any situation—job or marriage—where I had to play a role of something I am not, such as being "Mrs. Organization," I would just chuck the whole thing and start over.

SK: That is where The Fool comes in: He is always ending one thing and starting another. But he is a fool only in the eyes of the world. To himself, he is sublime.

Okay, let's look at the cards for the middle Cycle, the one you started about seven years ago. Now according to your chart, you began life in a 1 Cycle, and now you are in a 2. Whatever problems or frustrations you may have suffered during childhood, adolescence or your twenties, you must have found considerable fulfillment because 1 is the predominant number in your chart and in many ways, this was a golden age for you, for there must have been numerous opportunities to develop your individuality.

Consultant: In many ways it was a golden age, but that makes it a rather difficult act to follow, doesn't it?

SK: It does, but as you are now in a 2 Cycle and the other half of your Persona is a 2, and 2 is also your Roof number—that is, the covering influence in your life—this could be a pretty fair sequel. In a 2 Cycle, the basic theme is partnership and the form that it will take in your case is indicated by the leadoff card for this Cycle, which is The Lovers.

Consultant: That seems fairly explicit.

SK: But in looking at the card, we see that the lovers are not together, they are apart, and there is actually a mountain to climb before they can come together. And looking at the Inclusion of your chart, we can see that 2 is one of your Karmic or missing numbers.

Consultant: So you're saying there might be some problems?

SK: Think of it as a school course. In the case of the 1 Cycle, you had all kinds of things going for you; you had acquired the basics in the earlier grades, so to speak. But the 2 Cycle is different. You are not going in cold exactly, for with 2 both as a Persona and Roof number there is a powerful inner motivation on your part to pass this course. But in another life, you apparently fell down in this area, and so it is a lesson that needs to be learned.

Consultant: You're saying I flunked out?

SK: That's both the beauty and the pain of karma: no one ever flunks out; they just keep repeating the course until they pass it. That also accounts for why you were born into Libra and why Justice—the Libra card—comes up as the key card of this 2 Cycle, and, in fact, the center card of the entire spread. And speaking of 2, the second card in this Cycle is the 2 of Swords and that suggests there will be some initial problems for there is a blindfold over the woman's eyes and at this point she can't really "see" her way. Also, look at the two swords the woman is holding and where they are pointing.

Consultant: One is to The Lovers.

SK: And the other is to the 5 of Wands, which is fulfillment in work. And since there are what appear to be children at play on this card, it looks like fulfillment in working with children.

Consultant: What about fulfillment in having my own children?

SK: The cards suggest that you will decide to have children. *When* you make that decision is up to you, your husband, and Mother Nature.

Consultant: I don't think I am ready to make that decision at this time. When you did my chart reading, you told me that next year would be a 1 Personal Year, and that would be a very good time to start anything new. That, of course, would include having a baby?

SK: Definitely! Although the 2 and 3 Personal Years, which follow the 1, would also be very good. So anytime in the next three years would be fine.

All right, now we go into your final life Cycle, which will start around your fifty-sixth birthday.

Consultant: If it's bad, I'm not sure I want to look that far ahead.

SK: Well, we already know it is not going to be an easy period for you. Remember when we went over your chart, we saw that it would be a 7 Cycle, which *has* to present special problems for not only is 7 one of your Karmic numbers, but, in addition, you have no 7s anywhere in your chart to help you cope.

So as I see it, the Tarot can be helpful here; it can aid in shedding some light on the nature of the problems you will face and help you prepare for them. Contrary to popular belief, 7 is not necessarily a "lucky" number; in fact, it can often be devastating as many people have problems handling this number. But once an individual understands what is being asked for and meets the exacting requirements of a 7, it can be the most uplifting and rewarding of numbers and time periods in one's life.

Are you ready to get a preview of your 7 Cycle?

Consultant: As ready as I'll ever be. Let me have it straight.

SK: The Cycle starts with two horsemen, the Knight of Cups and the Knight of Swords. One is brandishing a sword, riding off hell-bent-for-election, while the other, clasping a cup, seems to be peacefully plodding along.

Consultant: But they're riding off in different directions, aren't they?

SK: Not only that, but the Knight of Swords is chasing the Moon, while the Knight of Cups is going aimlessly off into empty space.

Consultant: The way the cards are facing, it looks like one horse with two heads and two riders.

SK: That's an excellent observation. It looks like our old friend, the balance again.

Consultant: Between work and marriage, or adventure and security?

SK: It could be some kind of combination of the two, but looking at the cards as a whole in this Cycle, I have a feeling that it goes deeper than that.

Consultant: What do you mean?

SK: I think the answer lies in the card of The Magician, which is the key to this Cycle.

Consultant: Ah, The Magician. He always comes up when I need him!

SK: Now, if we look at the three cards to the right of The Magician, we see a kind of unholy trinity—two horses riding off in different directions and The Moon of illusion.

But when we look at the three cards to the left of The Magician, we see a very different pattern: Look at these three cards—the 6 of swords, The Hanged Man and The Empress—and tell me what your overall impression is.

Consultant: For some reason, I get a wonderful sense of peace.

SK: Yes, that is exactly what I get, too. Part of it is what I think of as "the Libra blue" of The Hanged Man's blouse, and the blue water of the 6 of Swords. Water, in fact, appears to be the major motif, for the three people on the 6 of Swords card are in a boat surrounded by water; a cool forest stream dances alongside The Empress, and the card of The Hanged Man is associated with water.

Why this emphasis on water? I think the message is beginning to come through for there comes to mind that wonderful healing passage from the twenty-third Psalm, "He leadeth me beside the still waters; He restoreth my soul."

And in this vein we notice something rather startling, for another dominant symbol on these three cards is that of a cross. The most obvious card is that of The Hanged Man who is suspended on a cross and whose body also forms a cross. On the card of The Empress there appears the Venus symbol—a mandala of wholeness atop a cross. But most amazing of all is the 6 of Swords card for the boatman dipping his pole into the water also forms a cross and the six swords on the boat have in some mysterious way been transformed into a field of crosses.

Consultant: At one time the Church was an important part of my life.

SK: I think it will be again. In fact, it *must* be again if you are to find fulfillment in this Cycle. It is not necessarily a church built with hands, but with spirit—the cathedral of your soul.

A 7 cycle is the Cycle of God and the emphasis must be placed on affairs of the spirit. That is what The Magician seems to be telling you; with his left hand he is pointing earthward toward material things and to the negative cards of The Moon and the two horsemen riding off in different directions. But his right hand is pointed toward heaven and the trinity of spiritual cards.

Consultant: Once again, The Magician has given me a new lease on life.

SK: It seems that even The Magician has been transformed for always before in your spreads, he represented will power, but here he seems to be operating at a higher level of consciousness and to be the Christ-bearer of Divine Will.

It is interesting that the final card in this Cycle is The Empress, whose number is 3. Since your Destiny numbers are 1 and 3, the message is fairly clear: Your 1 Path is that of The Magician, but The Magician operating on the highest level of awareness. By following that Path and being The Magician, you will become The Empress and achieve your 3 Goal. The Empress has learned the lesson of independence—the 1 of The Magician—and also the lesson of dependence—the 2 of The High Priestess—and as the 3 The Empress has achieved a new synthesis and is now a fully integrated and creative person.

But she is creative in a very special way. And whether it is an idea, a book or a baby, The Empress brings the wonders of heaven into the ways of earth.

9

Eros and Eden:
The Numbers of Love

One of Freud's more profound assertions is that "constitution is destiny." That is to say that the particular physical envelope within which one is contained has built into it a program of feelings, desires, motivations and predilections.

Another basic theorem of Freud's is that the wellspring of personality is the *libido*, a mass of undifferentiated energy, primarily sexual in origin.

Today many neo-Freudians as well as non-Freudians would take issue with that statement. But the discovery by scientists of the DNA genetic code must give us pause. On the basis of this discovery the open-minded person is forced to conclude that a considerable portion of his or her physical-psychological-emotional makeup has been *pre-determined*. It is not necessary to reach agreement as to how or when or why this cosmic pre-packaging was done; what is significant is that, to science, at least, the DNA code may be classified as a fact of life.

Numerologists and astrologers—as well as practitioners of other ancient arts—are not displeased with this finding; it lends impressive support to the growing body of evidence for a cosmic plan for each individual. What so many believe to be free will is, to a large extent, pre-programmed behavior.

No one is denying the existence of free will. Free will exists, but it may not work in exactly the manner many people believe that it does. Let us take a chess board and set of pieces as analogy. Pretend for a moment that these chess pieces have a life of their own as well as a psychological bundle of needs, wishes and aspirations. Now, these chess pieces have had their life programmed: Bodily shape, potential and mode of action have all been pre-determined. Whether a lowly pawn or a regal queen, the piece has the free will to move, to advance and to achieve *but only in accordance with the eight-by-eight rows of squares that comprise the individual's physical universe and by the type of movement ascribed at birth.* Both the boundaries of the physical board and of possible modes of action were determined before the pieces came into being. It is not possible to overstep these boundaries or move in a way contrary to these designations for to do so is to break the law, and lawbreakers, both great and small, invariably initiate their own destruction. The wise chess pieces use free will to learn the individual laws of nature and of the physical universe. Thus, they act within the law rather than trying to go against it. It is only in this way that ultimate freedom may be attained. Before we leave that chess board analogy, let us keep in mind that freedom can be gained or lost. Patience and adherence to The Law can result in the elevation of a pawn; impatience and arrogance combined with a failure to "move properly" can result in the entrapment of a king or the downfall of a queeen.

Let us return to the libido. We may not all share Freud's belief that raw sexual energy is the be-all and end-all of our existence, but few would doubt that it has a significant role. It is futile to argue its importance even in the case of a single individual. We have no reliable measure for determining to what extent erotic wishes and needs, rooted in the unconscious, result in patterns of behavior and significant life actions.

If, however, one accepts the notion that personality makeup and desire for expression are to some extent pre-determined, the first step has been taken along the road of self-knowledge. The traveler on that road is asking the question, "Who am I?" And an important part of that identity is one's sexual nature. Once that is fully understood, self-actualization becomes possible.

Numerology provides a working blueprint of destiny. In the realm of sexuality the "numbers of love" in a chart can be quite revealing. And when one combines number analysis with certain cards of the Tarot's Major Arcana, an extra dimension is opened up.

Each of the root numbers from 1 to 9, along with the Master Numbers, has something to say about the individual's sexuality and capacity for love. In making this type of assessment, there are three basic areas to look at in a chart and they are the Inclusion, the Planes of Expression and the 9 Keys. (The Inclusion and Planes of Expression will be discussed in the following chapter.) Both *where* and *how often* in the chart the number appears have to be taken into consideration. And if the number *fails* to appear, that is also important. Before making this type of analysis, the reader should complete Chapter 10, for a number that fails to appear among the nine Keys may figure prominently in the Inclusion or Planes of Expression, and the chart has to be considered as a whole. The number, "7," for example, might appear nowhere among the Keys, but if found on the Planes of Expression, could be quite significant. Among the Keys, the principal numbers are those of Persona, Inner Self and Destiny. On the Persona, a number indicates the sexual role that the individual appears to play and usually does, while a number that appears on the Inner Self reveals a sexual role that the individual would like to play; whether or not that desire is realized depends on the rest of the chart. On Destiny, the interpretation alters somewhat and indicates either that the sexual role implied by the Path or Goal is the role the individual will ultimately play or that he or she will become associated with people who play that role.

1 as Dominance
2 as Submission

The numbers of primary importance are 1 and 2; they serve as the indicators of one's sexuality. The other numbers provide additional information, but 1 and 2 essentially describe the sexual lifestyle of the individual. We know that 1 is a masculine number while 2 is feminine, and, of these two, the number highlighted in the chart tells whether the person's attitude, approach and overall style in regard to sex and love are essentially active or passive. It matters little whether the individual is a biological man or woman; what determines sexual expression is the masculine 1 and the feminine 2. A woman with a chart rich in 1s, for example, is going to play a "primary" role in a relationship, while, conversely, a man with many 2s in his chart is going to essay a passive role. That does not mean that a "1-woman" and a "2-man" are going to be gay—homosexuality is suggested more by the confusion of the 7, often in combination with a "hang ups 4" or a "go either way 11." It merely indicates that the woman, however stereotypically feminine she may appear, is going to take an active, aggressive, "masculine" role in a relationship, while the man, however stereotypically masculine, is going to assume a more passive "feminine" role. And if other factors in the charts are in harmony, this pairing of a 1-woman and a 2-man could be an ideal romantic partnership.

As most people have a sprinkling of both 1s and 2s in their charts, roles are rarely defined so that one partner is always 100 percent submissive. In most relationships, one partner may be dominant only 90, 70 or 51 percent of the time, but the point is that he (or she) is prepared to play the dominant role when it becomes psychologically necessary to do so.

It should be made clear at this point that the discussion is centering not on some bizarre form of psycho-sexual behavior but rather, what mountains of psychiatric clinical findings have shown to be the norm in a happy, healthy relationship. Often the dominant-submissive needs and desires of two partners in a love match will not be articulated and in a large number of cases they remain rooted in the unconscious. But consciously or unconsciously, where there is awareness and understanding, each partner knows the other's needs.

On the physical-erotic level in a love relationship, one of the ways people play games is for the dominant partner to force the other to submit. In some cases this may be accompanied with a mock battle and the employment of fetish objects and "instruments of torture" such as whips and paddles. But in the majority of cases, the roles are played out on more subtle emotional and psychological planes.

In sum, the dominant-submissive roles in a relationship take a great variety of forms and this type of role-playing is not necessarily good or bad—it is only human. In any type of love relationship these roles must be played. This is best done when each partner chooses the role that is most natural. The role that is *natural*—that is, according to one's own nature—will be found in the chart.

The first two numbered cards of the Major Arcana tell essentially the same story as the opening pair of numbers: The Magician, who holds high the wand of power, exudes masculine dominance; The High Priestess is seated and submissive. The Magician's wand has considerable utility value, for in addition to being phallic, it can also be converted into a "rod of correction."

The dominance of The Magician is further emphasized by his red cloak—red being the color of the planet Mars and aggression. But Mercury is the planet with which the card is directly associated, and Mercury is the god of knowledge. That this knowledge is, in part, sexual may be testified to by the serpent belt that The Magician is wearing—the serpent representing the world's first sexual counselor in the Garden of Eden. For obvious reasons, serpents are considered phallic symbols and that serves to remind us that the card of The Magician has a surfeit of phallic symbols. Quite clearly, this card is related to the sexual experience and the role The Magician plays is that of the dominant partner.

While The Magician card is associated with the masculine planet, Mercury, The High Priestess is associated with the Moon, which represents femininity. In fact, its monthly orbit of 27.3 days approximates the menstrual cycle in women. In contrast to the active red cloak of The Magician, The High Priestess wears a gown of blue, the color of passivity. Phallic symbols predominate on the card in the form of two pillars on either side of her, but unlike The Magician who commanded and controlled the phalli, The High Priestess appears to be hemmed in and overpowered by them. She wears a somewhat furtive look, much in the manner of a child who has been sent to her room to do her lessons. The "lesson," by the way, is headed, "Tora," possibly referring to the Torah, the body of Jewish law. She knows also that she needs to learn the law of her own nature.

The numbers 1 and 2 differ from the other numbers in that they reveal masculine and feminine roles in a relationship. The other numbers to be taken up will indicate sexual attitudes and preferences.

3 as Pleasure

People with a chart strong in 3s are going to enter a relationship in a free and easy manner with a joyful feeling of abandon. They will succeed also in experiencing every nuance of erotic stimulation. They are extremely creative and they work in a romantic endeavor in much the manner that a sculptor works in clay.

The card of The Empress is associated with Venus, the goddess of love. In astrology, Venus is an indicator of one's sexuality. Unlike The High Priestess who was learning about sex in secret, The Empress is practicing it out in the open. A phallic symbol in the form of a sceptre appears on the card, but far from being frightened, The Empress holds it lovingly in her hand and is eager to gratify any and all sexual desires—both her own and those of her partners. The stream flowing by her suggests the eruption of orgasmic fluids. In her spontaneous, natural and playful approach to lovemaking, The Empress is the supreme representative of people under the 3 vibration. But the influence of Venus has the same effect on The Empress as it does upon the signs ruled by Venus—Libra and Taurus. Venus suggests gentility rather than rowdiness. All 3s share this trait and thus can enter into a love relationship with great zest, but always in a highly refined manner. Negatively, they may remain somewhat detached emotionally and expect to receive more than they give.

As a rule 3s make good marriages, but a relationship will be sustained only so long as it continues to give them pleasure. And they can start and end an affair in record time. Should difficulties arise, they will move on quickly. But whether the relationship is an enduring one or only a brief encounter, they can always be counted on to treat their partners with tact and consideration. In short, 3s have class.

4 as Hangups

From our earlier discussions in this book it must be clear that 4 is a somewhat ominous number. Not always of course, for no number is totally lacking in redeeming qualities. Because 4 is associated with work, it can be quite helpful for some people—particularly those under the 1 vibration—and can, in fact, be the best of all numbers to have as a residence, place of work or telephone number.

But on the level of love, too great an emphasis on work and petty details can mar a relationship. The fourth card of the Major Arcana is that of The Emperor and in this context, we see him in an entirely different light. In fact, he is revealed in much the manner of that sad fellow in the fairy tale, *The Emperor's New Clothes*—and we find that behind the regal facade beats a heart with sexual problems.

Take a closer look at The Emperor. The first thing we notice is the rams-head throne and we are reminded of The Emperor's association with Aries, the sign that is forever ramming its head into brick walls. Notice how tightly he grasps the symbols depicted—the phallic sceptre of material power in his right hand and the orb of spiritual power in his left. The fact that the orb of spiritual power is in his *left* hand is in itself significant for that indicates that spiritual power is "not right," or at least, less important than material power. Notice how tense he appears and remember the game played by children called "King of the Mountain" in which one kid battles to the top of a small hill and everyone else tries to throw the child off.

Let's face it, The Emperor has problems! His empire has always been shaky because of his association with Aries, which is ruled by Mars, for both the sign and planet are noted for rash, impulsive action and violence, and what is gained in this fashion, can be lost in the same way.

But The Emperor's ultimate undoing is his affiliation with the number 4 because 4 is the number of neurosis. It is also the number of masochism. Once The Emperor and the people who are reacting to the lowest level of the 4 vibration realize that the hurt and humiliation that they suffer at the hands of others are primarily the result of their own neurotic fears and negative thought-forms, which they project into the atmosphere, they are at least on the road to coping with the problem.

5 as Action

Five is the number of the senses—sight, smell, hearing, touch and taste—and thus is the number of the human race. Five is also the half-way house of the root numbers for there are four numbers above, and four below. As there are four elements—fire, earth, air and water—representing the physical world, 5 may be said to stand in between earth and heaven, and actually act as the central station or coordinator between the numbers below and the numbers above.

This idea of a cosmic connection may be seen also on the fifth card of the Major Arcana. On this card two figures kneel at the feet of The Hierophant; therefore, he stands above them. But in giving his blessing, The Hierophant's right hand is pointed toward heaven while the sceptre in his left hand points to earth. As is the case with Number 5, The Hierophant bridges the gulf and is the connecting link between the two. The card's association with Taurus further reinforces this idea. The astrological symbol for Taurus is ♉. The circle representing the Sun is connected to a half-circle representing a crescent moon. Here again is depicted a cosmic connection between "above" and "below."

The Hierophant can be seen as a spiritual figure, but the association with Taurus, the most earthy of the earth signs, provides an additional link between the spiritual and physical.

In some decks, this card is labelled The Pope, which is misleading for we then respond to the card in terms of our own cultural conditioning and think of him as totally removed from the realm of sex. But in the Eleusinian Mysteries there was a ceremony celebrating the death and resurrection of Osiris in which The Hierophant engaged in a "sacred marriage" and copulated with a priestess. As "the revealer of sacred things," in the ceremony, The Hierophant was using his own phallic member to demonstrate the connection between the physical and the spiritual. This theme is underscored by the two phallic pillars on either side of The Hierophant. Neither the top nor the bottom of these pillars can be seen. They are rooted in earth but reach up to heaven. Also, one could be thought of as the world of the physical, the other as the realm of spirit. And as The Hierophant stands in between them, he connects the two.

In reference to this, perhaps the key symbol on the card is the triple sceptre. This glorious union of spirit, mind and body finds additional support in the triple crown worn by The Hierophant and from the fact that he and his followers form a triangle on the card, the symbol for creation and perfection.

What does all this say about the number 5? Just this: Five is the number of the human race and sensory gratification, but on this level sexual activities are not an end in themselves and serve as a means of transcendance. Because 5 is the number of humanity, and in the case of The Hierophant, the bridge between Above and Below, the number may be considered to have a rather special significance. But for our purposes, the most telling clue is the fact that 5 on an Inclusion Chart is The Sun of the root numbers, and is, in effect, the generator or energy system for the rest. What it boils down to is that a chart strong in 5s will find a way to manifest energy—sexual or otherwise; a chart with few or no 5s will not. Sexually speaking, 5 is where the action is; without 5s there is no action.

In addition to the Persona and Inner Self numbers, the main indicator will be the number of 5s in the name. In an average name of 14 letters, most people have two or more 5s. If—again, using an average fourteen-letter name—a person has but two 5s and none elsewhere in the Keys or Planes of Expression, sex will play a relatively minor role. With one or no 5s, the person would have an ascetic temperament and possibly refrain from sex altogether. But with three 5s there would be more than a little activity; with four a sexual marathon; and with five or more, there would be time for little else.

The Keys also have to be looked at and one set of factors weighed against another. A person might, for example, have only two 5s in his or her name, but if he or she has two or more 5s among the Keys, that could change the picture considerably. This would be particularly true if he or she has one or more 5s on the Persona. On Inner Self, the Psyche number is perhaps the most erotic portion of the chart and a 5 there would give powerful motivation indeed for engaging in sexual activity. Of the Inner Self numbers, one 5 in that slot would indicate a strong fantasy life, while two would reveal a person for whom virtually every life experience would be imbued with sexuality. With a 5 Roof, every major step in life, including career, would have an underlying sexual motivation behind it, although this would be rooted in the individual's Unconscious. On Destiny, a 5 would suggest a person caught up in sexual encounters not of his or her own making. Two 5s on Destiny would indicate a member of the world's oldest profession, or, at least, a person who was constantly being used and/or abused for his or her sexual favors. Because of the gift of transcendance that is built into 5, it would be difficult to assess the sexual meaning of the 5s in a given chart without knowing what stage of evolvement the person had reached.

Five is the central number of the roots and it invariably plays a pivotal role on the level of sexual expression. The other numbers describe what an individual's sexual preferences are; the number of 5s (or lack thereof) tell how often and in what mannner these desires will be met. People strongly under the 5 vibration will unquestionably be sexually active. The lesson of The Hierophant, however, is that when operating at one's upper potential, physical union with another can also be a way of experiencing Spirit.

6 as Devotion

Six is the number of responsibility and this also applies to affairs of the heart. We know from our previous discussion of Personal Years that a 6 Year is the very best time to launch a marital partnership. The reason is that people strongly under the 6 vibration tend to take considerable enjoyment in the pleasures of love partners and the family circle.

A person with a 6-oriented chart is not interested in transient affairs or a great variety of love partners. The interest in sex is definitely there, but as part of an ongoing love relationship—one that will lead to a permanent union.

In the Tarot, Arcanum VI is the card of The Lovers and therefore has to have special significance in the context of the present discussion. In most Tarot decks this card depicts a man and two women. But the Rider deck, to which we have referred consistently throughout this work, is admirably suited to our purposes. It shows a man and a woman standing naked and unadorned before each other. The serpent-entwined tree leaves little question but that this is the trysting site of the world's first and most highly publicized love affair. That this love match has a powerful physical basis may be testified to by both the serpent and the suggestive phallic mountain in the background.

What is important to realize about the card is the time—it is before the young people have tasted of the Tree of Knowledge of Good and Evil and therefore they stand before each other in complete abandonment and innocence. Sexual hangups have not been invented yet and so they dine at each other's table unburdened by what society thinks or what society says. They *are* society and they haven't had time yet to develop bad habits such as living in the past and worrying about the future. The harsh truths of reality symbolized by the Sun are being shielded from them by their guardian angel hovering above. And so in the eloquent silence of twilight the man approaches the woman and they know each other in the best Biblical sense and it is good. That Eve wasn't hard to woo may be evidenced by the fact that history tells us that it was she who offered Adam "the fruit." And then there is the matter of her name: Although there are only three letters, two of them are 5s and the Expression is also a 5!

And it is that "before the Fall" state of innocence that characterizes a 6 relationship. They love open-heartedly and until "death do us part." As in Eden, their lives are not problem-free and it must be noted that the card of The Lovers is associated with Gemini. This suggests some fickleness and conflict in a relationship, but as 6 is not only the number of responsibility, but also of adjustment, they can usually live happily ever after. Generally speaking, 6s make the most enduring marriages and it is the number more than any other that represents a full and happy family life.

7 as Confusion

The essentially spiritual vibrations of 7 are difficult for many people to handle and they tend to react in a variety of ways. Some get themselves to a nunnery or mountaintop, some take to the bottle, some become more aloof and introspective and some join the Gay Liberation Movement.

No number has a monopoly on homosexuality. There are a great many factors at work here—genetic, environmental, astrological and perhaps most important of all, karmic, for an entity who has lived several recent past lives as a woman, and suddenly finds itself in a man's body, is going to have problems adjusting to the situation.

It is not that 7 produces more practicing homosexuals than any other number, but rather, that as a group, they tend to agonize more and undergo greater confusion about their sexual roles. As in the case of most numbers, it is the Inclusion—that is, the number value of each letter in the name—that counts most, along with the physical Plane of Expression and certain of the Keys, mainly the numbers of Persona and Inner Self. A 7 on Destiny would suggest that the individual would be destined to have an active relationship with someone of the same sex in which he or she might play the role of counselor or confessor. For highly evolved souls, a Destiny 7 would suggest someone who would lead a highly introspective or spiritual life.

This sexual confusion of Arcanum VII in the Tarot is suggested by the man driving The Chariot. If The Chariot may be said to symbolize the vehicle of personality, it is apparent that the two sphinxes pulling The Chariot are different for one is black, the other white, suggesting conflicting sexual energies. This duality is further suggested by the two faces of Janus that appear on the charioteer's shoulders.

He not only holds a spear—a phallic symbol—but the red-tipped castles and red-tipped crest on The Chariot all add up to an embarrasssment of phallic riches.

The card is associated with the sign of Cancer, which commences at the solstice with the burning Sun of summer. The charioteer has often been identified with Apollo, who drove the Sun in its blazing march through the heavens. Of all the heavenly bodies, the Sun most clearly symbolizes masculine energy.

But the association of the card of The Chariot with Cancer adds to the enigma; Cancer is said to be ruled by the Moon, the planet associated with feminine energy.

In the mannner of the charioteer, those strongly under the 7 vibration have to decide with which of their sexual energies to identify. That the problem is not insurmountable is indicated by the meaning of the card on any level: Victory.

8 as (Im) Balance

Power is the path of 8 and those under its vibration seek power in all things, including sexual activities. But the force that impels one to command a company or a state can be destructive in human relationships. The 8 knows what he or she wants and knows how to get it but isn't always overly considerate about the feelings of others. The 8's motto is "I want what I want and I want it *now!*"

Masterful in the art of love-making, the 8 has little patience with the wishes or shortcomings of others. And when the 8's desires are thwarted, he or she can be quite unbending and even ruthless in achieving his or her ends.

The eighth card of the Major Arcana in most Tarot decks is Justice (see note on page 28), associated with the sign of Libra, symbolized by The Scales. "The Libra problem" is also shared by Justice, who attempts to balance its life, but rarely succeeds. It is significant that the Justice figure holds the scales rather ginerly with her left hand while the all-powerful right hand firmly grasps the avenging sword. She sits between the two phallic pillars, which in this case suggest selfishness and lack of consideration for others. But while the intent to mete out justice is there, it does not look like she is going to succeed for the figure of Justice herself represents a scale with the balance in one hand and the sword in the other. Quite obviously, the sword hand is higher than the other. There may be an attempt to achieve harmony with a mate, but the need to control every aspect of the relationship creates an uneasy balance.

The relationship between 4 and 8 has been discussed elsewhere in this book—8 being an exalted version of 4—and because of its impatience and failure to understand human frailties, Justice is capable of social sado-masochism. But where The Emperor was the neurotic masochist, Justice is the sadist for she is continually giving pain to partners and loved ones by judging them by her sexual standards.

There is some degree of hope in an 8 match because of the awareness of the need to balance. And there is further hope in the design: 8 is the most balanced of all the root numbers. But those under its vibration are much like Olympic figure skaters who must prove themselves again and again by cutting perfect figure 8s. They possess the skill necessary to accomplish this and on the days when they have that perfect figure 8 in the inner state they "put it on ice."

9 as Knighthood

Nine is the highest of the root numbers and those under it seek a love relationship that is predominantly spiritual in orientation. They don't always find it but they keep looking. Their inner world is that of the Middle Ages when knights set off on their white chargers in quest of damsels in distress.

Those under the 9 vibration still believe that a perfect person-in-need awaits them, and ride off to find that person murmuring "Somewhere—somehow . . . ."

It is not that 9s are uninterested in sex. They are interested, but it has to be combined with something spiritual, something higher. This is clearly indicated by the ninth card of the Major Arcana, The Hermit. His interest in sexual activity may be readily confirmed by that elongated phallic staff that he carries. But it is also clear that sex is secondary for the staff is in his left hand, while in his right hand he bears a lantern. But unlike Diogones, who was searching for an honest man, The Hermit is searching for an honest woman. Those individuals influenced by the 9 are searching for compatible partners.

Another interpretation for the lantern is that it is the light of truth. It represents the culmination of a spiritual odyssey and a readiness to "let the light shine before all." But in the process this individual hopes to find the type of partner who is also on this path and will "live in the light."

Another dimension is added by the card's association with Virgo. Virgo, like The Hermit, often chooses the solitary path. One reason for this is that the center of Virgo's existence is the life of the mind, and if Virgo cannot find a like-minded mate, this sign does not particularly care for it has its own inner resources and is quite content to go it alone.

This is where 9 differs. Nine often winds up as a solitary traveler but is never happy about it. And a 9 rides off each morning murmuring, "Somewhere—somehow . . . ."

11 as Role Exchange

Eleven is 2 raised to mastership. In a relationship, not everyone is happy to take on the sexual role of 2, which is submission. If, however, they are operating under the vibration of $11/2$, things can be changed. Once again, the clue is in the number itself; 11 is two 1s, suggesting equality in a relationship.

Arcanum XI, The Enchantress (see note on page 28), goes a step further for the woman is taming the lion. And what is more, she is doing it calmly and gently. She doesn't have to throw temper tantrums or use undue force for she possesses self-confidence and commands authority. As the card is associated with Leo, "King of the Beasts," the lesson here is quite dramatic: A frail maid can tame the passions of a virile male and exchange sexual roles with him when she, like The Enchantress, schools herself in the sexual arts.

As always, however, the real name of the game is her inner state. The woman subdues the lion only after she has licked her own fears and self-doubts. And this she can only do after she accepts the responsibility of operating on the upper level of the $11/2$ vibration. If she fails, she may sink down to the negative 2 level and can become engaged in perverse relationships.

22 as Serendipity

Under the powerful 22 vibration an individual would find it difficult to confine love to a single individual. This is the love that is global in scope. Much depends on whether anyone can live at the upper reaches of the $22/4$ vibration, because as a 4 he or she is going to suffer from hangups, but as a 22 he or she is going to love and be loved.

The card of The Fool is instructive here for it is associated with the element of air. What a difference from The Emperor whose tie-in with 4 restricts him to things of the earth such as empires, power, glory, success—and hangups. The Emperor can't make it sexually because he is too busy trying to hold on to his throne. He does not realize that he is only the Emperor of Ice Cream and come summer, all will melt away.

The Fool, however, has but one ambition: he wishes to remain unencumbered with material things and to live in the moment. He responds to nature with all of his senses. That having sex is one of his pleasures can be seen by the phallic rod held in his right hand and casually slung over his shoulder. He wants it, he enjoys it, but he doesn't worry about it for he is a practitioner of serendipity and thus a past master in the art of entertaining the unexpected. He lives in the moment with every fiber of his being.

Conventional thinkers looking at the card of The Fool are likely to view The Fool's position with scorn for "obviously" he should look where he is going as he is about to step off the precipice and break his fool neck. But that is where they are different from The Fool for he is living in the present while they are worrying about the future.

The book, *Inner Skiing*,[1] comes to mind here for the authors point out that success in skiing is much like success in any other aspect of life (which would include sexual activity) that depends upon skill and achievement with no fear of losing.

The book talks of each of us as having two selves: Self 1, the rational, thinking self; and Self 2, our upper potential. It is also our non-thinking, non-rational or instinctive self. When Self 1 is in control we *think* about our mistakes of the past and worry about imagined mistakes in the future. When Self 2 is in control we *live* in the present and react to the environment with the instincts Mother Nature has been shaping into us over the centuries. In short, in any type of physical activity that requires agility and courage, we go out of control when Self 1 is in control. When Self 2 is in control, we trust our instincts and flow freely through time and space.

In the context of our discussion, The Emperor's problem is that he is forever at the mercy of Self 1 and continues to bind himself in the psychological chains of Arcanum IV, whereas if he could relate to Self 2, he could ascend to the 22 level of vibration and travel high, wide and handsome like The Fool. With Self 1 his outer empire gives him no joy for he has an inner empire of hangups. Maybe if some reader would be kind enough to give him a copy of *Inner Skiing*, The Emperor could let Self 2 blossom forth, and living at the upper level of his potential as The Fool, could enter with abandon on the slope of sexual skiing and be free to love openly, easily and wholeheartedly.

Casebook—The Private Lives of Sherlock Holmes and John Watson

With discretion the good Dr. Watson has told virtually everything about Sherlock Holmes during the Baker Street years with one significant omission: His love life. Did he ever know romance? Have an affair? Was he married?

These are important questions and it seems curious indeed that Watson chose to keep his readers in the dark on this vital area of life. It is possible, and even likely, that Watson simply didn't know. Holmes certainly had the ability to keep things under his deerstalker cap. Most of what Watson tells us about Holmes in his chronicles is that which he himself observed while working on a case with him or when they rattled arond their lodgings on Baker Street. But far from telling Watson everything, Holmes seems to have told him almost nothing.

What then may we infer about the private life of Sherlock Holmes? And for that matter, what about Dr. Watson? Their lives were so closely intertwined for so many years that it would be interesting to know more about both of them. In short, what facts do we have to go on, and what may we surmise on the basis of those facts?

Best we start with the doctor for he has seen fit to include a great deal more about himself than he has about his colleague and companion. Going to the Sacred Writings, as Dr. Watson's journals are known to the initiate, one of the first things we learn about John Watson is that he had a compelling desire for companionship. It will be remembered that as a young man he was wounded in Afghanistan by a bullet he received in the shoulder while serving a tour of duty as an Assistant Surgeon with the Fifth Northumberland Fusiliers—and that while recuperating at the base hospital in Peshawur, complications set in when he contracted enteric fever.[2] Upon gaining a discharge from the British Army and with the knowledge that regaining his health would be at least a matter of months, Watson set out for London. Living by himself in a hotel on the Strand proved to be "a comfortless, meaningless existence,"[3] and when informed by an acquaintance of his, Stamford, that there was a young man employed as a chemist in a hospital laboratory who was seeking someone to share rooms he had found on Baker Street, Watson's unhesitating reply was, "By jove!...if he really wants someone to share the rooms and the expense, I am the very man for him. I should prefer having a partner to being alone."[4]

The young chemist is of course Mr. Sherlock Holmes, and Watson's statement is indeed interesting in that the two had not yet met. The implication is clearly that Watson would prefer living with someone—anyone—to living alone. Watson is introduced to Holmes by Stamford and in no time at all an agreement is reached and the pair establish themselves in Baker Street. But this rooming arrangement was to end abruptly early in 1884,[5] when Watson made a trip to the United States to look after an ailing brother in San Francisco. It is in that city that Watson effects a new partnership, this time with a patient, Miss Constance Adams.[6] He proposes to her, is accepted, and on November 1, 1886, the pair are married in England.[7]

But the marriage is to be short-lived. We learn later of the young Mrs. Watson's death in December of the following year.[8]

Once again the partnership with Holmes is reactivated. Two years later, Watson marries again, this time taking as his bride Miss Mary

Morstan,[9] whose father had been a captain in the 34th Bombay Infantry. The marriage ceremony takes place on May 1, 1889.[10]

But once again tragedy was to strike for before another two years had passed, she too was to have shuffled off this mortal coil.[11] And in 1894, following Holmes' three-year absence from England, the two friends are once again sharing rooms in Baker Street.[12] This time they remain together for eight years, when in 1902, Watson marries for the third time.[13] As Watson almost never afterwards refers to his third wife, we can only guess as to the longevity of Mrs. Watson number three.

That is what we have to go on. And certainly we have to share in Watson's sorrow to some extent for it is quite a misfortune to lose not one, but two young attractive wives by early death.

Let us now take a look at Watson's chart and see what we may deduce:

```
   6            1        6        13
J  O  H  N   W  A  T  S  O  N
1  8  5      5  2  1     5   27
                            40 = 4
```

Watson's Expression number then was 4. The other thing we need to know is the birthday, which was August 7, 1852.[14] Here are Watson's Keys:

Roof 8
Secret Passion 1, 5
Inner Self 9, 4
Persona 7, 4
Destiny . . . . $^{22}/_4$, 6
Cornerstone 1

The first thing that strikes us about Watson's chart is the predominant 4—the number of sexual hangups. And there is a 4 on each of the three levels of Inner Self, Persona and Destiny! It is true that the 4 on Destiny is actually $^{22}/_4$ but it would be doubtful if he could attain the vibrations of the Destiny 22 and its accompanying freedom in the realm of sexuality due to the crushing weight of the 4s on Inner Self and Persona.

And that combination of a 7/4 Persona would have to prove deadly for no matter how you slice it, the end result is a sexual life role of hangups and confusion. Either of these numbers by itself would not necessarily be a serious handicap, but in tandem they are an explosive combination, particularly when the 4 gets reinforcement throughout the chart, which is capped by an 8 (two 4s) Roof.

That sex was important to Watson is evidenced by the fact that he has 5 as his Secret Passion. The motivation is there but only serves to thicken Watson's psychological fog. His other Secret Passion is a 1 so that the desire to dominate his partner would be there also, but his weak Persona does not really allow him to do that. Also, considering he has a short name—only 10 letters—the strong 1 and 5 are out of proportion and indicate that in sexual matters he would be overly demanding of his partner.

Now we are ready to draw some conclusions about the first and second Mrs. Watsons. One very important feature is that "the facts" of the matter have been given to us by Dr. Watson, for with the exception of two cases penned by Holmes and two of disputed authorship, Watson was the sole chronicler of information about Holmes and himself. Is it not possible that the good doctor found himself in a sticky situation and rather than lay the bald facts before his readers, maybe decided to fudge things a bit? After all, the coincidence of two young women dying in the prime of life after a few months of marriage creates something of a credibility gap. It seems more likely in each case that the marriage died, and Watson, thoroughly humiliated and ashamed, knowing he had to tell Holmes something, chose "death" as the easiest way out. Also, in Victorian England, might not tongues begin to wag following the disclosure that a man has divorced his wife and then gone off to live with another man? But, if Watson's wife had "passed over" the whole situation changes, and anyone could understand the man's natural need for companionship following his "loss."

Watson probably worked very hard on his third marriage because by that time he and Holmes had really come to a parting of the ways. Holmes was not an easy man to live with, and affable and understanding as Watson was, he eventually reached the end of his tether, for significantly enough, he packed up and left Holmes in the summer of 1902, *several months before his third marriage.*[15] But the final straw for Watson was the telegram Holmes sent him in September, 1903, which read, "Come at once if convenient—if inconvenient come all the same. SH"[16]

Bitterly, Watson took up his pen and wrote, "The relations between us in those latter days were peculiar. He was a man of habits, narrow and concentrated habits, and I had become one of them. As an institution I was like the violin, the shag tobacco, the old black pipe, the index books and others perhaps less excusable."[17]

This is one of the few revealing insights that Watson ever gives us about himself and we catch an air of finality in his tone. Whatever the nature of the invisible bond that had existed between the two, it had been irreparably severed.

So, for John Watson, there could be no return to Baker Street and Sherlock Holmes. That third marriage would have to work. Hopefully, by this point, the old boy had finally gotten it together and was able to live happily every after with the third Mrs. Watson.

We speak of three marriages for Dr. Watson but that of course is incorrect. The "third Mrs. Watson" was, in reality, the doctor's fourth marriage. And the marriage we have not spoken about lasted off and on for some twenty-three years; it was the marriage to Sherlock Holmes.

Before some reader cries, "Foul!" let us define terms. The American Heritage Dictionary offers as its third definition for "marriage" the following: "Any close union: *a true marriage of minds.*" And two people who are associated by a bond of affection over a period of time are "married" in the purest and deepest sense of the word. Thus in the case of Holmes and Watson, it might be closer to the mark to say that it was not so much "a true marriage of minds" as it was of psychological temperament: In the family of numbers, 1 and 4 are of the same house and will seek each other out; the Expression numbers of Holmes and Watson were respectively 1 and 4.

But while 1 and 4 are drawn together, the dominant member of the duo is invariably 1, and 4 must play a subservient role. So in a very real sense then, this was a sado-masochistic relationship, with Holmes as the dominant partner and Watson as the submissive one. There is, however, no reason to suppose that it was a homosexual relationship for there is no evidence in Holmes' chart or elsewhere to support that. In any sado-masochistic relationship, there are always sexual overtones, but by and large, it seems to have been largely on the psychological plane.

What is noteworthy is that in terms of the two charts, this was a perfectly healthy and happy relationship; each filled the needs of the other: Holmes liked to have someone to dominate; Watson enjoyed being dominated.

In any kind of sharing relationship—and not all relationships fit neatly into the pigeonholes of heterosexual or homosexual—there are always deep feelings of affection. That Holmes was hit harder by Watson's leaving than he let on may be evidenced by the fact that it was the very next year—1903—that Holmes gave up his career and retired to the Sussex Downs to become a bee-keeper.[18] Taking up bee-keeping makes little sense in rational terms, but considered symbolically, it makes excellent sense: Could a few bee stings be any more bitter than the sting of a partner who has run off?

It is not exactly customary for a man in his forty-ninth year who is at the top of his profession to suddenly chuck everything and become a hermit. To be sure, there were other reasons (to be taken up in Chapter 11) for Holmes' flight from London, but one suspects that it was the traumatic break with Watson that served as the trigger.

The question arises: Why did Watson leave Holmes? There is no easy answer. Perhaps the best one is because Watson was Watson. As his chart indicates, he was a highly complex man with all kinds of conflicting drives. There is, however, one significant piece of evidence: In the summer of 1902, at age fifty, Watson moved from a 2 (submissive) Pinnacle to a 6 (marriage) Pinnacle and he took his third wife just two months later.[19] There is added hope that this marriage worked out in that 6 was also Watson's Goal number.

And speaking of 6s, we know from our prior study of Holmes' chart that he was strongly under the 6-vibration. Was there no one else in his life? There is some evidence to suggest that there was. To start with, there is a tantalizing entry in the London Post Office Directory for 1878, which records changes of address for the previous year. There is listed at 24 (which reduces to "6") Montague Street a "Mrs. Holmes."[20] Who the husband was we can only guess but it is a matter of record that "our Mr. Holmes" was living on Montague Street at that time.[21]

We do not know if Sherlock was the husband of "Mrs. Holmes," but we do know that it is unlikely that he would have been for long because at age twenty-three (in 1877) he was still in a 1 Cycle facing a 7 Pinnacle, and in a 4 Personal Year. Any marriage undertaken at that time would almost surely have been doomed to failure.

According to Dr. Watson, Holmes was not a man given over to romance and sentiment and was more or less a human calculating machine. That, at least, is what Watson would have us believe.

But that calculating-machine image does not hold up very well when we consider the encounter that Holmes had with a certain lady of the theatre. It was with "the" woman in Sherlock's life—Miss Irene Adler. And even Watson was forced to admit that "to Sherlock Holmes she is always *the* woman. I have seldom heard him mention her under any other name. In his eyes, she eclipses and predominates the whole of her sex. It was not that he felt any emotion akin to love for Irene Adler. All emotions and that one particularly, were abhorent to his cold, precise, but admirably balanced mind . . . And yet there was but one woman to him and that woman was the late Irene Adler . . . ."[22]

Holmes had good reason to remember *the* woman for she was involved in a case in which Holmes' client was none other than the King of Bohemia. It appears that Irene Adler had in her possession a certain photograph involving the King, which could very well have had repercussions in Bohemia should the lady have chosen to publicize it. Holmes was at the top of his form on the case, but it turned out in the end that this proved to be one of the very rare occasions in which the dean of sleuths was outfoxed by Irene Adler.

Watson insists that whatever Holmes' feelings were toward the woman, it was definitely not a love match.

But how can he be so sure? He tells us that although Holmes was unhappy with the outcome of the case, the King of Bohemia was delighted with the way Holmes had managed matters and asked him to name his reward, taking an emerald snake ring off his finger as a possible means of payment. According to Watson, Holmes took no interest in the ring and said, " 'Your Majesty has something which I should value even more highly . . . this photograph.'

"The King stared at him in amazement.

" 'Irene's photograph,' he cried. 'Certainly, if you wish it.' He bowed and turning along without observing the hand which the King had stretched out to him, he set off in my company for his chambers."[23]

If that wasn't love, it sure came excitingly close. Some light is shed on the mystery when we take into account that this case occurred in 1887,[24] the year when Watson's first marriage was going on the rocks. Watson's observations about his friend's incapacity to love may well have been a projection of his own inadequacies in this department. Fortunately, Watson was a better biographer than he was a psychologist and the closing words he pens to the case give the lie to his opening remarks, for any man who acted as Holmes did in the presence of royalty would have to be pretty badly smitten. Watson's myth about Holmes has been forever shattered: The truth of the matter is that the logical, unsentimental, hard-nosed realist, Sherlock Holmes, was capable of being reduced to the emotional state of a love-sick schoolboy!

But the definitive evidence comes from Holmes' chart, for in 1887 he was thirty-three years old, which reduces to a "6." And he was also in both a 6 Cycle and a 6 Pinnacle. If ever Sherlock Holmes was ripe for a grand passion, that would have been the time!

But as usual, Watson was wrong: Irene Adler was unquestionably something rather special but she was *not* "the" woman in Holmes' life. If endurance of relationship is any criterion, "the" woman was not Miss Adler at all, but someone else that he had known for almost the entire time that he lived in London.

Who was she? The answer may come as a shock to some, for it was the woman Holmes took with him from London when he retired to the Sussex Downs. Of course Watson was aware of Holmes' new mate when he visited the pair on occasion, but quite possibly, for reasons of discretion, he chose not to inform his readers. So it is instructive that we learn of the relationship *from Holmes himself* when in his laconic style he tells us of his new mode of life in the country: "My house is lonely. I, *my old housekeeper*, (emphasis added) and my bees have the estate all to ourselves."[25]

His "old housekeeper"? That phrase is all Holmes utters to describe his bride, but it hits us with the impact of a thunderbolt for it could be none other than the woman who had cooked and cared for him throughout the Baker Street years, his landlady—Martha Hudson!

As Holmes provides no further details, we can only speculate on the exact nature and intensity of the relationship, but it is reasonable to assume that there must have existed a strong bond of affection between them. And considering that Holmes has a double 7 on his Destiny, it is interesting to note that Martha Hudson also has strong 7s: Seven is both her Expression and Core number.

Truly then, Martha Hudson was The woman in the life of Sherlock Holmes for as their chart numbers indicate, she was the Expression of Holmes' ultimate Destiny.

The Spread: Sex and the Single Number

There are nine cards in this spread, each one geared to one of the Keys in the consultant's chart. Only the twenty-two Major Arcana and sixteen Court Cards are used, and they are interpreted on the plane of sexuality, love and marriage.

The consultant chooses every card that appears in the spread. After the cards have been cut and shuffled, fan them out face down on the table, forming a circle, asking the consultant to hand you cards, one at a time, face down. When nine cards have been collected in this fashion, hand them back and ask the consultant to shuffle only those nine cards.

Then throw the spread as follows:

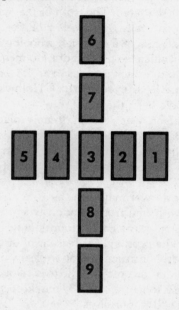

Card 1—Cornerstone: This gives the foundation of the individual's sexual nature.

Card 2—Roof: This may be likened to the id and expresses the individual's romantic instincts and drives.

Card 3—Secret Passion: This means exactly what it says.

Card 4—Persona (Birth Number): This tells us the type of sexuality or romantic expression that is intimately bound up with the consultant's life style.

Card 5—Persona (Expression): This should be compatible with Card 4, but if at variance with that card, it would indicate the possibility that the Birth and Name numbers are not in harmony and this would cause a conflict in the sexual nature. A change of name might well be in order—particularly if the Birth and Expression numbers are not in harmony—and the consultant should be counselled accordingly.

Card 6—Inner Self (Psyche): This indicates the type of sexual fantasy the individual subscribes to.

Card 7—Inner Self (Soul Urge): This reveals the individual's most deep-seated sexual motivation. Again, if this card does not square with Card 6, and the numbers are not harmonious, a name change might be in order.

Card 8—Destiny (Path): This describes the manner in which sexual desires will be met.

Card 9—Destiny (Goal): This should serve as the culmination of all the other cards in the spread and suggest the consultant's sexual destiny.

The Tape:

Chart		Tarot
Cornerstone 11		Card 1—Queen of Cups
Roof 4		2—Knight of Cups
Secret Passion 2, 9		3—The Fool
Persona (Birth) 9		4—The Hieropant
Persona (Name) 7		5—King of Coins
Inner Self (Psyche) 1		6—The Hermit
Inner Self (Soul Urge) 6		7—Page of Wands
Destiny (Path) 6		8—Day of Judgment
Destiny (Goal) 8		9—The Enchantress

The consultant is a handsome, intelligent man in his late twenties. At the time of the reading, he was single and had started to pursue a theatrical career.

SK: The Cornerstone of your chart is an 11, which is a Master Number and one of great strength and spirituality. The first card in this spread represents the cornerstone of your emotional life. It is the Queen of Cups and as I have done your mother's chart, and know that this is her significator card, the implication is that she has given you much warmth and affection and that she is—to borrow some Jungian terminology—the archetypal Woman of your Unconscious.

Consultant: It sounds more like Freud than Jung.

SK: Well, there's a bit of both there. But as I see it, the kind of mate you are searching for is a woman who is both very cultured and high on the passions, and who, like your mother, has great depth of feeling.

Consultant: That's an interesting way of putting it and I would certainly have to agree.

SK: The Roof number of your chart is 4, the number of work and details, which certainly goes along with your Virgo Sun. The card for the Roof number is the Knight of Cups, suggesting that much of your work energies is directed toward matters of the heart.

Consultant: Sometimes, I think they *all* are.

SK: Well, in your case, that's probably a good sign for Virgos often go the other way and live almost entirely on the mental plane. A 4 Roof number is excellent for details and this suggests that you will not overlook the smallest detail in pleasing a partner and making a marriage work. Although, there is a danger here of working too hard on a courtship and being fearful that it won't work. The combination of a 4 Roof and a Virgo Sun would make you more than a little of a perfectionist, and in a love relationship, at least, it might be better just to relax more and not worry so much about the details.

Consultant: But don't forget, I am on the cusp of Leo. Isn't Leo sort of lazy about details?

SK: Leo can be lazy, and likes to paint with a broad brush. I think that Leo influence is helpful as it tends to soften the picture. Also, we have to consider *both* your chart numbers and the Tarot counterparts, and taken together—the number 4 and the Knight of Cups—there's a nice balance of the practical and the romantic.

Consultant: Does that mean I am romantically practical or practically romantic?

SK: Moving right along, as they say, we get to your Secret Passion numbers, 2 and 9, which are another odd couple, for 2 is the number of close association with one partner, while 9 is the number of the person who belongs to the world.

Consultant: That's me all right.

SK: Which one?

Consultant: Don't you mean which *two*?

SK: Speaking of duality, your Secret Passion card is The Fool, which says it as well as anything for he is looking back at the girl he left behind while off in quest of fresh adventures. But more than anything else, The Fool doesn't like to be tied down; he wants to live spontaneously, and he cherishes his freedom.

The numbers of Persona in your chart are 7 and 9, which is another version of our old friend, Duality. For 7 is the loner and 9 prefers to be with the masses. And don't look now but the number 4 and 5 cards, which represent Persona, are The Hierophant and the King of Coins.

Consultant: Even without knowing the meanings I can see that they are yin and yang.

SK: You really couldn't ask for much more of a contrast than these two. The Hierophant is not married and cares for mainly spiritual things, while the King of Coins enjoys the pleasures of the flesh and is married to the Queen of Coins.

Consultant: Where does a schizo go to register?

SK: It is really the Leo-Virgo duality all over again. You are going to have to decide which "you" you're going to be.

Consultant: I'm afraid whoever comes along is just going to have to take both of me.

SK: I think you are going to have to do it yourself first. For in your chart, your numbers of Inner Self are 1 and 6, which represent the loner on one hand and the happily married man on the other. Interestingly enough, Sherlock Holmes had a 1/6 split in his chart.

Consultant: How did he solve it? On second thought, don't tell me; I think I know.

SK: The Tarot picks up this split, for your Inner Self cards are The Hermit and the Page of Wands. Interesting also is the fact that The Hermit is the card in the Tarot associated with Virgo, who often is a party of one, while Wands go with fire signs—including of course, Leo—and the Page here seems to suggest a marriage with children.

Consultant: Again, that is both of me.

SK: But of the two, I would pay more attention to the card representing the Soul Urge, because deep down inside of you, that is what you want more than anything else.

Consultant: And that's the one with the wife and kids?

SK: Yup. And that ties in directly with your chart; your Soul Urge number is a 6 and that is the number of marital bliss.

Consultant: Now I am more confused than ever.

SK: Hopefully, the cards of Destiny will shed more light on the matter for your Path tells you the road you must take in life and the final card is the Goal you must reach.

The Path card is the Day of Judgment, which is about as explicit as you can get. Not only does it mean taking a major step such as marriage but it actually depicts a man, woman and child.

Consultant: What is the coffin doing there? Does that mean, if I get married I'm dead?

SK: I think you have to look at your chart numbers. You've got a 6 there, which means you're dead if you don't. There are some numbers in a chart you can fool around with, but the only thing you can do with Destiny numbers is follow them. So let's say that these people on the Day of Judgment card had a 6 Path, like you, and they were dead to the world until they woke up and followed it.

It is this final Destiny card that is really heavy for it is The Enchantress. And in some magnificent way, she combines all the characteristics of the people cards in this spread, but in a way that is absolutely beautiful.

Consultant: I think I am going to like her.

SK: You need someone strong, and another name for this card is Strength. Anyone who can tame a Leo as she is doing here—it could be you as you're sort of an honorary Leo—and still keep that fresh sweet smile, has got to be a woman who knows what she's doing.

This reading then is all of a piece for it started with a warm affectionate person and ends with the same type of woman. There isn't much question but that you are going to fulfill that 6 marriage Path you are on. And what is more, it looks to be a solid marriage for The Enchantress is the eleventh card of the Major Arcana—and 11 is your Cornerstone number, what you build the life upon.

And what is really interesting is that in the Rider-Waite Deck, The Enchantress is not the eleventh but the eighth numbered card of the Major Arcana—the same number as the Goal of Destiny that you must reach. So there you have it: Any woman who represents your Cornerstone and your Goal of Destiny is going to be both the beginning and ending point of your life.

----

[1]Timothey Gallwey and Bob Kriegel, *Inner Skiing*, Random House, New York, 1977, *passim*.

[2]John Watson, M.D., (amanuensis: Arthur Conan Doyle), *The Adventures of Sherlock Holmes* ("A Study in Scarlet"), The Heritage Press, New York, 1950, p.3.

[3]*Ibid.*, p. 4

[4]*Ibid.*, p. 5

[5]William S. Baring-Gould, *Sherlock Holmes of Baker Street—A Life of the World's First Consulting Detective*, Bramhall House, New York, 1962, p. 299.

[6]*Ibid.*

[7]*Ibid.*, p. 300.

[8]*Ibid.*, p. 302.

[9]John Watson, M.D., (amanuensis: Arthur Conan Doyle), *op. cit.*, "The Sign of The Four," p. 237.

[10]William S. Baring-Gould, *op. cit.*, p. 305.

[11]*Ibid.*, p. 308

[12]John Watson, M.D. (amanuensis: Arthur Conan Doyle), *The Later Adventures of Sherlock Holmes* ("The Adventure of the Empty House"), Heritage Press, New York, 1952, pp. 767, 770.

[13]William S. Baring-Gould, *op. cit.*, p. 316.

[14]*Ibid.*, p. 293.

[15]*Ibid.*, pp. 315-316.

[16]John Watson, M.D. (amanuensis: Arthur Conan Doyle), *The Casebook of Sherlock Holmes* ("The Adventure of the Creeping Man"), Berkley Publishing Corporation, New York, 1955, p. 163.

[17]*Ibid.*

[18]William S. Baring-Gould, *op. cit.*, p. 318.

[19]*Ibid.*, p. 316.

[20]Michael Harrison, *The World of Sherlock Holmes*, E.P. Dutton & Co., Inc., New York, 1975, p. 86.

[21]William S. Baring-Gould, *op. cit.*, p. 295.

[22]John Watson, M.D. (amanuensis: Arthur Conan Doyle), *The Adventures of Sherlock Holmes* ("A Scandal in Bohemia"), p. 241.

[23]*Ibid.*, p. 263.

[24]William S. Baring-Gould, *op. cit.*, p. 301.

[25]Sherlock Holmes, "The Adventure of the Lion's Mane" (included in *Casebook*), p. 187.

10

Personality's Map: Planes of Expression— The Inclusion

When an individual enters a library that person knows it is not possible to read everything and so decides what he or she is interested in at the moment and then hunts for a book fitting that description. In a very real sense, a chart is a human resources library. And just as many books may be read on several levels—psychological, erotic, religious, to name but a few—the same holds true for the "book of numbers."

Love is the single most important question on the minds of many people, but a question of equal, or even greater importance to many others is career. "What am I fitted for?" "Would I be wise to enter that profession?" "Will I succeed in such and such a field?" "Will I find fulfillment in that calling?" These are some of the questions people ask themselves. A careful reading of the chart can point the way.

As always, there are certain numbers that are important in any context. There are, for example, the Persona numbers. As the term implies, they represent the *person*—his or her skills and potentialities—and will apply in all areas of life. The Destiny numbers also must be borne in mind for the Path is the road we must take and the Goal is the place we must reach. And this holds true for everything we are and do, including of course, our work.

Two methods for obtaining guidelines in this vital area of life are the Planes of Expression and the Inclusion. When set down in the manner prescribed, they form what is, in effect, a bird's-eye view of the personality and its strengths and limitations. When read and interpreted in conjunction with the Tarot spread, the Plane of Expression and Inclusion can be most informative.

Planes of Expression

Each letter of the alphabet operates on a Mental, Physical, Emotional or Intuitive plane. In addition, each letter also operates on a plane of Creation, Continuation or Completion:

	Mental	*Physical*	*Emotional*	*Intuitive*
Creation	A	E	IORZ	K
Continuation	HJNP	W	BSTX	FQUY
Completion	GL	DM		CV

Meaning of the Planes

Mental—People operating largely on this plane are well-organized and often have executive ability. This is the plane of the person who thinks in large terms and can convey ideas to others. Many letters here would indicate an individual with leadership ability or one who takes pleasure in executing tasks of a mental nature.

Physical—People found on this plane take enjoyment in the physical nature of a job. The type of work could vary considerably, but whether the individuals are farmers, generals or football players, the one thing they would have in common is a conservative, practical, down-to-earth quality.

Emotional—Those with a majority of letters on this plane are people who tend to be highly creative. They work with their hearts rather than their minds. They can, of course, work with both, but essentially they are people who are all heart. What appeals to them in a given task is the emotional satisfaction that they derive from it.

Intuitive—Spiritual types, psychics and dreamers are found on this plane. It would be rare for anyone to have a majority of letters here, but an individual with two or more would be one in tune with some form of higher consciousness.

The Mental, Physical, Emotional and Intuitive Planes indicate the type of work that appeals to a given person. The horizontal planes—Creation, Continuation and Completion—suggest the kind of self-discipline a person brings to work.

Creation—Geographically, this is the highest plane and a majority of letters here would indicate a creative individual, an idea person, one who is proficient in initiating new ideas and who is capable of creative self-expression.

Continuation—Once the seed is planted, it must be watered and looked after. This is more a plane of consolidation. A majority of letters here suggests someone who can continue with a task once it has been started. If this is the dominant plane in a chart, it would indicate a plodder, the person who is good at routine, but lacks initiative or inspiration. Also, there is another meaning for this plane as it is one of duality, and so indicates a certain amount of stopping and starting. But basically, it is one of follow-up.

Completion—This is the "ground level" plane and a majority of letters here indicates someone who perseveres and one who has his or her feet on the ground. The top plane *creates*, the middle one *continues*, but this plane is important for it sees the job through and *completes* the task. As only six letters of the alphabet operate on this plane, it would be a rare person who would have a majority of letters here. In an average name of fourteen letters, one or two on this plane would be par for the course; three or more would be considered high. But in a name of any length, no letters at all on this plane would indicate someone who has trouble getting the job done.

To erect a Planes of Expression chart, be guided by the one for Sherlock Holmes shown below. Using the name by which the person is known, place each letter in the appropriate slot. Then, add up the letters on each plane and place the tally alongside or under the row.

	Mental	Physical	Emotional	Intuitive	
Creation		EE	ROO	K	6
Continuation	HH		SS		4
Completion	LCL	M			4
	5	3	5	1	

Sherlock Holmes

It is no surprise that the Mental Plane is strong in Holmes' chart but what is interesting is that equally strong is the Emotional Plane, which also has five letters. After what we learned in the preceding chapter about Holmes losing his heart to Irene Adler, we shouldn't be too surpirsed to learn that he was a man of deep emotions. This is yet further ammunition, if any be needed, to provide the death blow to Watson's perennial fantasy about Holmes being a human calculating machine.

That combination of five letters on the Mental Plane and five on the Emotional Plane is a rather happy one for it describes an individual of deep mental powers and organizational ability, but nevertheless, one who will give himself emotionally to the task at hand so that whatever he does, it will be a labor of love.

The deeper that we get into Holmes' chart, the clearer it becomes that we are dealing not with some thinking robot but with a complex individual who has *both* human strengths and human weaknesses.

On the horizontal planes, the word that comes to mind is "balance," for while Holmes' main asset is creativity, with six letters in that slot, he has four letters each for following up and finishing a task. This appears to be an accurate depiction of Holmes' overall performance for he was creative in a number of areas, but once the game was afoot, he would drive himself for days and weeks running until justice had been served.

A further clue to sexuality—in fact, the leading one—is obtained by looking at the letters on the Physical Plane. The number of letters is added together and the total is suggestive of the individual's overall love nature. Holmes has three letters on that plane, and as 3 is also his Secret Passion number, what we already know about his refined and expressive attitude toward sex is reinforced.

Sherlock Holmes, we know, sublimated his desires in a variety of ways, including music and drugs. However, with a chart so strong on the passions, it is unlikely that he was ever able to succeed in subduing those desires for very long.

The Inclusion

Volumes could be written about the Inclusion, and in some important ways, it is the single most informative aspect of a chart. It is found by looking at the number value of each letter in the name by which a person is known and then setting up a grid picturing the repetition of each number by "clothing" the grid. First, the grid is set up unclothed:

3	6	9
2	5	8
1	4	7

The method customarily employed is to figure out the total of 1s, 2s, 3s and so on, and then convert the grid in the following manner, and once again we are using the name of Sherlock Holmes:

3	2	1
1	2	2
2	1	0

Sherlock Holmes

Translated, this means that in the name by which he was known Holmes has two 1s, one 2, three 3s, one 4, two 5s, two 6s, no 7s, two 8s, and one 9.

A much more dramatic method, however, is the one used by the innovative numerologist, Austin Coates, and that is to keep the original grid but to place a circle around each number every time it appears.[1] Employing that system, Holmes' Inclusion chart looks like this:

Sherlock Holmes

We shall return to Holmes' chart later to see what further we may learn about his personality and career potential, but first we need to learn what the numbers mean in this regard.

In reading the "numbers of work," the Tarot will again be our chief couselor.

Table of Number Interpretations in the Inclusion

1

The Magician, associated with Mercury, the planet of communication, suggests a writing or speaking career. Preeminently, 1 is the number of literature. It is also the number of teaching, and of intellectual, creative, executive and innovative pursuits.

2

The High Priestess, associated with the Moon, suggests a career where emotions predominate—particularly in the theatre. As the Moon rules motherhood, 2 is also the number of the home or anyone who works at home. As it is dual, it has to do with professions having to do with deception such as diplomacy and spy work.

3

The Empress, associated with Venus, primarily represents creation, so this would relate to any of the creative arts and sciences, or a profession requiring much creative expression.

4

The Emperor, associated with Aries, is very mindful of details, and so 4 is the number of clerks and bookkeepers or any type of profession requiring detailed work. As The Emperor suffers from neurotic fears, 4 is also the number of psychotherapists, or any vocation involving health.

5

The Hierophant, associated with Taurus, indicates a job that one is committed to both body and soul. Often 5 represents an adventurous calling or glamour job, and almost always, an occupation that is people-oriented such as politics, or any position where there is much travel and communication.

6

The Lovers, associated with Gemini, refers particularly to occupants centered around products for the home. Also represented are all types of professional homemakers, sales and commercial jobs, antique dealers and certain types of teachers, particularly those whose subject matter is business-related such as commerce.

7

The Chariot, associated with Cancer, is indicative of God's heavenly messenger heralding the divine. It thus suggests a religious calling or profession dealing with the occult or anything that requires investigation or research. Because Cancer rules the stomach, any type of work involving food would also be indicated.

8

Justice (see note, page 28), associated with Libra, is indicative of law, banking or any type of government profession.

9

The Hermit, associated with Virgo, is mainly concerned with service and humanitarian enterprises on a global scale.

The final step in the Inclusion before attempting an analysis is the stress line. This offers one of the main clues to the career and is found by looking at the rows—vertical, horizontal and diagonal—and placing a line connecting the numbers on the row or rows with the greatest number of circles. There are eight possible stress lines and the interpretation is suggested by the Tarot cards in a line:

1–3 Vertical Row—The Magician, The High Priestess, The Empress. This indicates someone who is highly creative and who is dedicated to a career, often in the performing arts.

4–6 Vertical Row—The Emperor, The Hierophant, The Lovers. The combination of The Emperor and The Hierophant—the rulers of the temporal and spiritual realms—along with the decision-making card of The Lovers, suggests an individual who is temperamentally suited to command. This is the line of the generalissimo.

7–9 Vertical Row—The Chariot, Justice, The Hermit. The combination of The Chariot and Justice is one that makes for power, but The Hermit wishes to gain power in order to serve humanity. This line indicates someone who is very much a part of the power structure, but who essentially *serves* humanity.

3–9 Horizontal Row—The Empress, The Lovers, The Hermit. The Empress represents creativity, while The Lovers and The Hermit are both associated with the mental planet, Mercury. The indication is someone who works with the mind, a true intellectual, but also one who is somewhat aloof and detached.

2–8 Horizontal Row—The High Priestess, The Hierophant, Justice. As Venus is associated with both The Hierophant and Justice, and The High Priestess with the emotional Moon, this line suggests someone in a career where the emotions predominate, particularly the theatre.

1–7 Horizontal Row—The Magician, The Emperor, The Chariot. This Tarot trinity of God-men indicates someone who wishes to transform the world in his or her own image and the individual who has a stress line here will be a reformer or revolutionary in spirit if not in action.

1–9 Diagonal Row—The Magician, The Hierophant, The Hermit. As The Hierophant is "the revealer of sacred things," and The Magician and The Hermit are both associated with Mercury, the God of Communications, this is the line of the writer, teacher and anyone involved in communications of any kind. But more than anything else, it is the line of success and usually the success will come through communications.

3–7 Diagonal Row—The Empress, The Hierophant, The Chariot. This is the line of popular acclaim for it begins with the creativity of The Empress, carries through with the communicative abilities of The Hierophant and then concludes with the smashing victory of The Chariot. It is, in short, the line of fame and adulation of the masses. This line will not be found very often in a chart and when it is, the indication is very strong that this is an individual "whose name will be known."

Professors, a Pair

Before moving on to the Inclusion of Mr. Holmes, let us have a look at his nemesis, the man he called the "Napoleon of Crime"—James Moriarty.

Taking the name by which he became known, this is one of those unusual instances where a title is used in lieu of a first name, for he was to become famous—or infamous—as "Professor Moriarty."

Taking this in a step-by-step fashion, we first set down his name and find the numbers:

```
        6   5   6       6   9 1
   P R O F E S S O R   M O R I A R T Y   33
   7 9   6   1 1   9   4   9       9 2 7   64
                                         ——
                                         97 = 16 = 7
```

The next step is to get a count of each number in the name:

    1s—3
    2s—1
    3s—0
    4s—1
    5s—1
    6s—4
    7s—2
    8s—0
    9s—5

and now we're ready to set up the chart:

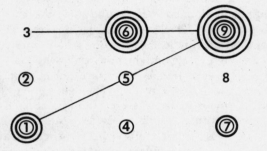

Professor Moriarty

One of the first things that strikes us about the chart of Professor Moriarty is the similarity with the one of Sherlock Holmes. We note in the Keys the 6/1 split and the strong 7. This is true also of the Inclusion, for, like Holmes, Moriarty has a stress line on the "head numbers," 3–9. But we see that the most powerful numbers in the Inclusion are 9, 6 and 1 with respectively five, four and three circles. The corresponding Tarot cards—The Hermit, The Lovers and The Magician—are *all* associated with Mercury, the planet of Mentality. As 9 is also the Professor's Secret Passion number, Mercury may be said to represent the governor of the chart.

The focus on the mental is further reinforced by the two stress lines—one on the head numbers, 9–6–3, and the other, the communications line of 9–5–1. It is clear that this is an introverted man, somewhat aloof, who in some way will communicate to the world at large, and as the 1–5–9 line is weighted in 9, all things will return to "Number 1."

This is a rather strong chart for all but two numbers are clothed, and one stress line deals with thought, the other with action. But mental and communicative powers are not intrinsically "good" or "bad"; all depends on how they are used and upon what energy and spiritual levels the individual is operating.

On one level, this could be the chart of a brilliant mathematician who would inspire with his teaching. One is reminded that the title, "Professor," was one that he earned as a scholar. During the summer of 1872, he served as tutor in mathematics to Sherlock Holmes.[2]

Is there anything in Professor Moriarty's chart to indicate that he would embark on a career that would prove so destructive to humanity? There are only hints, but taken together they are suggestive. There is, for example, the weak 2, the number of cooperation and association, which has only one circle. Then there are the missing "Venus numbers," 3 (The Empress) and 8 (Justice, see note on page 28), indicating a lack of feeling and refinement. In the Professor's case, the missing 8 may be seen as a lack of regard for the law. The 2–5–8 horizontal row is considered the "heart line" and that is the weakest one in the chart as there are only two numbers with one circle each.

Moriarty's chart is quite similar to another individual that the world also knew by the title of "Professor," and his chart looks like this:

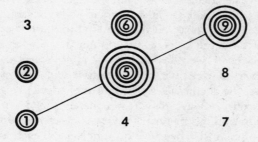

Professor Einstein

Note that Professor Einstein also has the 9–5–1 stress line and strong head numbers. He too is missing the Venus numbers, 3 and 8. Perhaps the principal difference is that while Moriarty has Mercury as the ruler of his chart (five circles around 9, the number of the Hermit, associated with Virgo which is ruled by Mercury), Einstein's Secret Passion is 5, the number of involvement in the world. Because the corresponding card in the Tarot is The Hierophant, the ruler of his chart is Venus, the goddess of Love. Mercury knowledge can go either way, but Venus love can only benefit humanity.

Casebook—The Hidden Career of Mr. Holmes

For those who have followed Sherlock Holmes in his many cases over the years, one of the more engaging things about him is his sense of showmanship and flair for the dramatic. Holmes' theatricality is evident in almost all his adventures. Take for example, that climactic scene in the case Watson chronicled as "A Study in Scarlet" where Holmes plays cat and mouse with two of Scotland Yard's finest, Lestrade and Gregson, who—baffled as usual—have paid a call on Holmes in the hopes of getting some small clue as to the name of the murderer. Holmes acknowledges that he is in possession of this information, but would prefer not to divulge it until the time is ripe. Then there comes a knock at the door and young

Wiggins, the street urchin leader of the Baker Street Irregulars, enters to tell Holmes that a cab is waiting for him downstairs. Holmes tells Wiggins to ask the cabman to come up and help with the luggage. Then brandishing a pair of handcuffs, he remarks to Lestrade and Gregson, "Why don't you introduce this pattern at Scotland Yard...See how beautifully the spring works. They fasten in an instant."

"The old pattern is good enough, remarked Lestrade, if we can only find the man to put them on."

The cabman then enters the room. " 'Just give me a help with this buckle, cabman,' he said, kneeling over his task, and never turning his head."

Watson states that "the fellow came forward with a somewhat sullen, defiant air and put down his hands to assist. At that instant there was a sharp click, the jangling of metal, and Sherlock Holmes sprang to his feet again.

" 'Gentlemen,' he cried, with flashing eyes, 'let me introduce you to Mr. Jefferson Hope, the murderer of Enoch Drebber and of Joseph Strangerson.' "[3]

A magnificent bit of stagecraft that, and in these little theatrical exercises, as Holmes might have called them, he was not only the chief actor but the director and dramatist as well. We realize that Holmes was also a past master of disguise and so artful were his impersonations that at times even Watson was taken in. Of course the doctor was well aware of Sherlock's singular gifts in this realm and in his phraseology, "It was not merely that Holmes changed his costume. His expression, his manner, his very soul seemed to vary with every fresh part that he assumed. The stage lost a fine actor, even as science lost an acute reasoner, when he became a specialist in crime."[4]

Let us now have another look at Holmes' Inclusion:

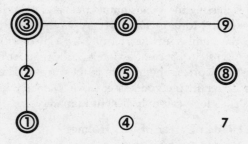

Sherlock Holmes

Looking at his chart we realize that Watson was probably speaking the literal truth for one of the stress lines is the 3–1 vertical, most often an indication of an actor or musician.

Actually, both of Holmes' professions are indicated in this chart. The other stress line is the 3–9 horizontal, which tells of a man who possesses strong mental powers. This line would, of course, account for his career as a consulting detective.

But primarily this is the chart of a performer. In addition to the artistic stress line, the Secret Passion is 3, which again suggests music or some other field of creative self-expression. And the "heart line" (2–8 horizontal) is also strong with all numbers circled and 5 and 8 in doubles.

Is it possible that Sherlock Holmes was ever on the stage? Several Sherlockian commentators are under that impression and have pointed to evidence that Holmes made a brief foray into the theatre before settling down to his better-known career. According to one biographer, Holmes made his first appearance on the London stage in October, 1879, taking William Escott as his stage name.[5] Because his baptismal name was William Sherlock Scott Holmes,[6] it can be seen that he kept two of his Christian names, William and Scott. And when "Escott" is pronounced, it sounds like "S. Scott," the "S" of course, being for Sherlock. We further learn that Holmes (as Escott) made his debut in the role of Horatio in *Hamlet*.[7] Escott-Holmes must have felt more than a tinge of irony when Horatio is asked by Hamlet to observe the King's countenance during the play within the play and the script compels him to deliver the line,

"Well my lord.

If 'a steal naught the whilst this play is playing,

And scape detecting I will pay the theft."[8]

Escott-Holmes' first role of consequence was that of Cassius, in *Julius Caesar*,[9] a part for which he was unquestionably right. In fact, it would almost seem that Shakespeare had Holmes in mind when he has Caesar say,

"Let me have men about me that are fat;

Sleek-headed men and such as sleep o' nights.

Yond Cassius has a lean and hungry look;

He thinks too much. Such men are dangerous.

...He reads much,

He is a great observer, and he looks

Quite through the deeds of men."[10]

When theatre people say someone is "right" for a role, they do not so much mean that an actor looks the part, but rather, that he *is* the part. Let us pause for a moment to take a brief glance at the numbers of Cassius and see how they match Holmes' chart. We note first that Cassius' Expression number is 1, the same as Holmes. When we set up his Inclusion, it looks like this:

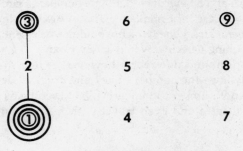

Cassius

Quite a different chart from Holmes in some respects, but the major trends are the same—a strong 1 and 3 and the stress line on the 1–3 vertical: Dedication to a career!

According to one of Holmes' principal biographers, "Critics are generally agreed that 'William Escott' made an amazing success as an actor."[11]

And small wonder. Look at his chart:

William Escott

There is only a single stress line in this Holmes-Escott chart and that is the one of the actor who lives only for his craft.

Let us set up Holmes' chart again and do a comparison:

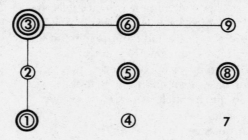

Sherlock Holmes

Although "William Escott" appears a rather different name from "Sherlock Holmes," we immediately note certain similarities in the charts. In addition to the "career dedication" stress line, we see that 3, the number of self-expression and hunger for applause, remains the (not so) Secret Passion. We see further that numbers 1, 4 and 5 have the exact same number of circles as in the original chart! And in both cases, the number 7 is bare. Also missing in Escott's chart is the "head numbers" stress line, which would not be essential for an actor, but one that a consulting detective would surely need.

The most profound difference, however, is that in Escott's chart, the number 8 is missing—the number of law and criminal detection. But, 8 had been Holmes' Roof number too long. William Escott was to continue tasting success in the theatre and even travel with his company on a triumphal

American tour. But upon his return to London he would take on the role for which he was superbly suited. A role that would prove to be one of the longest running hits of all time. And that role, of course, was to be Sherlock Holmes—The World's First Consulting Detective.

Casebook—Sherlock's Smarter Older Brother

On an April evening Holmes and Watson are discussing the origins of Holmes' remarkable powers of ratiocination. Watson believes that he has acquired them by self-training while Holmes insists that they are hereditary. To make his point, he reveals to Watson the existence of an older brother, Mycroft, whom he considers his superior in both observation and deduction. In a rare instance of modesty, Holmes admits that on the really tough cases he goes to his brother, and invariably Mycroft's solutions prove to be correct. When Watson inquires why he has not heard of him as a detective, Holmes tells him that sleuthing is not Mycroft's profession. He has the gift, states Holmes, but not the energy or desire. We learn also that Mycroft is seven years Sherlock's senior and that he has a post in the British Government.

Sherlock Holmes has, as we have seen, an extraordinary chart, and if, by his own admission, his older brother is actually his superior in intellect, it might be instructive to study Mycroft's Inclusion:

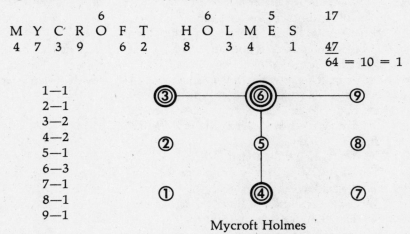

$$
\begin{array}{ccccccc}
& 6 & & & 6 & & 5 & & 17 \\
\text{M Y C R O F T} & & \text{H O L M E S} & & \\
4\ 7\ 3\ 9\quad 6\ 2 & & 8\quad 3\ 4\quad 1 & & \underline{47} \\
& & & & & & & & 64 = 10 = 1
\end{array}
$$

1—1
2—1
3—2
4—2
5—1
6—3
7—1
8—1
9—1

Mycroft Holmes

A cursory glance at his brother's chart tells us that Sherlock was indeed telling the truth. We note first those powerful Inner Self numbers of 8 and the Master number, 11; and like Sherlock, a 1 on the Persona. In the Inclusion itself we see that even though the name is somewhat shorter than average (13 letters) all numbers are clothed, indicating one who has no Karmic Lessons to learn.

Then, wonder of wonders, Mycroft has what is known as the Cross of Destiny—the 4–6 center vertical stress line supporting the 3–9 crossbar.

That 3–9 stress line is the mark of a mental type and is the same line we observed in the charts of Professors Einstein and Moriarty, and of course, Sherlock Holmes. But looking at Mycroft's chart in comparison with Sherlock's, we note that Mycroft's "head numbers" are somewhat stronger. While Sherlock's Secret Passion was 3, the number associated with Venus and the arts, Mycroft's Secret Passion is 6, the number associated with Mercury. It is also a more harmonious chart than Sherlock's—note the perfect balance of one circle each on the 1–9 diagonal, the 2–8 horizontal and the 7–9 vertical. In an Inclusion chart, balance is of tremendous significance and will indicate abilities of a very special order. In Mycroft's case, the abilities would lie in communications (1–9 diagonal), feeling (2–8 horizontal) and power to influence others (7–9 vertical). As good as Sherlock's chart is, there are no balanced rows. Holmes was correct; Mycroft would have the edge over him in the arts of observation and deduction. And this is borne out in Watson's initial meeting with Mycroft in the Strangers' Room of the Diogones Club in London. At that time the mentally acrobatic brothers engage in a cerebral tennis match, for as Watson relates, "The two sat down together in the bow-window of the club.

" 'To anyone who wishes to study mankind this is the spot' said Mycroft, 'Look at the magnificent types. Look at these two men who are coming towards us for example.'

" 'The billiard-maker and the other?'

" 'Precisely. What do you make of the other?'

" 'The two men had stopped opposite the window. Some chalk marks over the waistcoat pocket were the only signs of billiards which I could see on one of them. The other was a very small, dark fellow with his hat pushed back and several packages under his arm.

" 'An old soldier, I perceive,' said Sherlock.

" 'And very recently discharged,' remarked the brother.

" 'Served in India, I see.'

" 'And a non-commissioned officer.'

" 'Royal Artillery, I fancy', said Sherlock.

" 'And a widower.'

" 'But with a child.'

" 'Children, my dear boy, children.' "[12]

Truly, there is the feeling we have witnessed a battle of mental giants, and as his chart suggests, Mycroft did succeed in one-upping his less intelligent brother.

Sherlock Holmes enjoyed two careers, one in the theatre, and the other in criminal detection—and rose to the top in both fields. Mycroft, however, shared but one of his brother's interests—detection—and only as a hobby. His primary occupation is indicated by the second stress line (6–4 vertical), the line of command. This is considered the line of The Prime Minister and it is significant that Mycroft was in the British Government. That he enjoyed preeminence there may be attested to by Holmes' remark to Watson to the effect that Mycroft was not only part of the British Government, but that there were times when he *was* the British Government.

Casebook—The Final Problem for Dr. Watson

In reference to the Sherlockian canon, one of the greatest unsolved mysteries concerning the doings of the Master is exactly *who* was the author of the narratives?

A word of qualification is perhaps needed here for of the four longer and fifty-six shorter accounts, there are at least three authors. Sherlock Holmes himself penned "The Adventure of the Blanched Soldier" and "The Adventure of the Lion's Mane." A brace of the later tales—"The Adventure of the Mazarin Stone" and "His Last Bow"—is of disputed authorship. But of the fifty-six remaining pieces, the narrator is ostensibly John Watson, M.D. For any soul who has cast so much as a sleepy glance at the canonical writings, this fact is so blindingly obvious that it would scarcely bear mention were it not for one rude item of recrudescence: In every work authored by Dr. Watson, there appears on the dust jacket and title page the name, "Sir Arthur Conan Doyle." Since everyone *knows* that Watson is the true author, the question continues to intrude: Exactly who and what is this Arthur Conan Doyle?

It is no good to ask a Baker Street Irregular, or one of the Hounds of the Baskerville—those being two of the guises under which Sherlockians travel—for at best you will be showered with an elfin smile and the enigmatic reply, "Doyle? Conan Doyle? Oh, *that* Doyle. He was the agent."

The logical inference, of course, is that he was acting as Watson's literary agent and helped the doctor to line up a publisher. But this seems unlikely for Sir Authur was himself a man of letters in the front rank of British authors. Why should a prestigious writer of medieval romances who had been acclaimed for such masterpieces as *Micah Clarke* and *The White Company* deign to moonlight as a publisher's errand boy for a part-time doctor involved in helping chase after criminals and then writing the cases up for public consumption?

One possibility is that Doyle identified in some way with Watson's mentor, Sherlock Holmes. But after a moment's thought, this thesis must be discarded as being too outlandish. For Doyle and Holmes were universes apart in just about every way. Holmes was a man of science and rationality. He placed criminal detection on a scientific basis and his theories and methods had a profound influence on Scotland Yard and other great criminal detection centers throughout the world. He was a hard-nosed investigator who began and ended with the facts; the feet of Sherlock Holmes were firmly planted on mother earth.

But Arthur Conan Doyle was a man of vastly different attitudes and temperament. Where Holmes was a man of earth, today, and this world, Doyle's inner universe was concerned with the Middle Ages and with the romance of chivalry when Knighthood was in flower. And far from being concerned with this world, his all-consuming passion was the next world and, in fact, he devoted the last twelve years of his life to lecturing on spiritualism. Spiritualists believe that not only do the dead have an existence on another plane, but that they can communicate with friends and relatives through a medium, and this is something that Holmes would have laughed to scorn.

And far from being an exponent of science and rationality, Doyle often inveighed against them by serving as a champion for trance mediums and other practitioners of the occult. His obsession with psychic phenomena was such that he accepted a paranormal explanation for something where a rational one would suffice, such as his explaining Houdini's escapes as psychic dematerializations.

If Sherlock Holmes would have laughed up his sleeve at Doyle's explanation of Houdini's feats, he would have doubtless been totally convulsed with merriment had his piercing gray eyes chanced upon the following exchange between Doyle and his friend, Houdini. Doyle writes, "I have something...precious, two photos, one of a goblin, the other of four fairies in a Yorkshire wood. A fake! you will say. No sir; I think not. However, all inquiry will be made. These I am not allowed to send. The fairies are about eight inches high. In one there is a single goblin dancing. In the other, four beautiful luminous creatures. Yes, it is a revelation."[13]

It is not our purpose here to comment on the validity of fairies or any other of Sir Arthur's theories or findings but only to note that here is a man who would seemingly have little in common with the clear-thinking, practical Mr. Holmes. Much more likely, he became involved as a service to Watson. We know that Doyle was an M.D., and in the days when he practiced medicine at Southsea, a colleague and friend of his was, in fact, a certain "Dr. Watson."[14]

Was this the same Dr. Watson who was later to turn author and trade on his friendship with Doyle in seeking out a publisher? The Great Detective was fond of saying that when one has eliminated the impossible, whatever remains, however improbable, has to be the truth. That ex-Doctor Doyle did it as an act of friendship seems the most likely explanation.

But one mystery still remains. For if our deductions are correct and we have some idea why Doyle became involved as "the agent" for Watson, we are no closer to knowing the extent of his involvement. Did he actually write the pieces about Holmes or only lend his name? History is silent on this but clues are available, and let us begin with the primary one, the Inclusion chart of Dr. Watson.

The first thing we notice about Dr. Watson's chart are the gaps. The numbers 3, 4, 7 and 9 are not circled and while most of them are compensated for elsewhere in his chart, there would still remain some problem with the energies they represent—creative expression (3), details (4), spiritual insight (7) and communicating with large groups of people (9).

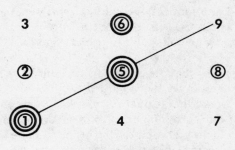

John Watson

It is rare to find 9 as a missing number in the Inclusion and this indicates someone who has much to learn about any project involving the larger community. Nine is also a number of completion and would suggest someone who has trouble finishing things. Florence Campbell has this to say about the person with a missing 9: "Life will offer jolt after jolt to the emotional nature until it is thoroughly awakened. The minus 9 will be called upon to relinquish all without personal satisfaction or reward."[15]

The karmic 9 in Watson's chart is partially atoned for in the Keys as he has it as one of his Inner Self numbers. But it is on the wrong side of the chart! As the Psyche it would be vague and undifferentiated, particularly with no other 9s in the chart to set it off. Had it been the Soul Urge number, there would have been an all-consuming drive to communicate freely and dive into the sea of humanity.

Dr. Watson has two Secret Passions, for 1 and 5 are each encircled three times. This begins to look promising then for 1 is the number of the writer and 5 is the number of involvement and reaching out and making connections. It begins, in short, to look like an author's chart. We note further that Watson's stress line is on the 1–9 diagonal, which is "the writer's line."

But closer inspection gives us pause. For one thing, 1 and 5 are equally weighted with three circles each so there is no real movement to the line. It could represent a balance between writing (1) and healing (5—remember the number's association with The Hierophant), but lacking a "weighted end," the arrow may not find its mark.

And worse still, if the direction of flow is seen as 1 to 9, we note that since 9 is uncircled, there seems to be no way to get there. Watson's stress line appears to say that something is started but that it never arrives at its destination, which in this case would be the reading public.

Our case is reasonably complete when we look at Watson's Planes of Expression. For we see that he has three letters on the Plane of Creativity, seven letters on the middle Plane of Continuation (and vacillation), but that on the Plane of Completion, he draws a complete blank! In itself, this would not necessarily be disasterous but combined with the other aforementioned shortcomings, it becomes clear that the final problem for Dr. Watson was that he could start the tales of his friend, Sherlock Holmes, but that someone else had to finish them.

We can guess now the role of "the agent," but let's check out the facts, my dear Watson, before we theorize further.

To begin with, Arthur Conan Doyle was born on May 22, 1859,[16] which would not only give him that Master Number on the Persona, but would also place him in a 22 cycle during his productive years. (His opening and closing Cycles were also strong as they were both 5, which tied in with his Expression and Path numbers.) Examining his Keys we find "the writer's 1" as his Cornerstone, Roof and Psyche number. Five, the number of verbal communication, is to be found on both his Persona and Destiny, while the Master Number, 22, which appears on his Persona, is re-echoed as the all-encompassing Soul Urge. And his Goal is 9—humanity at large. In short, he starts with 1 and ends with 9—the writer who conveys his message to the people. This communicating power is further borne out in his Inclusion:

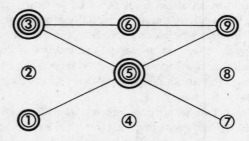

Arthur Conan Doyle

Simply looking at this chart intuitively makes us gasp with awe at the power and beauty of Sir Arthur's numbers. First, we note that all numbers are clothed, the mark of an old soul. The Secret Passions are the communicative expression numbers of 3 and 5, while the numbers of the writer (1) and the people (9) are both strong.

And something rather unusual, we find not one stress line, or two, but three. And as everything radiates from 5, this suggests a man of many interests and immense energies.

One of the stress lines is that of the writer, 1-9, but as 1 and 9 each have two circles, more than one career is indicated. And with both a 3-9 horizontal and a 3-7 diagonal stress line, the intelligence to do the job is there; fame and success are assured.

The picture is completed by the Planes of Expression for Doyle has seven letters on the Creative Plane, six on the Plane of Continuation, and three on the Completion Plane. Here is the chart of a writer's writer and quite clearly what

Maxwell Perkins was to Thomas Wolfe, Sir Arthur Conan Doyle was to Dr. Watson. While it is true that without Watson, the world may have never heard of Sherlock Holmes, it is no less true that without Doyle, the world may jolly well have heard of *neither* Holmes nor Watson.

It is time to give credit where credit is due and I say hurrah for Arthur Conan Doyle, the man who gave Sherlock Holmes to the world!

The Spread: Talent and Career Potential

This spread is used when the consultant wishes guidance in selecting or changing a career.

Throw the spread as follows:

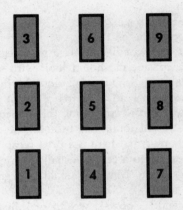

After the cards have been cut and shuffled, lay out nine cards according to the diagram. Begin by reading each card individually according to the "job slot" it is in. The first slot, for example, has to do with the communications field, so that The Wheel of Fortune in that slot would be extemely encouraging, whereas the 2 of Swords would suggest looking elsewhere. Here is a brief description of the career potential for each number:

1—Writing, teaching, communications, innovative career.

2—The theatre, diplomacy, service occupations.

3—The creative arts and sciences, particularly music, anything expressive or creative, including parenting.

4—Clerks, bookkeepers, psychotherapists, health-related vocations, detailed work of any kind.

5—Politics, guidance work, bartending, glamour jobs, work involving much travel or adventure, any job where there is tactile gratification.

6—Commerce, garden-variety jobs, selling, collecting, home management.

7—Religious, spiritual or occult calling; research, any profession involving food.

8—Law, banking, The Power Structure.

9—Humanitarian service, social work, people-oriented enterprises on a grand scale.

If any of the following cards appear in their designated slots, it would indicate a particular proclivity or talent for the line of work indicated:

1—The Magician
2—The Star
3—The World
4—The High Priestess
5—The Fool
6—The Lovers
7—The Hermit
8—Justice (see note, page 28)
9—The Angel of Time

Aces are significant and would indicate a new beginning in a particular line of work. Also, the consultant should look with special interest at the cards that tie in with the Inner Self, Persona and Destiny numbers.

After each card has been read in terms of talent and career potential, interpretation is made of the row containing the invisible stress line, that is, the row with the highest point total. The meanings are essentially the same as stated earlier in the chapter, but here is a brief recap:

1-3 Vertical—Dedication to a career, usually in the arts or sciences.

4-6 Vertical—The Prime Minister, skillful organizer, enterpreneur, generalissimo.

7-9 Vertical—Tremendous power, wealth or influence, or combination of all three.

3-9 Horizontal—The Scholar.

2-8 Horizontal—The theatre, any line of work involving powerful emotions.

1-7 Horizontal—Reformer, any line of work involved with changing the status quo.

1-9 Diagonal—Line of success. Skill in communications, particularly writing.

3-7 Diagonal—A person of great magnetism, often a public figure.

The Tape:

Chart		Tarot	
Roof	5	Card 1—The Chariot	
Secret Passion	9	2—The Star	
Inner Self (Psyche)	9	3—The Magician	
Inner Self (Soul Urge)	2	4—7 of Wands	
Persona (Birth)	8	5—Wheel of Fortune	
Persona (Expression)	1½	6—8 of Wands	
Destiny (Path)	3	7—5 of Wands	
Destiny (Goal)	1½	8—The Lovers	
Cornerstone	9	9—Knight of Wands	

The consultant is a scintillating woman with a large number of interests and abilities. She is active in several fields related to the arts and sciences and has much solid experience in communications.

SK: You have what I would call a writer's chart. It is most interesting that the Number 1 slot signifies writing, for the card there is The Chariot. It is clear that you have been quite successful in this field.

Consultant: I have, as you know, a number of interests, but you're quite right, writing has been "my" field.

SK: The card in the Number 2 spot should be important because both your Expression and Goal number is the Master Number 11, and because there are only nine cards in this spread, we have to reduce it to 2, but I think of 11 as a career in the limelight and 2 is the number of the theatre.

Consultant: I know what I think but what does the Tarot say?

SK: Well, I would say that you and the Tarot are of one accord in this respect for the card here is The Star, and it is especially significant in this case as it is the precise card designated for this spot.

Consultant: Does that mean I might have been another Katherine Cornell?

SK: Had you gone into the theatre, Miss Cornell would have probably measured herself by your standards. The Tarot is really shouting at this point and what it is saying is that had you pursued a theatrical career, you would have been a star of the first magnitude.

Consultant: That is certainly nice to know!

SK: Not only do you have The Star in the theater spot, but since it is Arcanum XVII, it reduces to 8, which is your other Persona number. And with The Star in the 1½ slot of this grid, it also ties in with both your Expression and Goal numbers. This means that it would be hard for you to miss in this field.

Consultant: I've always believed that, but I may be prejudiced.

SK: You may be, but the Tarot clearly is not. So we'll just have to accept it as a fact of life.

Consultant: I won't argue.

SK: We said before that you had a Destiny–Goal number of 11. Your other Destiny number is 3, which is the Path you must take in order to reach the Goal. Now, I'm turning over the Number 3 card, and in hockey parlance I would say that you have just pulled the hat trick for this is the card of The Magician.

Consultant: Believe me, there have been times when I had to pull some rabbits out of hats.

SK: The point is that you had the ability to make them materialize. This does offer added insight into your chart for ordinarily the 3 Path is strewn with red carpets and garlands of roses.

Consultant: There have been plenty of roses but I had to go out and pick them.

SK: Yes, that is what the Tarot is saying. You have had, I am sure, an interesting life with plenty of high spots but things did not exactly fall into your lap. You brought them about for you are The Magician.

Consultant: If you only knew how true that is.

SK: But even more to the point, 3 is the number of creativity and The Magician is associated with Mercury, the ruler of communications. So not only have you enjoyed success in this field, but there is a considerable amount of native talent there.

Consultant: This is really incredible. You told me that the 1–3 line of my chart had to do with the arts and was very powerful and here the Tarot seems to be saying exactly the same thing.

SK: With regard to astro-numeric charts, that is really the way of the Tarot—to reinforce and add to what we have learned. Now the fourth card is the 7 of Wands, which is the card of The Writer. Do you have something in the works right now?

Consultant: There's a book that wants to get started, but I am torn between that and the counselling work that I am involved in at the moment.

SK: Well, 4 is the number of details and hard work, so I guess what the Tarot is saying is that the book is going to take lots of hard work.

Consultant: I guess I can take a hint. In other words, the only way I am going to get the book done is to sit down and do it.

SK: Right. But now is the time to do it as you are in an 8 Personal Year, which is a power year for you. Any projects undertaken this year should pay off. Whatever you do, don't start the book next year or you'll never finish it as you will then be in a 9 Year and that's no time to start anything. Things don't start in a 9 Year, they finish.

Consultant: Didn't you say before that a 1 Year was a good time to start on something creative?

SK: Absolutely right! On second thought, it might be best to stick with what you're doing now and wait for the 1 Year before you pick up that pen. Looking at your chart, I see that what is known as the Essence of your chart for that 1 Year is the Master Number 22—so it should prove to be a fantastic year not only for getting the words on paper, but also for getting the book into the hands of the world.

Consultant: That does look good!

SK: I can't believe all these Major Arcana cards—the fifth card is The Wheel of Fortune! Five is the number of involvement in a number of projects and, financially, they are apparently doing very well.

Consultant: That's true right now but there have been some rough periods.

SK: Right, but as this is a spread for the overall pattern of the life, I think that in general you live a kind of enchanted life. Also, 5 is a number of travel and I think of the Wheel of Fortune as a traveling card, so I suspect that you have managed to see something of the world.

Consultant: That does seem to fit. I've always loved going to romantic places.

SK: The Number 6 card is the 8 of Wands. Since 6 is the number of home, I am wondering if there is somebody in your family that you have to handle with kid gloves.

Consultant: That would be Mummie. You know about the problem with her from the other spreads we did. So, yes, that is true. It has been a very tight situation and I need all the tact I can muster to deal with my mother right now.

SK: The seventh card is the 5 of Wands. So far, Wands is the only suit in the Minor Arcana that has come up for you, which is appropriate as this is a work spread and Wands do deal with work. But the implication here is that you work not because you have to but because you want to. Apparently, work—that is, creative work—has always been important to you.

Consultant: I have always known that.

SK: But Number 7 has to do with spiritual things so this card seems to be saying that there is a kind of spiritual fulfillment that you derive from creative work.

Consultant: That is extremely true.

SK: The eighth card we want to look at with particular care as 8 is one of your Persona numbers. Eight is also the number of law, banking and balance, and the card of The Lovers in this spot seems to indicate that there is an imbalance somewhere. We go back to your chart and note that your Persona numbers are 8 and 11, and I think that is where the imbalance begins as the number 8 has to do with responsibility and material things, while 11 is a Master Number indicating creative and spiritual pursuits. There probably have been times when this polarity presented a real dilemma for you, no?

Consultant: You have just hit on the story of my life! I have often thought of going into a convent. One day I say who needs material things? And the next day I say, "I do." But it is an ongoing battle.

SK: I guess it all depends which number is on the ascendant at a given point—8 or that Master Number, 11. And don't forget, you are in a 8 cycle right now and will remain in it for some time.

Consultant: I guess the convent will have to wait.

SK: The ninth card is the Knight of Wands. This makes the spread all of a piece for 9 has to do with emotional intensity and you apparently are a person who puts a good deal of yourself into anything you do. And since 9 is a number of humanitarian enterprises, and the Knight of Wands is thoughts about work, you tend to think of your work as a way of reaching out to humanity.

Somehow, too, this card seems to go with your sign, Pisces. For I think of natives of Pisces as being knights-errant riding off to fight the good fight for humanity's sake. Edgar Cayce would just be the most obvious example.

Or, come to think of it, the second most obvious example, for you are about as knight-errantish as a person can get.

Consultant: It was sweet of you to say that.

SK: There is one final thing, and that is to find the strongest row by point total. You remember, when I first completed your chart and spoke to you on the phone, I said you were probably talented in the arts, but were involved in communications as a career. I said that because the strongest row in the Inclusion was the 1–9 diagonal. Let's see if the Tarot agrees. Isn't this something! The 1–9 diagnoal, which might be called Writers' Row, is one of the stronger ones in this spread going by the number of total points in a row. But there is one row that is even stronger and that is the 2–8 horizontal line, which is the heartline of the chart and the row of the theatre. And with The Star as one of the cards, you might just reconsider.

Consultant: Are you trying to tell me that the convent's loss...

SK: Would be the theatre's gain...exactly!

[1]Austin Coates, *Numerology—The Meaning of Numbers*, Citadel Press, Secaucus, N.J., 1975, *passim*.

[2]William S. Baring-Gould, *Sherlock Holmes of Baker Street—A Life of the World's First Consulting Detective*, Bramhall House, New York, 1962, p. 62.

[3]John Watson, M.D. (amanuensis: Arthur Conan Doyle), *The Adventures of Sherlock Holmes* ("A Study in Scarlet"), Heritage Press, New York, p. 62.

[4]*Ibid.*, ("A Scandal in Bohemia"), p. 256.

[5]William S. Baring-Gould, *op. cit.*, p. 48.

[6]*Ibid.*, p. 13.

[7]*Ibid.*, p. 296.

[8]William Shakespeare, *Hamlet*, Act III, sc. 2.

[9]William S. Baring-Gould, *op. cit.*, p. 49.

[10]William Shakespeare, *Julius Caesar*, Act I, sc. 2.

[11]William S. Baring-Gould, *op. cit.*, p. 48.

[12]John Watson, M.D. (amanuensis: Arthur Conan Doyle), *op. cit.*, ("The Greek Interpreter"), p. 696.

[13]As quoted in Martin Gardner's essay, *The Irrelevance of Conan Doyle,* included in the Sherlockian Anthology, *Beyond Baker Street,* edited by Michael Harrison, Bobbs-Merrill, New York, 1976, p. 129.

[14]John Dickson Carr, *The Life of Sir Arthur Conan Doyle,* Vintage Books, New York, p. 70.

[15]Florence Campbell, *Your Days Are Numbered,* Gateway, Pa., 1976, p. 150.

[16]John Dickson Carr, *op. cit.,* p. 10.

11

Tomorrow and Tomorrow and Tomorrow: The Letters of Transit—Alternate Methods of Prediction

Yesterday. Today. Tomorrow. They are time's trinity as revealed by the chart. And, while "all our yesterdays" may "have lighted fools the way to dusty death," they have enabled the wise man to gain the inner light of self-understanding.

To the numerologist, the Yesterday of a chart is of profound significance for therein is revealed the foundation of the life. It is well and good to know the future but of what use will it serve if we have overlooked and failed to understand the Morning of our life. The early years of childhood that some call maturity, and others, youth or middle age, are the formative ones for the Evening and our lives to come. Only by fully understanding our Yesterday ". . . ye shall know the truth and the truth shall make you free."[1]

Next in importance is our Today, for that is the moment of time in which we live and move and have our being. By knowing our Personal Day, Month and Year, along with our current Cycle and Pinnacle, we can more fully comprehend our influences of the moment, the better to cope with them.

We understand the past; we cope with the present; but we *prepare* for the future. From what we have already learned, we can do this with some degree of accuracy by studying our coming Cycles and Pinnacles and the personal vibrations we will be under during a given time period.

But while a Pinnacle or Cycle may be quite informative in describing a pattern of a decade or more, it may not say very much about a specific year. We know what Personal Year we are in at any given time, but that is not a complete picture either. We could, for example, be going into a 3 Personal Year, and thus know that it will be a rather pleasant time period and one where we will not be overly burdened with responsibilities. And while a 3 Personal Year is a fairly good time for marriage, what are the prospects, if any, that the *opportunity* for marriage will be there? How does the year look from a monetary point of view? Does it seem likely that there will be a promotion or change of job in the year ahead? You say you want to move to another part of the country; is it likely that you will have the chance to do so sometime in the twelve months following?

There are a number of ways of forecasting along rather precise lines but the one that might be considered the Old Faithful of numerology is what is known variously as the Immediate Period Table, the Excursion or the description preferred by this author—the Letters of Transit. As indicated, it is based upon the transits of each letter in your name. In a manner not unlike that of an astrologer, a numerologist can progress an individual chart ahead for any year in the life and predict occurrences, opportunities and influences based upon the particular name letters in transit during a specific twelve-month period.

In order to predict with some degree of accuracy, however, it will be necessary to go against a rule that was stated earlier concerning setting up a chart using the name by which a person is known. This is one of those instances in which best results are obtained by using the full name that you were given at birth. If humanly possible, obtain a copy of your birth certificate as "something may have gotten lost in the translation," and you may not be who you think you are. The reason for using the "birth certificate name" is that if you are setting up a chart that looks ahead (or back) ten, twenty, fifty years or more, the starting point or "birth time" of the name must be correct. Looked at another way, an astrologer can erect a chart of planetary transits by house for some time in the future only if the true time of birth is known, for one follows from the other. And while a woman who has had her name changed by marriage could tell you the birth time of her new name, most people who are known by names other than the ones that appear on their birth certificates would probably be hard pressed to tell you exactly what day, month and year they made the name change, or had it made for them.

Also, if the truth be told, the vibrations under which we were originally born will always be there in some fashion or other. They are the basic underlying vibrations of the life and while we can intensify or alter them, we cannot obliterate them. The "birth name" is not unlike our physical body in that we can effect substantial changes to it. If we have a body we are not overly happy with and start early enough, we can, through affirmative thinking, exercise, proper diet and training, strengthen or streamline it. But only to a degree. For the frame we were born with is the one we must carry with us throughout life. We can alter it to some extent but we cannot trade it in for a different model.

By changing our name, or having it changed for us, we intensify or weaken the original vibrations, and sometimes succeed in altering them drastically, but they still remain. Depending on how you have changed your name, and more importantly, how you have changed your thinking and your actions, the transits will be felt with greater or lesser force but they will still be felt. However much an individual has succeeded in altering his or her material, psychological and spiritual state, that person remains responsive to original birth influences. Essentially, transits reveal *energies* we will be under and *opportunities* for change that will be in operation. And transits can be rather precise: An opportunity to move, or marry, or do or undo any number of things, can be foretold with considerable accuracy.

Once the transit chart is set up, it can be progressed ahead to any year of the life. So if you are now twenty-one and wish to see what specific influences will be in effect at age twenty-two or age ninety, it will be possible to do so. Or if you wish to look back and see why you went slightly crazy at age sixteen, the chart will tell you that also. You may look backward or forward and in fact should do both for the future is no more than the sum total of the past.

To erect the transit chart, begin by printing the full name that appeared on your birth certificate at the top of a piece of paper. If, for any reason, you cannot lay hands on your birth certificate, simply put down what you have been told from childhood is your *full name*, and keep your fingers crossed. Below that, forming a horizontal line, write the numbers 1 to 9. As you are going to write the transiting letters of each name on separate lines, leave sufficient space below the numbers for that purpose. So, two, three, or four spaces (depending on the number of middle names) below the first horizontal line, make a second horizontal row of the numbers 10 to 18, and a row several spaces below that of 19 to 27, and so on until you have progressed the chart ahead to the desired age.

Immediately below the number "1" print the first letter of your first name. The numbers represent years of transit and the number of years in transit of a particular letter will depend on the number value of that letter. Let us say your birth certificate name is "Thomas." As T has a number value of 2, it will be in transit for two years. To show that on the chart, write the T twice, under the numbers 1 and 2. The next letter is H and as that has a value of 8, start under the number 3 and print it eight times. When you have finished, the last H will be on the line below the second row of numbers 10 to 18, under the number 10. Continuing in the same manner, write O six times, M four times, and A and S both once. This will take you to the twenty-second year. If you wish to go further, simply start over again with T and continue the same process until you reach the year you have in mind. Age twenty-three, incidentally, will be an eventful year for "Thomas" as that marks the commencement of a new first-name cycle. (See chart page 204.)

Do the same thing with your middle and last names until you have completed the process. The Letters of Transit is a most informative chart, and once one has learned how to interpret it, it is possible to piece together the essential pattern of a life and to single out key years simply from the transiting letters.

The Essence

For a given year, there are two ways to interpret the transits. First, look up the number value for each letter in transit and add the numbers together. If the total comes to a compound number between ten and twenty-six, do not reduce it just yet, but rather check it against the corresponding number of the Letters of Transit Table and read that description. Then reduce it to a root, except in the case of Master Numbers, and look up that meaning in The Essence Table. Both meanings will apply, but it is the compound meaning that will be the more important for a given year.

The other method of interpretation is to look at the individual letters and check their meanings when in transit by consulting The Letters of Transit Table. The number value of the letter in transit is the primary indicator. And here, too, one discovers another direct connection with the Tarot, for in most instances the transiting letter number has much the same meaning as its corresponding card in the Major Arcana. As a further guide to interpretation the number and card of the Major Arcana relating to each letter appears in the Table. The Tables follow:

The Essence Table

In the main, the root number for the Essence will have much the same meaning as for a Personal Year, and what follows is basically a capsule version of the Personal Years.

1—New starts, change of job or home, launching of creative project.

2—Time of consolidation; partner, mate, friends, all important this year.

3—An excellent time for involvement in theatrical and musical activities, an active social period, good marriage vibrations.

4—Work important this year—both around home and office. Guard health. Make no unnecessary changes.

5—Many new developments, particularly in regard to friendship and romance. Active and exciting period socially. Travel indicated.

6—Family responsibilities increase, excellent time for marriage or any changes in relation to home.

7—A quiet time and one for spiritual growth. Not good for making changes regarding business or family. Not a good marriage vibration.

8—A very good year for making a job change, gaining a promotion, speculating, or anything to do with finances.

9—A finishing cycle and some loss and sacrifice may be expected. Not a time for initiation with regard to business or social life. Good time for travel and also good for large-scale projects.

11—A creative period, but best utilized by furthering spiritual or occult studies. A somewhat difficult period socially but a first-rate one for learning and inner growth.

22—A milestone year. Anything touched this year will turn to gold, particularly projects benefitting the larger community.

The Letters of Transit Table

1   A   The Magician

As The Magician begins the numbered cards of the Major Arcana, and 1 begins the root numbers, A's transit is a sign of beginnings or changes, particularly in regard to residence.

2   B   The High Priestess

Since The High Priestess is an emotional woman who is guarded and alone, the transiting B is usually a period of strife in a marriage or relationship. Often it denotes lowered health and finances. On the positive side, it can often mark a period of spiritual growth.

3   C   The Empress

The Empress radiates creativity, health, happiness and thus C is a most pleasing letter in transit. The Empress card may also indicate a marriage.

4   D   The Emperor

As 4 is a number of work and The Emperor is overtaxed with burdens of state, it is not the season for love. Also, it is a time to look after one's health. A happier feature of the D in transit is that it can denote travel, although the trip is not always one taken for pleasure.

5	E	The Hierophant

The Hierophant is concerned with spiritual matters, and because 5 is a number of change, there will often be spiritual changes. And while there may be changes also in the material realm, it is the inner changes that will be most important.

6	F	The Lovers

As 6 is the number of responsibility and The Lovers deals with a decision affecting family matters, there will be adjustments and added problems pertaining to the home.

7	G	The Chariot

Seven is a number of aloneness and The Chariot is a card of victory. Thus, the transiting G is a mixed bag: Not a good time socially, but a victorious one for money matters.

8	H	Justice (see note page 28)

This letter has to be looked at in conjunction with the other letters in transit for as in the case of both the number 8 and the Justice card, the H in transit can represent balance or imbalance, depending on surrounding influences. Often, it will signify a period that is all the way up or all the way down.

9	I	The Hermit

As 9 is a number of endings and The Hermit is starting out on a new path by himself, this is often the time of tensions, afflictions, separation or divorce. Much will depend on how the emotions are handled during this transit for they act as the trigger.

10	J	The Wheel of Fortune

With such boon companions as the Special Number 10 and The Wheel of Fortune, this letter in transit marks a turn for the better in one's affairs, and is particularly good for financial dealings.

11	K★	The Enchantress (see note page 28)

Strength, the other name for this card, is most descriptive here, for this is a period of tension and emotional upset, but if the individual is up to the vibrations of the Master Number, 11, he or she will be able to manage and may even find this to be one of the more rewarding periods of his or her life in regard to understanding truths of the inner and outer universes.

★ In a transit chart, K, which ordinarily appears as $1\frac{1}{2}$, is in transit for two years. The same rule holds for V, which is usually written $2\frac{2}{4}$, and is in transit for four years.

12   L   The Hanged Man

In divination, The Hanged Man is not a good card, but on another level of meaning, he is quite happy that he has reversed his old values. That is the interpretation pertaining here. And the number 12 reduces to 3, the number of conviviality and pleasant experiences. So, in all, this is a time of change, but a happy time indeed.

13   M   The Reaper

Both the number 13 and the Death card are somewhat awesome and are considered either very "lucky" or "unlucky." So, too, with this letter in transit. It will inevitably bring about major changes, either for better or worse. Often a time of marriage. As the real significance of the card of The Reaper suggests, this can be a period of total transformation.

14   N   The Angel of Time

The Angel of Time is a card of regeneration; the number, 14, reduces to 5, signifying change. Changes will come about during this transit, but they will be harmonious ones and often they will coincide with a period of psychological and spiritual growth.

15   O   The Devil

In this case, there is little similarity (fortunately) to The Devil card, although because the letter O is entirely enclosed, it can be somewhat overprotected and unduly apprehensive. The number really provides the basic clue, for 15 reduces to 6, which has to do with responsibility, particularly around the home and in connection with mate and family. During this transit added responsibilities will be taken on, but usually they will be self-imposed and highly agreeable. This is also a good period for finances, and a strong indicator for travel or change of residence.

16   P   The Lightning-Struck Tower

It is possible that the expression, "seven years' bad luck" is derived for the time of transit of this letter for 16 reduces to 7, the number of loneliness and secrecy, and the card of The Lightning-Struck Tower connotes accidents, disasters and catastrophes. Obviously, not everyone with this letter in transit is numbered among disaster victims, but it would be well to take every necessary precaution during this period. It is also a difficult time emotionally and therefore does not favor romance.

Q

17   The Star

The Star is a card of hope and optimism and 17 reduces to 8, the number of power and wealth. The transit of this letter, then, is a most beneficial one both materially and spiritually.

R

18   The Moon

Emotions are what the transiting R is all about for 18 reduces to 9, which has to do with emotional turmoil and The Moon also suggests emotional maladjustments, along with deception and delays. This can also be a time of accident or loss.

S

19   The Sun

This might be referred to as the "Glory, Glory, Hallelujah" transit for the combination of the card of The Sun and the number 19, which is the optimum octave of 1, is a most happy omen. Marriage or a change of job or residence for the better will often come about under this radiant transit.

T

20   Day of Judgment

In transit, this letter has much the same meaning as The Day of Judgment card, for it will almost always be a time of decision prior to taking a major step regarding marriage or career.

U

21   The World

This letter indicates a rather dismal period for it is generally accompanied by loss. Seemingly, there is little correspondence to the card of The World signifying joy and happiness or to the reduced number, 3, which suggests much the same. But one must keep in mind that The World card is associated with the planet Saturn, which is considered forbidding and known as "the headmaster." Looked at this way, the transiting U in a three-year period could be likened to a prolonged visit to the office of the principal. The student in this case has been taken down a peg or two, forced to confont his or her own shortcomings and while it has been an agonizing experience, there is a cleansing effect.

V

22   The Fool

Victory in most matters is a virtual certainty during this four-year transit, which marks a time of new starts. There is a need to guard against inner conflict as that is the only real obstacle to success during this period.

W

23

Change is the key word here as the 5 suggests, but as 23 is a most fortunate vibration of 5, it will almost always be a change for the better.

X

24

The letter itself is the prime indicator here for it is formed by two lines going in opposite directions. This translates to, "There is some good news and some bad news." Often the good news has to do with material things such as career or finances and the bad news with nerves or health.

Y

25

Seven is oftentimes an "either–or" situation: Either the individual undergoing its vibration is drinking of the riches of spiritual wisdom, or the individual is drinking, period. Either could happen during this transit. It will mark an important cycle for it will be a time of decision. Oftentimes, the decisions will not be easy ones to make, but if the individual rises to the occasion, much soul wisdom can be acquired.

Z

26

In accordance with the number 8, this can be a very good period financially, but it can also be a period when karmic debts fall due and there can be much unhappiness and frustration in dealing with loved ones, friends and associates.

The Duality

When the Essence is the same number as the Personal Year, it is known as the Duality. This situation will make for problems. Generally, the difficulties will have to do with nerves, inner conflict and a scattering of energies. If the rest of a progressed chart so indicates, the person can be quite self-destructive during this period, particularly in regard to drugs.

Another form of the Duality is when two letters in transit are the same. The effect is much the same as the Essence–Personal Year Duality, although there is an added possibility of accidents, afflictions or loss during the time of transit.

Alternate Methods of Prediction

The Synthesis

The Letters of Transit Table is the meat-and-potatoes of forecasting, and the Essence, along with the Personal Year number, can say quite a bit about what one might expect during the time period under study. There are, however, a number of other ways of predicting and an entire book could be written on this vital phase of numerology. The student who wishes to go further into this is invited to pick up texts by numerologists who have made a special study of forecasting. Recommended particularly are the works of Dr. Kevin Quinn Avery such as *The Numbers of Life*, or for the advanced student, that author's monumental four-volume study, *The Cycle of Man*.

Let us now take up a trio of alternate methods based on the birth data alone. The first, the synthesis, is to take an individual's age before and after a birthday, in each case reducing to a root number if necessary and then adding them together. If the result of this addition is a compound number, reduce again so as to get a single digit. Then add the Personal Year number. Let us say, for example, that a person is now thirty-nine years of age and has a birthday coming up in March. And while it is true that many people borrow a leaf from the late Jack Benny and remain thirty-nine long after they are past forty, if they are honest with themselves, they will be thirty-nine before their birthday, and forty after it. The steps would be as follows:

Age before birthday $39 = 12 = 3$
Age after birthday $40 = 4$ $\underline{4}$
                                    7

To this result, add the Personal Year number and then reduce. If, for example, the individual is in a 2 Personal Year, the Synthesis would be 9 ($7 + 2 = 9$). The Synthesis number for the year will be revealing in regard to the person's *mental* outlook for that twelve-month period. Often, it will indicate the innermost desire for the immediate future, and above all, it will indicate wherein one is most likely to find fulfillment during that period.

Table of Synthesis Numbers

1—Initiate an important project or career change.

2—Get closer to a spouse, family member or friend; join an organization.

3—Take a more active interest in the arts and whatever you do creatively; get out more into the social swim.

4—Roll up your sleeves and get to work on whatever needs doing.

5—Make needed changes.

6—Take on added responsibilities, or do what needs to be done with regard to home, family and community; buy or sell a house.

7—Delve deeply into spiritual and occult matters; go off to a desert island.

8—Push!

9—Adopt a philosophical attitude and stay loose.

11—Put the idea down on paper or canvas.

22—Take a much larger role in the (world) community.

The Higher Consciousness Digit

This figure is obtained by adding the Goal and Personal Year numbers and reducing to a root digit, except in the case of Master Numbers.

Much of the time a person is interested in looking into the future to see how the prospects appear for romance, marriage, career or other matters of a material nature. The value of the Higher Consciousness Digit is that it suggests what needs to be done in the year ahead to help one achieve what must be achieved to reach the Goal of Destiny in this life and find fulfillment. After you have found the Higher Consciousness Digit, refer to the Synthesis Table, but in each case, mentally insert the word "spiritual." A Higher Consciousness Digit of 5, for example, would indicate that what would be called for in that year would be *spiritual* changes.

Future Time and the Tarot

One antique method of prediction is a marriage between the Tarot and numerology. Since this method has to do with the Major Arcana and the Major Arcana has to do with psychological states, this will say something about the individual's psyche for the time in question.

To find the number and the Tarot card corresponding to it, take the present calendar year and age of an individual *after* the birthday. Add them together and reduce to a number between 1 and 22. The number will indicate the corresponding card of the Major Arcana and the *psychological* characteristics of that card in relation to the individual's present affairs. Take, for example, the year 1891 when Sherlock Holmes took a three-year leave of absence to travel in the East, following his near-fatal confrontation with Professor Moriarty. As Holmes was thirty-seven in that year, the two numbers are added together:

$$
\begin{array}{r}
1891 \\
\underline{37} \\
1928 = 20
\end{array}
$$

Thus, according to the Tarot card for the year—Day of Judgment—this would be a milestone year, and psychologically, Holmes would have been prepared to make major changes in his life.

Casebook—The Case of the Dancing Detective

In a sense, we all dance to the music of time, and Sherlock Holmes, however original, however independent, however unique, found himself caught up with the rest of suffering humanity, tapping his slippered foot to Destiny's tune.

Here is Mr. Holmes' Letters of Transit chart for the first sixty-three years of his life from 1854 to 1917. (In practice, always start with the year *after* birth when the letters have been in transit for one full year.)

Letters of Transit
for
William Sherlock Scott Holmes

	1855	'56	'57	'58	'59	'60	'61	'62	'63
	1	2	3	4	5	6	7	8	9
1	W	W	W	W	W	I	I	I	I
2	S	H	H	H	H	H	H	H	H
3	S	C	C	C	O	O	O	O	O
4	H	H	H	H	H	H	H	H	O

	1864	'65	'66	'67	'68	'69	'70	'71	'72
	10	11	12	13	14	15	16	17	18
1	I	I	I	I	I	L	L	L	L
2	E	E	E	E	E	R	R	R	R
3	O	T	T	T	T	S	C	C	C
4	O	O	O	O	O	L	L	L	M

	1873	'74	'75	'76	'77	'78	'79	'80	'81
	19	20	21	22	23	24	25	26	27
1	L	L	I	I	I	I	I	I	I
2	R	R	R	R	R	L	L	L	O
3	O	O	O	O	O	O	T	T	T
4	M	M	M	E	E	E	E	E	S
					29		19		18

	1882	'83	'84	'85	'86	'87	'88	'89	'90
	28	29	30	31	32	33	34	35	36
1	I	I	A	M	M	M	M	W	W
2	O	O	O	O	O	C	C	C	K
3	T	S	C	C	C	O	O	O	O
4	H	H	H	H	H	H	H	H	O
						21			

	1891	'92	'93	'94	'95	'96	'97	'98	'99
	37	38	39	40	41	42	43	44	45
1	W	W	W	I	I	I	I	I	I
2	K	S	H	H	H	H	H	H	H
3	O	O	T	T	T	T	S	C	C
4	O	O	O	O	O	L	L	L	M
	19								

	1900	'01	'02	'03	'04	'05	'06	'07	'08
	46	47	48	49	50	51	52	53	54
1	I	I	I	L	L	L	L	L	L
2	H	E	E	E	E	E	R	R	R
3	C	O	O	O	O	O	O	T	T
4	M	M	M	E	E	E	E	E	S
				19					

	1909	'10	'11	'12	'13	'14	'15	'16	'17
	55	56	57	58	59	60	61	62	63
1	I	I	I	I	I	I	I	I	I
2	R	R	R	R	R	R	L	L	L
3	T	T	S	C	C	C	O	O	O
4	H	H	H	H	H	H	H	H	O
						29			

As Sherlock Holmes was so strongly under the 7 vibration with regard to his personal destiny, let us look at seven significant years in his life and examine the influences he was under in each case. Our major area of focus will be the Essence and Letters of Transit, but we shall also take into account other vibrations such as Personal Years, Months and Days, along with Cycles and Pinnacles. Any abbreviated list of key events in a life is bound to be somewhat arbitrary, but most Sherlockians would probably agree that the following seven were central episodes in the life of the Great Detective. Biographers differ on some of the dates for major events in the life of Sherlock Holmes, and while there is perhaps no way of resolving this problem to everyone's satisfaction, the procedure here has been to stick with one source throughout, and that is Baring-Gould. There follows a listing of seven significant events, after which we shall look at each one in some depth in terms of what is revealed by the chart:

(1) July, 1877—Takes rooms in Montague Street in London and begins career as a consulting detective.[2]

(2) October 13, 1879—Makes his debut as an actor on the London stage.[3]

(3) January, 1881—Historic meeting with Dr. Watson; agreement reached to share lodgings at 221B Baker Street.[4]

(4) May, 1887—Meets and is smitten by *"the* woman"—Irene Adler.[5]

(5) May 4, 1891—The fateful confrontation with Professor Moriarty over the abyss of the Reichenbach Falls, that Watson mistakenly called "the final problem."[6]

(6) October, 1903—Says good-bye to all that and leaves London to take up bee-keeping on the Sussex Downs.[7]

(7) August 2, 1914—Makes "his last bow" as a counter-espionage agent for the British Government.[8]

(1) July, 1877:

Upon leaving Cambridge the young Sherlock Holmes went to London and took rooms in Montague Street. There can be little disagreement that this was a key period in the life of Mr. Holmes for this is when he commenced his extraordinary career as the world's first consulting detective. This period may have been doubly important in that there is reason to believe that he had taken a bride at this time. Conclusive evidence is lacking for this but Sherlockian scholar Michael Harrison considers that a distinct possibility (see Chapter 9).

Refer to the Letters of Transit chart of Mr. Holmes and examine the major influences for that period. Before going further, one highly important detail needs to be pointed out. At the beginning of the chart, where the first nine years are listed along with the accompanying Letters of Transit, note that "1" is not 1854 but 1855, the time when Holmes celebrated his first birthday. It follows then that the first letter of his birth certificate name, "W," (for "William") *concluded* its transit on January 6, 1859 when Sherlock marked his fifth birthday. The second letter of that first name, "I," begins then at age five. At age six it had been in transit for one year and would continue for eight additional years. It is important that this point be understood before attempting to set up a chart. If the chart is not erected in the prescribed manner, the calculations will be a year off.

Looking at Mr. Holmes' chart for the year 1877, we find that the Essence for the year was 29, which reduces to the Master Number, 11. Thus, we realize that Holmes was under great emotional strain at this time, but in view of the fact that he did begin his consulting career, appears to have been operating at the upper levels of his numbers. Eleven is a tricky vibration, particularly for a young person to be under, but as we know from previous examination of his chart, Holmes has the moral fiber to respond in a positive manner.

Emotional strain is further reinforced by the transiting I and R, and possible change of residence and marriage by the transiting O and E. The emotional problems were somewhat alleviated by the fact that he was in a 3 Personal Year, but only to a degree, for a 3 Year is often a time of duality as far as the emotions go. It is significant that Mr. Holmes commenced his venture in July, the time when he was in a 1 Personal Month.

(2) October 13, 1879:

At this time Holmes begins a new career although it is to be of brief duration. Does his chart so indicate? We see that the Essence for the year was 19, which corresponds to the card of The Sun in the Tarot and the optimum octave of the number 1, a vibration encouraging initiation and creativity. This suggests a rather happy period and an excellent time for starting a new creative venture. As Holmes was in a 5 Personal Year, it would almost certainly mark a time of change.

The Letters of Transit also reinforce this. The I and E are "old transits," but the L began the previous year, and the T that same year; they both indicate changes, particularly in regard to career. Of further significance is the fact that Holmes opened in *Hamlet* on October 13, which was a 1 Personal Day.

(3) January, 1881:

Late in the month Holmes and Watson have their first meeting and immediately agree to share rooms in Baker Street. Quite frankly, the relationship was not launched under the best circumstances as Holmes was in a 7 Personal Year, which is not a good time for establishing relationships. Also, the Essence of this period was 18, a period of intense emotions and a better time for endings than beginnings. Although the partnership was to last for over twenty years, there were a number of separations and emotionally trying periods, and this may well be due in part, at least, to the high-strung vibrations under which the union began.

(4) May, 1887:

Irene Adler, who was forever to be *the* woman in Sherlock Holmes' life, made her debut at this time while Holmes was on assignment for the King of Bohemia. It is clear that Holmes was in an extremely down period at the time for he was under a 21 Essence, a grim period indeed, and was in a 4 Personal Year, easily the dreariest of the nine-year cycle. At such a time, even an independent type will look for someone to care for him, usually a life mate. And when added to that, we see that three of Holmes Letters of Transit (M, C and O) are all strong indicators of marriage and since he had recently gone into a 6 Cycle facing a 6 Pinnacle, the will was definitely there. But for better or worse, the match was not to be.

(5) May 4, 1891:

Can one ever begin to comprehend the heartache and sense of loss in that closing decade of the nineteenth century when the readers of Dr. Watson's narrative, "The Final Problem," came upon the opening statement, "It is with a heavy heart that I take up my pen to write these the last words in which I shall ever record the singular gifts by which my friend Mr. Sherlock Holmes was distinguished."[9]

We now know what Watson did not, that the meeting of meetings in that melancholy vale by the falls of Reichenbach was not to be the last, but rather the first in a new series of adventures for Holmes. He was to journey to distant places in a three-year absence from London. Outwardly, the prolonged period of travel was necessitated by the vengeance sworn by Colonel Sebastian Moran, when Holmes dispatched his comrade in arms, Professor Moriarty, into the swirling inferno. But looking at the numerical vibrations affecting Holmes that year it is clear that there were cosmic reasons for Holmes' journey to the East.

For one thing, Holmes was under a 19 Essence, the "Glory, glory, hallelujah" transit indicating a marked change in the life and a change for the better. All the Letters of Transit for that year suggest change, but the O–O Duality indicates that the changes will be accompanied by great tension with accidents a distinct possibility.

What is perhaps most significant of all is that the first name by which Holmes was known to the world—Sherlock—had just completed its thirty-seven-year transit, and the completion of an entire cycle. Invariably, this marks the end of a chapter in a life—sometimes the life itself. This was certainly true for Sherlock Holmes and what is more, the travels he embarked upon during this period were not only travels in outer space, but travels in inner space as well.

(6) October, 1903:

This year was unquestionably one of primary significance in the life of Sherlock Holmes; it was at this time that he formally retired as a London-based consulting detective and took up bee-keeping on the Sussex Downs.

Physically, there were certainly reasons for Holmes to feel profoundly alone for the year before, his long-time roommate and companion in adventures had left Baker Street to take rooms by himself, and later married for the third time. During the early part of the month Holmes received the sad news of the passing of *"the* woman"—the great not-so-secret love of his life, Irene Adler.

Yes, the physical events were real enough but once again the major clues are to be found in the vibrations of transit. For we see that the Essence of his chart for 1903 was that pioneering number, 19, reducing to 1, a vibration Holmes had not been under since 1891, the year of "the final problem," and the start of his travels in the East.

Once again it will be noted that Holmes' Letters of Transit indicated either travel or major changes. Of particular significance is the E–E Duality, the first time in Holmes' forty-nine years that he had been under this extremely heavy vibration. Added to that, Holmes was in an 11 Personal Year. Those combined influences gave added fire to the 19 Essence, which helps to explain Holmes' dramatic exit and total change in lifestyle.

(7) August 2, 1914:

It was at this time that Sherlock Holmes emerged briefly from retirement to have, in the eyes of many, his finest hour as a counter-espionage agent in His Majesty's Service at the outset of The Great War. Ever the perfectionist, Holmes' career as "Altamount" had taken two years of intense training before he was able to achieve his spectacular coup over the master spy, Van Bork.

Again, it is the Essence that tells the story for it was in 1912, shortly after the Second Moroccan Crisis when the threat of a war with Germany suddenly became very real to the British people, that Mr. Holmes offered his services to the new king, George V. The Essence of each of those three years of Government service was 29, which reduces to the Master Number, 11. And in 1914, the year of Holmes' magnificent triumph, he was in a 22 Personal Year. A 22 Year facing an 11 Essence has to be a year of years and this was certainly true for Sherlock Holmes, who helped to turn the tide of victory for the Allies.

When Van Bork has been outwitted and overpowered by Holmes, he and Watson have what may well be their final conversation on earth. Holmes speaks:

"There's an east wind coming, Watson."

"I think not, Holmes. It is very warm."

"Good old Watson! You are the one fixed point in a changing age. There is an east wind coming all the same, such a wind as never blew on England yet. It will be cold and bitter, Watson, and a good many of us may wither before its blast. But it is God's own wind nonetheless, and a cleaner, better stronger land will lie in the sunshine when the storm has cleared."[10]

Yes, that is certainly Sherlock Holmes talking all right; it's the voice we know so well with that unmistakable air of authority and conviction. And yet, there is something different. We have an instant playback and upon hearing the words again, we penetrate the inscrutable mask, and for the first time catch a glimpse of The Real Sherlock Holmes.

And it is this Sherlock Holmes whose acquaintance we shall make in the final chapter.

The Spread: Inner and Outer Space

This is not a spread one would use in ordinary divination, but is rather one of self-discovery. This spread is begun with the assumption that the soul returns many times and each life is in some way a continuation or result of thoughts and actions taken in previous lives.

The spread consists of a significator plus twenty-two cards arranged as follows:

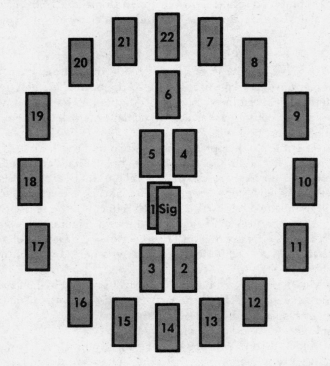

A significator is chosen and is placed face-up in the center of the table.

1—The Hidden Self—This card is placed face down *underneath* the significator and is not turned up and read until the very end and only then if the consultant wishes and the rest of the cards so indicate. The major guideline here is the twenty-first card—the one at the eleventh hour of the clock of life. Should it turn out to be a 6 or 7 of Swords, or any other ominous card, it would be best *not* to turn the first card over as it represents what might be likened to the dark side of the Moon of one's personality. It is what Jung called the "shadow," that unknown entity that the individual needs to confront and integrate if one is to be a whole person. However, one needs time to prepare for this confrontation. Some are ready early, some later, some never.

2—Inner Self: Psyche—Although the meaning is somewhat different, this card and the one following may be compared with the Inner Self numbers of the chart. Each person plays many roles not only in a given existence, but from life to life. But when the makeup and the costumes have been removed, the card of the Psyche is the basic entity, that is, the essential *you* throughout the ages.

3—Inner Self: Soul Urge—This card differs from the card of the Psyche in that it does not so much tell you what you have been and what you are, but rather what you aspire to and what you can be if you continue to advance upward on the evolutionary path.

4—Persona: Zodiac Card—This card depicts the astrological program designed for you at your time of birth and will supplement the Birth number of the chart.

5—Persona: Expression—This represents the life program as expressed by your name and will supplement that number of the chart.

6—The Total Self—This card represents the culmination of the Inner Self and Persona cards and is an indication of how you have integrated your personality.

The remaining cards in this spread represent "outer space"—that is, people, incidents and events—and the card of the Total Self serves as the bridge between the two. The first card in outer space—card 7—represents The Path and the twenty-second card is The Goal. Both should be compared with the Destiny numbers of the chart. After reading the card of The Path, continue in sequence as cards 8–21 will be a picture of the life, from earliest childhood on.

The Tape:

Significator—The Empress

Consultant's Keys

1—The Hidden Self: Queen of Wands
2—Inner Self: Psyche: Ace of Cups   5
3—Inner Self: Soul Urge: Page of Swords   6
4—Persona: Zodiac Card: 5 of Swords   1
5—Persona: Expression: Page of Cups   1
6—The Total Self: The Chariot
7—The Path: Wheel of Fortune   3
8—The High Priestess
9—Knight of Wands
10—10 of Coins
11—7 of Swords
12—King of Wands
13—3 of Wands
14—The Lovers

15—The Lightning-Struck Tower
16—The Hierophant
17—The Reaper
18—Day of Judgment
19—Page of Coins
20—The Moon
21—3 of Cups
22—The Goal: King of Cups   4

At the time of the reading, the consultant was preparing for a career as an opera singer.

SK: The first card is that of The Hidden Self, but we leave it face down underneath the significator, for it is actually the last card we will read.

Consultant: Yes, I understand.

SK: So we start by turning over the two cards below your significator, The Empress, which is one of my favorite cards and a very good one for a creative person.

Consultant: I have always liked her.

SK: I think she is particularly apt in your case as she is the third card of the Major Arcana, and as you know, you are on a 3 Path. Okay, so we begin by turning over the cards of the Inner Self. Well, here we go again. I'm looking at your chart and your Inner Self numbers don't really see eye to eye, for the 5 wants to get out into the world, go to Europe, and sing on the stage, while 6 wants to stay home and raise a family.

And lo and behold, the cards are saying the same thing for you have the Ace of Cups and the Page of Swords. The Ace of Cups wants to stay in and play house while the Page of Swords wants a life of adventure and likes to be in the thick of things.

Consultant: I can see they're saying the same thing as the chart, but they seem to be in reverse order.

SK: Ah, the Tarot is nothing if not subtle. You see, the card of the Psyche is really a card of the past—that is, past lives—while the Soul Urge card pertains to the future and is what you know, deep down, that you need to do in order to evolve spiritually. The Ace of Cups is your Psyche card because apparently in other lives you were mainly concerned with being a loving wife and mother. And that is why 6 is the Soul Urge number of your chart. It is really the remembrance of things past.

Consultant: So you're saying that raising a family gave me a lot of pleasure and I want to go back and do it again?

SK: That's it, exactly. But you see the difference between the Soul Urge of your chart and this spread is that the chart tells what you want to do now, but in the spread, the information is really coming from your higher self. It is not so much the physical you but rather, the cosmic you.

Consultant: I'm glad we're putting this on tape because I'm going to need time to chew this over, but I think I see what the Tarot is saying.

SK: It's really that there are different levels of "I-ness." And these next two cards of Persona seem also to be talking about different aspects of I-ness for you have two 1s, which makes you a strong individualist, but according to the cards, it's more like two individualists rather than one. I think what they are saying is that the inconsistency in your nature is consistent. That is, you may be divided about your desires, but you are essentially the same person without as you are within. Sometimes you're the Page of Cups; at other times, the 5 of Swords.

Consultant: Yes, anyone who knows me at all, knows that I am both and often at the same time. I am wondering if the fact that the Page of Swords and the Page of Cups both came up means that I have a split personality?

SK: You're painting the picture blacker than it is. I think of a split personality as someone who is two spearate people and neither one know anything about the other. Your problem is a division of desire because you want with equal fervor to be a singer *and* a loving wife and mother.

The Page of Swords was in the Inner Self section, the Page of Cups in the Persona part. What this suggests is that while you may think of yourself as being the aggressive adventurer, the self the world sees is someone who is all heart.

Consultant: I'm sure that's very kind of you to say so.

SK: It's not kindness so much; I'm just trying to be accurate. You have two 1s on the Persona, which would suggest some kind of unity. And the person the world sees is the Page of Cups.

Now, we're coming to a very important card, the one of The Total Self. This is the one that connects inner space with outer space. It's where you are right now, but in some mysterious way. It is everything you have been and everything you can be. I would say you just hit the jackpot because it is the card of The Chariot, one of the most powerful cards in the Tarot. It appears that you have some pretty good karma working for you.

Consultant: Is the fact that The Chariot is Number 7 of any importance?

SK: No, I don't think—whoa, wait a minute. Looking at your chart, I don't see too many 7s, but what I do see is that your Path is a 3 and your Goal a 4. And together they add up to 7! The Chariot spells victory, but what is being suggested here is that your Total Self calls for you to follow *both* your Destiny numbers: 3 is self-expression, but 4 is plain hard work. But you combine the two and you get 7 and The Chariot and victory.

Consultant: But, when you were reading my chart, didn't you say something about it being a bit tricky to reconcile a 3 Path with a 4 Goal?

SK: Tricky, yes, but impossible, no. Take a look at the card of The Chariot. Let's say the creatures which are pulling the chariot are the numbers "3" and "4." Now, you notice those sphinx-like creatures are very different for one is black, the other is white. So these creatures carrying the chariot of personality are literally as different as night and day. But the charioteer doesn't seem to be having any problem as they are both going in the same direction at the same time. And what is more, he doesn't even need to hold the reins.

Speaking of your Path, let's turn over the next card for that is the one referring to your Path. It is the Wheel of Fortune, which is just about the perfect card for a 3 Path.

Consultant: When I think of wheels, I think of traveling. Is that one of the things the card is saying?

SK: I would say so. I always think of travel in connection with the card. Now, the rest of the cards are going to get into your past, present and future. The first card of early childhood is The High Priestess. This woman seems troubled about something. What is the first impression that comes to mind about your early childhood? Were you sort of lonely?

Consultant: I think perhaps I suffered from some feelings of insecurity.

SK: Yes, that may be true, but I think you got over those fairly early for the next card is the Knight of Wands. Here's a person who seems to have a real sense of freedom and self.

Consultant: Somewhere about seven or eight, I began to come out of my shell.

SK: This next card is the 10 of Coins and I see a mother and father, children and dogs, and it appears to be a very happy family scene indeed.

Consultant: That card seems to describe my later childhood years exactly.

SK: Your teens, however, must have been something of a rude awakening, for on this card, the 7 of Swords, I see a youth carrying a burden that is heavy and painful. But there is a rather pleasant man who turns up on the following card—the King of Wands. He is very kind and understanding. Possibly he is your father, and maybe he is helping you to ease the burden.

Consultant: Actually, I think he is the main reason for the burden. But I do identify with him very strongly. The problem is that we are just too much alike.

SK: The next card is the 3 of Wands. The suit of Wands has to do, as you know, with work, career, school, that kind of thing. This is probably about the time you started college. But the interesting thing is that this person is holding on to a rod symbolizing work, but he appears to be looking out at the wider world suggesting thoughts of a career that would take one out into the larger world of humanity.

Consultant: I majored in psychology but it was at this time that I began to think of an operatic career.

SK: The next card is that of The Lovers and it looks as if your 6 Soul Urge won out and you married. But I don't like the looks of the card that follows it at all, for that is the Lightning-Struck Tower, and it may be that figuratively speaking, your house of marriage was struck by lightning?

Consultant: This spread is blowing my mind. As it happens, that is *literally* true, and it was around this time that my house was struck by lightning and burned to the ground.

SK: Now my mind is being blown. That might account for The Hierophant over here. After one literally gets hit by lightning one literally gets the call from on high. Did you find yourself becoming more religious at this time?

Consultant: For the first time in my life, I really got into it very deeply.

SK: Don't tell me that the next card, Death, is literal too?

Consultant: Well, I'm not sure. That could have to do with the end of my marriage. But then, come to think of it, one of my best friends was killed in an automobile accident at that time.

SK: Sometimes one card may be saying several things at once. But in this instance no card could have been more explicit than the Death Card. Speaking of death, the following card is Day of Judgment; a coffin has been opened up and three people have returned to life for they have heard the trumpet of The Holy Messenger. Since everything seems so literal in this spread, I think what reawakened you to life after the death of your friend and of your marriage was the trumpet of Michael—maybe not a trumpet necessarily, but at least, the sound of music. Following so soon after The Hierophant, this suggests that music for you became your rock and your fortress. In short, a religion.

Consultant: I must admit I never thought about it that way before, but I think you have something there.

SK: But what is really heavy is that you are on a 3 Path, and the first card we turned over relating to career was the 3 of Wands. Now we come to a card which seems to signify your decision to go into music, and rising out of the grave of the buried life is not one person, but three!

Consultant: In psychology, three is the number of personality. In Freudian terms—Id, Ego and Superego. And so three would represent psychological wholeness, and I certainly felt very together after making the decision.

SK: Three is also an important number in regard to religion—the trinity is one obvious example—and I think you were not only psychologically together but spiritually as well.

Consultant: I know I felt that even though I never got around to putting it into words.

SK: Around this time it seems that a young man has come into the picture, namely, the Page of Coins.

Consultant: There was—and is.

SK: He seems to be a serious young man, a hardworking fellow. But I don't like the looks of The Moon card that follows him. At present it may be a relationship where things are not very clear and it may be a while before the Sun comes up and sheds some light on things.

Consultant: We both hope so but you're right; there are a lot of things that have to be cleared up.

SK: It looks like they will be, for the following card is the 3 of Cups and it appears to me as if these people are at a wedding, drinking champagne. It is a marriage card in any case, but as it is preceded by The Moon, it may be a while before it takes place.

Consultant: That is nice to hear—not that it will be a while but that it will take place.

SK: The last card we turn up in outer space is the one of the Goal. I don't think there is much question about this for it is the King of Cups. He is a very warm, affectionate man and he follows the marriage card.

Consultant: I have had some doubts in my own mind whether I would get married again, and so I am rather glad to hear that.

SK: But keep in mind your Goal number is 4. What is being said is that marriage will come your way but you're going to have to work to make it a success.

Consultant: Yes, I think I learned that from my first marriage.

SK: Now we have covered all of your inner and outer space cards except for this one beneath the significator, which is a most important card for it represents The Hidden Self—an essential part of you but not something of which you are fully conscious. Are you ready for the encounter?

Consultant: By all means.

SK: With the cards that have come up for you in inner space, I don't think you need be apprehensive. Yes, I was right. It is the Queen of Wands. Pardon me while I hallucinate, but if there is any card that would tie in all the numbers of your chart, that would be it.

Consultant: How is that?

SK: Well, for openers, your Persona numbers are both 1, and a queen is usually considered the Number 1 lady in the land.

Then, your Path number is 3, which suggests a person very much involved with other people in a rather pleasant way, which certainly fits this queen. But your Goal number is 4, which means that your mission is to work and Wands is the suit that deals with work. This card suggests that you will not only accomplish your goal, but that you will be queen of your profession.

And finally, your Inner Self numbers are 5 and 6, which make for a somewhat indelicate balance, as 5 wants to become involved with the universe while 6 wants to stay home and raise nine. The Queen of Wands does both, you see. She is very much involved in the world of work and people but she is also married—her husband is the King of Wands. Only in this case, it will be the King of Cups.

Consultant: I'm glad that we taped this, because there is an awful lot here that I want to remember and think about.

SK: What is perhaps most interesting about this spread is the light it sheds on your chart. For, while your Persona numbers are the same, your Inner Self and Destiny numbers are not and there was some question whether they could be reconciled. And this spread makes it clear that they can. It is simply a matter of living all the way up to your potential. If you do, you will be the Queen of Wands and I hope you will have a reign of many long and happy years!

------

[1]St. John, *The Bible*, VIII, v. 32.

[2]William S. Baring-Gould, *Sherlock Holmes of Baker Street—A Life of the World's First Consulting Detective*, Bramhall House, New York, 1962, 295.

[3]*Ibid.*, 296.

[4]*Ibid.*, 298.

[5]*Ibid.*, 301.

[6]*Ibid.*, 307.

[7]*Ibid.*, 318.

[8]*Ibid.*

[9]John Watson, M.D. (amaneunsis: Arthur Conan Doyle), *The Adventures of Sherlock Holmes* ("The Final Problem"), Heritage Press, New York, 1950, 746.

[10]There is a question of authorship here and while some attribute this narrative to Sherlock's brother, Mycroft, it is just possible that it was penned by Watson's "agent," Sir Arthur Conan Doyle; *His Last Bow* ("His Last Bow"), Berkley Publishing Corp., 1964, 191.

12

Requiem for a (Very) Private Eye

A Note Concerning Chronology

Wherever possible, the dates given in this chapter are to be found in the Sacred Writings, *i.e.*, the biographical chronicles of Dr. Watson. In all other instances, the source is Baring-Gould.

When Sherlock Holmes exchanged dressing gown and slippers for his deerstalker cap and told Watson, "The game's afoot," the law-abiding citizens of London knew they had no worries, for soon the mystery would be solved. However, one mystery that has never been solved is why the master sleuth, at the very summit of his career, at age forty-nine, should decide to retire from his profession and become a bee-keeper on the Sussex Downs.

We can guess. We can surmise. We can speculate. But can we ever really know? Certainly, not without data. For as Holmes was so fond of telling his companion, "It is a capital mistake, my dear Watson, to theorize before one has the facts."

But on a moment's reflection, we realize that we do have "the facts" for staring us in the face is the chart of Sherlock Holmes. The clues of a life are there; all that is necessary is the correct interpretation.

Let us review the facts:

```
Roof....................8
Secret Passion ............ 3
Inner Self ............. 6, 22/4

Persona................6, 1
Destiny ...............7, 7
Cornerstone ..............1
```

First of all, this is a man who is a decided individual. One who will take the lonely road of leadership and let his light shine before all (Cornerstone, Core and Expression all 1). Home, however, will play an important part in his life (6 as a Birth and Psyche number), although both his Path and Goal will compel him to find secret knowledge (7/7 Destiny). And pervading his existence will be law (8 Roof). But it is the Soul Urge we look at particularly and there we find 22, the Master Number and often the number of *the* master.

The numbers are beginning to talk now, and noting the month and day of birth: January 6—That date gives us pause. January 6—We know we have come across this date before. But of course: To Christians it is known as "Twelfth Night" or "the twelfth day of Christmas." It is the time for the celebration of the Epiphany, which means "manifestation."

There is no common agreement among Christians as to why this date should be important, but if the famed seer, Edgar Cayce, is correct, as he invariably was when giving information in a trance state, the true significance of the date is that it marks the birth of Jesus![1] Biblical scholars have long realized that December 25 was a symbolic rather than an actual date for commemorating the birth of Jesus. Considering that Cayce's clairvoyance was amazingly accurate, there is good reason to accept the January 6 date as the actual birthdate of Jesus.

There were probably several motives for the moving of the date but symbolical reasons would have clearly been foremost. That final week in December marked the feast of Saturnalia, the most joyous period of the year to the Romans. It was the time of the Winter Solstice, and after the Sun went into Capricorn, the days would become longer. Physically there would be more *light*. What could be a more appropriate time of the year to celebrate a "birthday" for the individual who had said, ". . .I am the light of the world: he that followeth me shall not walk in darkness, but shall have the light of life."[2]

But what does all of this have to do with Sherlock Holmes? Even if Cayce's statement about the birth time of Jesus is accepted as fact, two men born on the same day centuries apart would not necessarily have very much in common with each other.

But when we think about it, some of the parallels are indeed striking: Both Jesus and Sherlock were born on Twelfth Night (January 6); both had "missing years" in which they journeyed in the East; both devoted their lives as "saviors" for humanity; both had a disciple called "John" who chronicled their words and deeds; both were known to their followers as "The Master"; and both were "killed" around their thirty-seventh year and rose again from the dead—Jesus on the third day, Sherlock in the third year after his "death" at Reichenbach. Both men "died" during the Jewish festival of Passover. Christians commemorate the resurrection of Jesus from the dead with the annual three-day period commencing on Good Friday and ending on Easter Sunday, and it is worthy of note that Sherlock "rose from the dead" just around Eastertime in the year 1894. It is not without interest that Watson called this account of the resurrected Sherlock, "The Adventure of the Empty House," which summons echoes of the empty tomb of Jesus.

In view of these parallels, let us make a bold assumption: Sherlock Holmes was a deeply religious man who had a keen sense of having a spiritual mission to perform.

Now, let us see if we can find anything in the chart and elsewhere to support this. It was stated earlier that a chart could be likened to a book which could be read on different levels. We have examined Sherlock's chart from several viewpoints; let us now approach it from the spiritual angle of vision.

The Cornerstone of the chart is 1, which is the number of concern with self. But for a pilgrim on the path, 1 is Self-concern; that is, concern for one's higher self. The Roof is 8, the number of law, but for someone who is Self-concerned, the interest could be in cosmic law. Six, which appears both on the Persona and Inner Self, has to do with home and responsibility, but on a higher level, the chief responsibility would be to seek out one's spiritual home. And this directly connects with the 7/7 Destiny, for only by choosing a more spiritual path can one arrive at "My Father's House," the ultimate spiritual goal. The 22 Soul Urge suggests the wise fool of the Tarot, who having lived through every experience, is now returning to the realm of Spirit.

Seen this way, Sherlock's chart is clearly a spiritual one, but is there any indication that he was living up to it? Is there any evidence to even suggest that he believed in God?

As in the case of Jesus, we cannot speak with authority about his childhood. It is not until his twenty-seventh year, in the winter of 1881, when he meets John Watson, that we have any idea about his religious position. But between 1881 and 1903 we have, thanks to the pen of Sherlock's Boswell, a fairly generous sample of his thoughts and utterances on a considerable variety of subjects—including religion.

It would be truly a Herculean task to attempt a rendering of every reference, allusion and implication made by Sherlock throughout the canonical writings, so let us content ourselves rather with a selection of his remarks over the years. What will be of particular concern to us is the order of the statements. Hopefully, this will give us some idea of the evolution, if any, of Sherlock's thinking with regard to the existence of a divine being.

During the early years that the famous pair worked together, John quotes Sherlock on many topics, but there is little bordering on religion until around 1888, which was significantly just seven years after the pair met. But in that year and the one following, the cosmos appears to be central in Sherlock's thoughts. It is more than likely that he was employing his singular deductive powers to unravel the mystery of the universe. In 1888 Sherlock was in a 5 Personal Year, which is one of change, and it is possible that he was going through inner change at this time.

It is the year after, however, in 1889, that Sherlock Holmes comes out with some of his weightier insights. This is easily explained by his chart: In 1888, his first name—William—had completed its first thirty-four-year transit, and so in 1889, a new first-name cycle had begun. In addition, the Essence of his Letters of Transit in 1889 was 22, the very special Master Number, which also tied in with his Soul Urge. What is more, 1889 marked the first year that Sherlock had a 22 Essence since reaching adulthood. From the point of view of numerology, this had to be an important year, but as the 22 Essence suggests, important for spiritual and global concerns rather than everyday matters.

In September 1888, he refers John to a book that was then enjoying wide readership called *Martyrdom of Man* by Winwood Reade, which according to Sherlock was a book that had to be "one of the most remarkable ever penned."[3]

As this work epitomized the skepticism of the age, it seems reasonable to infer that Sherlock at this point in time was not a firm believer in any religious creed, or for that matter, any explanation of the universe that failed to meet the test of science and the hard-nosed logic of post-Darwinian thought. If there was any church in late nineteenth-century Europe at which a thinking man could worship, it was clearly the Temple of Science. Considering that it was Sherlock Holmes who put the practice of criminal detection on a scientific basis, he appears to be not only part of the congregation, but one of its high priests as well.

The Search

In a conversation with John, Sherlock has occasion to refer to Reade's work again, and in a philosophical mood he states, "A strange enigma is man," to which the doctor replies, "Someone calls him a soul concealed in an animal."

To this, Sherlock offers a pragmatic response: "Winwood Reade is good upon the subject. He remarks that while the individual man is an insoluble puzzle, in the aggregate he becomes a mathematical certainty. You can, for example, never foretell what any one man will do, but you can say with precision what an average number will be up to."[4]

What is of interest in that exchange is John's remark, for he is the one who mentions the word "soul," a concept that seems to be foreign to Sherlock at this state of his development.

But nevertheless, an existential search appears to have been triggered in Sherlock's psyche, for a couple of months later at the conclusion of another case, he remarks to John, "The ways of fate are indeed hard to understand. If there is not some compensation hereafter, then the world is a cruel jest."[5]

In the Spring of 1889, a slight but significant change may be detected in this statement of Sherlock's: "God help us! Why does Fate play such tricks with poor helpless worms? I never hear of such a case as this that I do not think of Baxter's words, and say: 'There but for the grace of God, goes Sherlock Holmes.' "[6]

Rarely before this has Sherlock ever invoked the name of the diety and here he does so twice in the same breath. He seems to have an understanding of the rule of law in the universe, although the workings of this law continue to elude him.

A month or so later, during the summer of that year, a cosmic breakthrough appears to have occurred. For at this time, while in the home of a client, Sherlock goes into what John describes as a "reverie" over a moss rose that he has spotted from the open window.

" 'There is nothing in which deduction is so necessary as in religion,' said he leaning with his back against the shutters. 'It can be built up as an exact science by the reasoner. Our highest assurance of the goodness of Providence seems to me to rest in the flowers. All other things, our powers, our desires, our food, are really necessary for our existence in the first instance. But this rose is an extra. Its smell and its color are an embellishment of life, not a condition of it. It is only goodness which gives extras, and so I say that we have much to hope from the flowers.' "[7]

Sherlock's thoughts here suggest a parallel with another commentator on plant life some time before who phrased it this way: "And why take ye thought for rainment? Consider the lillies of the field, how they grow; they toil not, neither do they spin: And yet I say unto you that even Solomon in all his glory was not arrayed like one of these. Wherefore, if God so clothe the grass of the field, which today is, and tomorrow is cast into the oven, shall he not much more clothe you O ye of little faith?"[8]

But later that same month—August, 1889—Sherlock in a sombre and pensive mood feels that he is no closer to the heart of the great mystery than he ever was, for he tells his companion, "What is the meaning of it, Watson?...what object is served by this circle of misery and violence and fear? It must tend to some end, or else our universe is ruled by chance, which is unthinkable. But what end? There is the great standing perennial problem to which human reason is as far from an answer as ever."[9]

Actually, as shall be demonstrated shortly, his human reason was much closer to an answer than he realized at the time. Let us now move ahead a few years to the summer of 1902. Sherlock says at that time, "The wages of sin, Watson—the wages of sin!... Sooner or later it will always come, God knows."[10]

Supposedly, Sherlock's remarks refer to Baron Gruner and what happened to him. But considering that there had been an attack on his life a few days before, it is possible to interpret Sherlock's remarks as also applying to himself—the "sin" in this case being a failure to follow one's spiritual destiny. This interpretation is reinforced with the knowledge that Sherlock left London the following year for the Sussex Downs where he would be free to read and meditate upon the mysteries of the universe.

In *Naked Is the Best Disguise*, Samuel Rosenberg points out that in the chronicles of John, houses are often described as "two-storied," suggesting that two stories are being told—one on the level of crime and adventure, the other on the level of allegory or some higher realm of meaning. This seems to hold in the dialogue quoted above and again in a case that took place a few days later, in the autumn of 1902. Sherlock is explaining a deduction to John that he has made about their current case when John asks, "But what is at the root of it?" Sherlock's reply is a most interesting one: "Ah, yes, Watson—severely practical as usual! *What is at the root of it all?*"

There seems little doubt that Sherlock is on an existential plane here for shortly afterwards he states, "Education never ends, Watson. It is a series of lessons with the greatest for the last."[11]

It was exactly one year later, however, in September of 1903 that Sherlock makes a most revealing statement. Commenting upon a scientist who attempted to concoct a potion for recapturing his youth, he says, "When one tries to rise above Nature one is liable to fall below it. The highest type of man may revert to the animal if he leaves the straight road of destiny."[12]

Is not Holmes here suggesting that our lives are pre-destined to some extent, that our destiny is mapped out for us, and to tamper with it is to court disaster?

Shortly afterwards, he makes an anti-Darwinian value judgment about those who would use such a potion to increase their life span with the admonition, "There is danger there—a very real danger to humanity. Consider, Watson, that the material, the sensual, the worldly would all prolong their worthless lives. The spiritual would not avoid the call."[13]

With this single statement, Sherlock shuns the Darwinian materialistic practical world of science. Clearly, Sherlock at this point had come around to the view that the most highly evolved man was the spiritual. That these words were well considered may be evidenced by the fact that it was the very next month—October, 1903—when at the peak of his career he retired to become a keeper of bees.

Looking back over the statements Sherlock made to John between 1888 and 1903, it is possible to discern a pattern of sorts: the negative, pessimistic Sherlock is mainly in evidence in the years before 1890; the Sherlock with a sense of Divine Purpose appears after 1890. True, there are exceptions such as the lesson on the flowers that Sherlock gives in 1889, but the basic pattern still remains. After 1890 the statements cited in this chapter appear to grow in affirmation, with the most resounding of all the one quoted at the end of Chapter 11, made in the summer of 1914 when Sherlock tells John that the east wind coming is "God's own wind," and that "a cleaner, better, stronger land will lie in the sunshine when the storm has cleared."

How do we account for this conversion of a pragmatic man of science to a seeker who has seen the light of spirit?

An excellent starting place is with the Master Number 22, which takes on added significance when it is remembered that it appears as the Soul Urge in Sherlock's chart. Anyone with a $^{22}/_4$ Soul Urge will have an all-encompassing desire for work (4) but operating on the highest level (22), it will be only the kind of work that would concern a Master. In Tarodic terms, the $^{22}/_4$ Soul Urge always possesses the potential of becoming the Magus or "Wise Fool," who has lived through every life experience and embarks on the journey-of-journeys in a quest of his Higher Self.

In the second chapter, the soul growth of The Fool was described in terms of a "night journey." Possibly, Sherlock Holmes underwent such a journey and if so, this would go a long way toward accounting for his spiritual rebirth.

To focus on what we are seeking, let us remember that a night journey is essentially a waking dream and that while it is generally accompanied by an actual journey through time and space, the essential journey is of the inner variety and goes to the core of one's very being. It is generally undertaken around sundown, proceeds into growing darkness ("the dark night of the soul"), and if successful, is marked by a return to light. As was explained earlier, in literature the commencement of a night journey is signalled by white-on-black. Though the duration of the night journey may be several years, the white-on-black symbolism recurs toward the end, symbolizing successful completion and the return to light.

The profoundly important thing about a night journey is that the individual learns some vital truth about him- or herself in relation to the universe and has become, in effect, "a new person." To use the classic terminology, someone who has been "born again."

The year 1888 is the time when Sherlock begins a sustained absorption with existential matters. It is early in the year, in January to be exact, when Sherlock, hearing of the sudden death of John Douglas, realizes that this was the work of Professor Moriarty. A man by the name of Barker asks, " 'Do you say that no one can ever get level with this king devil?'

'No, I don't say that,' said Holmes, and his eyes seemed to be looking far into the future. 'I don't say that he can't be beat. But you must give me time—you must give me time.' "

Watson follows this statement with the thoughtful words, "We all sat in silence for some minutes while those fateful eyes strained to pierce the veil."[14]

It is important to realize that in a literary night journey, the characters operate on several levels and while they usually serve as real people doing real things, they may also by symbolic or allegorical. Professor Moriarty, for example, is, on the first level, "the Napoleon of crime" and the villain of the piece. But Barker's use of the term, "king devil," suggests that he might be employed as an allegorical figure, representing all the forces of evil and darkness.

A train of thought triggered by an incident in January begins to take a more active form in September while Sherlock and John are working on "The Sign of the Four Case." The companions are pursuing their quarry in a motor launch on the Thames and John describes the scene thus: "As we passed the city the last rays of the sun were gilding the cross upon the summit of St. Paul's. It was twilight before we reached the Tower."[15]

Considering that it is at this time that Sherlock makes the statement, "A strange enigma is man!," this could signal the beginning of a night journey. That the night journey will be a search for God is suggested by the dual imagery of St. Paul's Cathedral (the house of God) and the Tower of London (the house of evil). We note further that the Church is in the light (faith and truth) while the Tower is in darkness (ignorance and emptiness).

Additional support for the night journey thesis is evidenced by the following scene in which Sherlock describes a white handkerchief fluttering in the blackness. And this is followed by his sighting of the launch, *Aurora*, which is a powerful symbol indeed, suggesting as it does, a brilliant blaze of lights in a polar sky. Also noteworthy is the fact that in Roman mythology, Aurora was the goddess of dawn.

We have sufficient data at this point to suggest, at least, that Sherlock has embarked upon a night journey. However, there may be even more clues we can find to substantiate that thesis.

Because of the dangers of a night journey—one can search for God and find only the devil or nothing at all—there is generally a period of being alone and introspective while the individual consciously or unconsciously weighs the pros and cons of such a risky venture. During this period the white-on-black symbolism will continue to recur, signalling to the questioner, "Hurry up please, it is time!" The individual will always have the free will to take the journey or not, but the signals will continue and become increasingly difficult to ignore.

Sherlock and John wrap up The Sign of the Four case in September of 1888. Later that same month, Sherlock takes on one of his most celebrated cases, which his biographer was to label *The Hound of the Baskervilles*.

What is significant in the night journey context is that the case takes Sherlock out of London where he literally lives in a cave for almost a month, suggesting the night journey of Jesus when he spent forty days in the wilderness. That this "wilderness period" of Sherlock's is a continuation of the night journey started earlier in the month is borne out by the recurrent white-on-black symbolism throughout. This is chiefly supplied by Barrymore, a servant at Baskerville Hall, and an escaped convict who signal to each other at night with lanterns across the dark moors.

Everything in the chronicle leads up to the confrontation with the fabled hound and immediately before this occurs there is a sharp intensification of the white-on-black imagery: "The night was clear and fine above us. The stars shone cold and bright while a half-moon bathed the whole scene in a soft uncertain light. Before us lay the dark bulk of the house, its serrated roof and bristling chimney harsh outlined against the silver-spangled sky. Broad bars of golden light from the lower windows stretched across the orchard and the moor. . . . So as the fog-bank flowed onwards we fell back before it until we were half a mile from the house, and still that dense white sea, with the moon silvering its upper edge, swept slowly and inexorably on . . . ."[16]

The beast itself can obviously be taken as a symbol for, "A hound it was, an enormous coal-black hound, but not such a hound as mortal eyes have ever seen. Fire burst from its open mouth, its eyes glowed with a smouldering glare, its muzzle and hackles and dewlap were outlined in flickering flames. Never in the delerious dream of a disordered brain could anything more savage, more appalling, more hellish, be conceived than that dark form and savage face which broke upon us out of the wall of fog."[17]

The hound can clearly be seen as a symbol, but less clear is what it symbolizes. In the manner of Melville's white whale the apparition eludes precise labeling. It could easily be a hound of hell, but could also represent a "hound of heaven" who causes his quarry to cry out,

"I fled Him, down the night and down the days;
 I fled Him down the arches of the years;
 I fled Him, down the labyrinthine ways
  Of my own mind . . ."[18]

By the Waters of Reichenbach

Considering that Sherlock is on a night journey, the hound as a heavenly messenger seems likely, although it is to be almost three years before he is to have that fateful meeting with the Prince of Darkness in the person of Professor Moriarty.

As in the case of the Baskerville apparition, which was "not such a hound as mortal eyes have ever seen," the sinister Professor Moriarty is considerably larger than life, for in Sherlock's words, "He is the Napoleon of crime. . . . He is the organizer of half that is evil and of nearly all that is undetected in this great city. . . . He sits motionless, like a spider in the centre of its web, but that web has a thousand radiations, and he knows well every quiver of each of them."[19]

Previously, we remember, Moriarty had been described by Barker as a "king devil," and thus he can be seen as the leader of the forces of darkness in this world. But the real nature of Moriarty was revealed to Sherlock in his "singular interview" when the door to his Baker Street rooms opened and Professor Moriarty stood before him. At this time we get our first picture of the Professor and we learn that he was "extremely tall and thin," and that he appeared "clean-shaven, pale and ascetic-looking."[20]

In short, he looked a lot like Sherlock Holmes! When we take into account that John was not present at the "singular interview," and is merely quoting Sherlock, we begin to wonder if Moriarty is a creature of flesh and bones. When we consider further that there is no evidence in the chronicles that anyone but Holmes has ever seen Professor Moriarty, we begin to suspect that Moriarty is Sherlock's *doppelganger*, that is, a ghostly double of himself. During that "singular interview" Sherlock Holmes apparently came to the realization that Professor Moriarty was not somebody totally dissociated from himself but rather, "the devil within" and this is why he proved so formidable an adversary. Slowly, Sherlock begins to comprehend that he had a potential for violence and destruction and that if he failed to come to terms with these dark forces, and learn to understand and integrate them, his destruction would be assured. That destruction would be ordered by the Moriarty within.

It is shortly after this penultimate encounter with Moriarty that Sherlock decides to flee to Switzerland although what he failed to realize was the lesson of the fifteenth card of the Major Arcana: One cannot flee The Devil for the devil dwells within the self. This was the truth that Jesus learned during his forty days in the wilderness, but for Sherlock the problem was still to be solved.

On the morning of the appointed day, John does not recognize his friend for Sherlock is in disguise and it is not totally lacking in significance that the costume he has affected is that of a "venerable Italian priest." One explanation for this is that veteran actor Sherlock Holmes realized that through makeup and costume, one gets a feeling for the role, and donning the rainment of a "man of God" might enable him to truly "see" God and experience His presence. This knowledge would help him to muster the courage he needed to confront his shadow self in that meeting by the roar of mighty waters in "Death's dream kingdom."

Together with John, Sherlock makes his pilgrimage to the falls of Reichenbach. John, however, is lured away by a ruse and Sherlock is left to face his inner adversary on the very edge of the abyss. On the level of literal reality the wrestling match with Moriarty on the precipice taxes credulity, but on a psychological level, it is the essence of parable. One is reminded of the Biblical account of Jacob's wrestling with "the devil": "And Jacob was left alone; and there wrestled a man with him until the breaking of the day."[21]

After Moriarty has fallen screaming into the chasm, Sherlock decides not to travel back by the path whence he had come for fear of detection, but instead, attempts to ascend the sheer rock face of the cliff. Spiritually, this could be seen as Sherlock's putting off the old man (Moriarty) and putting on the new by ascending ever higher to the divine source.

As Sherlock describes the experience, ". . .I struggled upwards, and at last I reached a ledge several feet deep and covered with soft green moss, where I could lie unseen in the most perfect comfort."[22]

This too is reminiscent of the story of Jacob: "And he lighted upon a certain place and tarried there all night, because the sun was set; and he took of the stones of that place to sleep.

And he dreamed and beheld a ladder set up on the earth and the top of it reached to heaven; and behold the angels of God ascending and descending on it."[23]

For Sherlock, however, no ladder was extended and the ascension was to be delayed. And the stones that he encountered were to be of the hostile variety, coming as they did from the hand of Moriarty's chief aide, Colonel Sebastian Moran, who had been overseeing all from his vantage point on the top of the cliff. Sherlock had no choice but to make a quick downward descent and in his words, ". . .I had no time to think of the danger, for another stone sang past me as I hung by my hands from the edge of the ledge. Half-way down I slipped, *but by the blessing of God*, I landed torn and bleeding upon the path."[24] (Emphasis added.)

Looking at that scene on the story level, it makes little sense, for if Colonel Moran is there to guard his master, Moriarty, why did he not come armed with something better than a handful of pebbles? Getting rid of an opponent in this fashion is at best a chancy business. It makes even less sense when one recalls that Colonel Moran was a big-game hunter, and in fact, a most expert marksmen with a high-powered rifle. On this day of days, why would he leave it home?

But on the night journey level, the presence of Colonel Sebastian Moran makes for sound logic indeed for as "a surrogate Moriarty," Moran—even the first three letters of his last name are identical—represents another face of evil. Sherlock's work is but half-over; he needs to probe deeper into his own subconscious until all inner adversaries have been met. Then, and only then, will he be ready for the "ascension." Up to this point the struggle has been a perilous one indeed and there are still stony paths to travel before it will be over for Sherlock. But in the meantime, although he is a little worse for the wear—"torn and bleeding"—he is, "by the grace of God," on the path to higher consciousness. For Watson and the world, the meeting with Moriarty spelled the death of Sherlock Holmes. But the world and the doctor were wrong and three years later The Master was to be resurrected.

The years following the incident at the Reichenbach Falls are a matter of some dispute among historians. Sherlock apparently talked very little about those years and his biographer wrote even less. Research, however, combined with educated guesswork, indicates that Sherlock spent some days in Egypt, Persia, Byzantium and Tibet, thus consciously or unconsciously following in the track of the man called Jesus.[25]

During this period, there are, in fact, a surprising number of parallels to the life of Jesus: the flight into Egypt, travels in the East, exposure to the doctrines of the ancient masters and most importantly, the raising of consciousness. Also, in the manner of Jesus, Sherlock was baptised in water by the Falls of Reichenbach. Of this, as in the case of Jesus, it might be said that he had a spiritual rebirth for as it is written, "Except a man be born again, he cannot see the kingdom of God.

"Nicodemus saith unto him, How can a man be born when he is old? Can he enter the second time into his mother's womb and be born?

"Jesus answered, Verily, verily, I say unto thee, Except a man be born of water and of the spirit he cannot enter into the kingdom of God."[26]

Light in April

Jesus achieved resurrection in three days; for Sherlock, the time needed was three years. The account is provided by John in "The Adventure of the Empty House," perhaps the most symbolic of all the canonical writings. Sherlock's "resurrection" takes place appropriately enough in early April, at the time of Easter. John, who is curious about the death of a nobleman by the name of Ronald Adair, visits the scene of the crime, and while milling among the crowd, chances to run into an "elderly deformed man" carrying a pile of books that he causes to be scattered on the ground. The ancient bookseller is, of course, Sherlock Holmes in disguise and newly returned to England. What is of interest here is that the title of one book John espies is *The Origin of Tree Worship*. Samuel Rosenberg has shown that tree worship was associated with Dionysus, a god who was said to have died and been reborn.[27]

There is also a direct link here to the Tarot; derived as it was from the Eleusinian mysteries, several of the cards of the Major Arcana deal with the resurrection myth of Osiris. And, according to the noted mythographer, Sir James Frazer, "the resemblance which his (Dionysus') story and his ceremonies present to those of Osiris have had some enquiries both in ancient and modern times to hold that Dionysus was merely a disguised Osiris, imported directly from Egypt into Greece."[28]

Another of the books that Sherlock is carrying, and later tries to press on John is also highly significant as it is John Bunyan's allegory, *The Holy War*, and signals that Sherlock's night journey is still continuing for it deals with the forces of light against the forces of darkness. In Sherlock's night journey, the forces of darkness are represented first by Professor Moriarty, and later, by Colonel Sebastian Moran. Moran operates on both the literal and symbolic planes and is the last enemy to be defeated before Sherlock can complete his night journey.

Sherlock has had a wax bust of himself created and it is silhouetted behind the blind in his Baker Street living room. Suspecting that Moran will make an attempt on his life that very night, he, along with John, waits in the darkened "empty house" behind his Baker Street residence. Sure enough, Moran also enters the house, takes a potshot at what he believes to be Sherlock Holmes and is then overpowered by the detective and the doctor.

The victory over Moran (and himself) marks the end of the night journey and this is signaled by three men (Inspector Lestrade and two uniformed policemen) with lanterns. Actually, it is the two policemen who have the lanterns; Inspector Lestrade lights two candles, which could be seen as a parody of the Holy Saturday Easter Mass of the Catholic Church in which a deacon carries a lighted paschal candle into the darkened church, symbolizing the Risen Lord.

But things get curiouser and curiouser. The Colonel, totally flabergasted at Sherlock's brilliant stroke, can only mutter over and over again, "You fiend—you clever, clever fiend!"[29] To this compliment of sorts, Sherlock makes a rather cryptic reply, for he says, "Ah, Colonel. . . 'journies end in lovers' meetings,' as the old play says."[30]

When one takes into account that Moran has been responsible for driving Sherlock out of London for three years, it strains credulity to imagine him as being quite so playful. It is, in any case, an unlikely remark for Sherlock Holmes or anyone in that situation to make.

That is, it makes little or no sense if we take it literally. But if we keep in mind that Sherlock is living in two worlds at this time—the outer world of so-called reality and the inner one of the night journey, we get a somewhat clearer picture. Remember that Sherlock has conquered the last enemy—the devil within—and is radiant with joy. By making an alteration or two, Sherlock's message becomes clear: Night journeys end in meeting hate with love.

But it is when we look at the "old play" that Sherlock alluded to we find ourselves with an embarassment of symbolic riches. The play is Shakespeare's *Twelfth Night*, and there is a Sebastian in the play who has a twin sister from whom he is parted for a time. After a series of adventures, the pair are reunited.

This is the second time in "The Adventure of The Empty House" narrative that Sherlock has made an allusion to a Shakespearian play. The first instance was after pointing out to his companion the wax bust of himself in the Baker Street window, and following a delighted exclamation from John, he says, "I trust that age doth not wither nor custom stale my infinite variety. . . ."[31]

The reference here is to *Antony and Cleopatra*, and in describing the Egyptian Queen's allure for Antony and why he will never leave her, Enobarbus says to Maecenas, "Age cannot wither nor custom stale her

infinite variety. Other women cloy
   The appetites they feed, but she makes hungry
   Where most she satisfies . . .'"[32]

What is of note here is not only is this the second allusion to Shakespeare, but that in both instances, Sherlock has likened himself to a female character! And in each case the identification is artfully concealed in the context of what he says.

Now at this point some reader is going to jump up and shout, 'I knew it! Holmes is a closet queen!" However, by this time it has become clear that Sherlock is nearing the end of his night journey and that many of the remarks he makes are intelligible only in the context of the voyage of self discovery that he is on. During the course of a night journey an individual gets in touch with the deepest levels of being including what Carl Jung called for men, the *anima,* or feminine side, and for women, the *animus,* or masculine side. Every person has some inner quality of the other sex and to deny or repress this causes the personality to become distorted. For a variety of reasons—particularly, the strong, masculine 1s in his chart—Sherlock has, up to this point, rejected this side of himself. Now, as a result of the night journey, he is beginning to acknowledge this facet of his character. By doing so, Sherlock is in the process of becoming a whole person.

Of special interest is the remark that John makes when Colonel Moran's features are illuminated by the policemens' lanterns. Noting that Moran had "the brow of a philosopher," John surmises that the man was born with "great capacities for good or for evil." Thus, Sherlock, in making an allusion to the twins—Sebastian and Viola—in *Twelfth Night,* is suggesting that he is Sebastian Moran's "twin" in that he too was born with this capacity for good or for evil.

And if we look at Moran's name and number, we find another link between the two:

5		1		9	1			6		1		23
S	E	B	A	S	T	I	A	N	M	O	R	A	N
1	2	12			5		4	9		5		$\underline{29}$
												52 = 7

Colonel Moran's Expression number is 7, which was also the Expression number of Professor Moriarty. Since 7 is both Sherlock's Path and Goal number, it could well be that he shared the capacity of his "twin" for good or evil, and that it was his Destiny to emulate the evil that Moran was expressing.

But 7 is the most mystical of numbers and lends itself to a variety of Expressions as witness this individual:

	5		3				9			17
J	E	S	U	S	C	H	R	I	S	T
1		1		1	3	8	9		1	2	$\underline{26}$
											43 = 7

The key as to which way Sherlock chose lies in the title of the play alluded to: *Twelfth Night*. We realize with a start that "Twelfth Night" is, of course, the birthday of Sherlock Holmes! But Sherlock has a birthday "twin" in that it is also the natal day of Jesus. And so for Sherlock "the enigma of man"—that is, the enigma of himself—was resolved with the knowledge that his destiny (7/7) was to follow what Jesus was expressing. In the autumn of 1903 he relinquished fame, wealth and success to settle on the Sussex Downs for the purpose of fulfilling that Destiny. And so the final problem for Sherlock Holmes was to find a solution to the Ultimate Mystery.

---

[1]Anne Read (under the editorship of Hugh Lynn Cayce), *Edgar Cayce on Jesus and His Church*, Warner, New York, 1970, 40.

[2]John, *The Bible*, Ch. VIII, v 12.

[3]John Watson, MD. (amanuensis: Arthur Conan Doyle), *The Adventures of Sherlock Holmes* ("The Sign of the Four"), Heritage Press, New York, 1950, 139.

[4]*Ibid.*, 205.

[5]John Watson, M.D. (amanuensis: Arthur Conan Doyle), *The Case Book of Sherlock Holmes* ("The Adventure of the Veiled Lodger"), Berkley Publishing Corp., 1964, 218.

[6]John Watson, M.D. (amanuensis: Arthur Conan Doyle), *op. cit.*, *Adventures* ("The Boscombe Valley Mystery"), 331.

[7]*Ibid.*, ("The Naval Treaty"), 725.

[8]Matthew, *The Bible*, Ch VI, v 28-30.

[9]John Watson, M.D. (amanuensis: Arthur Conan Doyle), *op. cit.*, *Adventures* ("The Cardboard Box"), 561.

[10]John Watson, M.D. (amanuensis: Arthur Conan Doyle), *op. cit.*, *Case Book* ("The Adventure of the Illustrious Client"), 38.

[11]John Watson, M.D. (amanuensis: Arthur Conan Doyle), *His Last Bow* ("The Adventure of the Red Circle"), Berkley Publishing Corp., 1964, 69.

[12]John Watson, M.D. (amanuensis: Arthur Conan Doyle), *op. cit.*, *Case Book* ("The Adventure of the Creeping Man"), 184.

[13]*Ibid.*

[14]John Watson, M.D. (amanuensis: Arthur Conan Doyle), *The Valley of Fear*, Berkley Publishing Corp., 1964, 174-5.

[15]John Watson, M.D. (amanuensis: Arthur Conan Doyle), *op. cit.*, *Adventures* ("The Sign of the Four"), 204.

[16]John Watson, M.D. (amanuensis: Arthur Conan Doyle), *The Later Adventures of Sherlock Holmes (The Hound of the Baskervilles)*, Heritage Press, 1952, 1204-5.

[17]*Ibid.*, 1206.

[18]Francis Thompson, *The Hound of Heaven*.

[19]John Watson, M.D. (amanuensis: Arthur Conan Doyle), *op. cit.*, *Adventures* ("The Final Problem"), 749.

[20]*Ibid.*, 750.

[21]Genesis, *The Bible*, Ch XXXII, v 24.

[22]John Watson, M.D. (amanuensis: Arthur Conan Doyle), *op. cit.*, *Later Adventures* ("The Adventure of the Empty House"), 774.

[23]Genesis, *The Bible*, CH XXVIII, v 11-12.

[24]John Watson, M.D. (amanuensis: Arthur Conan Doyle), *op. cit.*, *Later Adventures* ("The Adventure of the Empty House"), 775.

[25]According to Anne Read's account (*op. cit.*, 70), Jesus as a young man traveled and studied in Egypt, India, and Persia.

[26]John, *The Bible*, III, 3-5.

[27]Samuel Rosenberg, *Naked Is the Best Disguise—The Death and Resurrection of Sherlock Holmes*, Penguin, N.Y., 1975, 80.

[28]Sir James Frazer, *The Golden Bough*, Macmillan, New York, 1958, 449.

[29]John Watson, M.D. (amanuensis: Arthur Conan Doyle), *op. cit.*, *Later Adventures* ("The Adventure of the Empty House"), 782.

[30]*Ibid.*

[31]*Ibid.*, 778.

[32]William Shakespeare, *Anthony and Cleopatra*, Act II, sc 2.

Afterword

In the beginning, this was not intended as a work about the Great Detective. But Holmes, old ham that he is, has a way of taking stage center. If the reader feels that "Sherlock's numbers" have provided a reasonably accurate portrait of the man, then the question inevitably arises, "Was he, or was he not, for real?" As is well known, there is a sizable group of disciples who claim that he was (or is) a real person, and perhaps an equally sizable group who maintain that he was not.

For the True Believer in the life and work of The Baker Street Saviour, there is surely no more mellow tribute than this unabashed hurrah by Sherlockian scholar Vincent Starret: "...there can be no grave for Sherlock Holmes or Watson....Shall they not always live in Baker Street? Are they not there this instant as one writes? Outside the hansoms rattle through the rain, and Moriarty plans his latest deviltry. Within the sea-coal flames upon the hearth, and Holmes and Watson take their well-won ease....So they still live for all that love them well: In a romantic chamber of the heart: in a nostalgic country of the mind: where it is always 1895."[1]

It is possible that this work will raise more questions than it has answered. The author admits that this is at least a "three-pipe problem," but feels that the probable possibilities reduce to two:

either

1) Sherlock Holmes was a real person and thus numerology offers a confirmation of this in that virtually every major instance he "followed his chart,"

or

2) There are Laws in the universe and because all entities are the product of Cosmic Mind, all entities—be they fleshly or otherwise—must obey these same Laws.

For, in the words of The Master, "When you have eliminated the impossible, whatever remains, *however improbable*, must be the truth."

---

[1]Vincent Starrett, *The Private Life of Sherlock Holmes*, Pinnacle, NYC, 1975, 73.

Acknowledgments

To my mother most adoring fan and severest critic—but always underlined with love and caring

To Mary P. Walker for providing the kind of haven where the muse could be entertained—but most of all, for *being* Mary P. Walker

To Karon Walker for "telling it on the plains"

To George Ziegler for toiling in the vineyards—but particularly for coming up with the brand of faith and early encouragement that made the difference

To those kind souls who aided directly in the preparation of this work: Rita Kip Ayer, Rose Marie Campagna, Francis Carpenter, Kristin Gersbo, Margaret Hitchcock, Pieter Huyser, Denny Koch, Kip Robbins, and Susanna Zukov

To those kindred spirits who aided indirectly in the writing of this book: Mark Twain, Finley Peter Dunne, George Ade, Stephen Leacock, Robert Benchley, Walt Kelly, Jean Shepherd, Al Capp, Charles Schulz, Russell Baker, Woody Allen, and especially, the airwaves' eternal custodian of The Brickbat and Bouquet, Henry Morgan—who all by example generated a healthy respect for The Word, artfully employed, combined with the masque of The Light Touch, thus enabling one to be serious without seeming so

To the Children of Light who helped point the way particularly Cheiro, Edgar Cayce, Florence Campbell, Austin Coates, Isabel Hickey, Gina Cerminara, and Arthur Conan Doyle

And finally, a very special "Thank you" to that first consultant—"Madame X"—whose innocent request for a "throw of the cards" culminated in the realization that there was more in this world than was dreamed of in the author's philosophy.

The Numerology Portrait

You were born on a certain date, at a certain hour and minute into the earth's field of energy. The conditions and vibrations of this energy field determine to a great extent those actions and reactions that will characterize your entire life. In addition to your birthdate and time of birth, your name is as individual as you are. It represents your personality and your potential to the rest of the world.

The Numerology Portrait presents an overview of your personality using the ancient science of Numerology. Through a series of calculations of the four personal numbers that affect you, this portrait can lead to a greater understanding of yourself and how you relate to the world.

The numerological analysis in your portrait is based on the concept of the Divine Triangle. In the sixth century B.C., the mathematician Pythagoras invented the equation, $c^2 = a^2 + b^2$, for the right triangle. Rather than simply use this elegant formula to solve geometric or physical problems, Pythagoras also considered the right triangle a map of the universe that incorporated all facets of human existence. In the same way, you can consider the Numerology Portrait a map or blueprint of your life.

The Numerology Portrait calculates the four personal numbers that you are endowed with at birth. The *Life Lesson Number* represents what you must learn in this lifetime and is derived from your full birthdate. Your *Soul Number* is your real personality, the underlying force that influences all your actions in life. This number is derived by assigning a numeric value to the vowels in your full name at birth and by adding those numbers together. The *Outer Personality Number* indicates how you appear to others and shows what people expect from you and is found by adding the values of the consonants in your full name at birth. The *Path of Destiny Number* indicates what you must do in this life and shows the contributions you are destined to make. This number is derived by adding your unreduced *Soul Number* and unreduced *Outer Personality Number* together.

All calculations and interpretations in the Numerology Portrait are done by the computer at Para Research. You receive an extensive computer printout that provides in-depth explanations of the meaning behind each of the four personal numbers. The explanations and analyses are based on the definitive book *Numerology and The Divine Triangle* by Faith Javane and Dusty Bunker, published by Para Research.

The Numerology Portrait will give you a diverse understanding of yourself and of how you function in the world. Use it as a map of the future that will make your upcoming experiences even more rewarding. To have your Numerology Portrait compiled, use the order form on the following page.

Your birthdate is more than a number

Your Numerology Portrait is all about you—the real you. It vividly reveals your inner potential, your key personality traits, and it helps you see your unique talents and abilities.

The Numerology Portrait results from a series of calculations based on your name at birth and the numbers in your birthdate. By using the concept of the Divine Triangle and proven mathematical derivations, Para Research has developed a clear and concise delination of the four personal numbers and the meanings they hold for you.

From the time you take your first breath, you are influenced by vibrations from the earth's field of energy. Your birthdate provides the pattern called the Life Lesson Number. Your name given at birth is translated into numbers using an ancient number-letter code. This code provides the three vibrations called the Soul Number, the Outer Personality Number and the Path of Destiny Number.

The Numerology Portrait provides an in-depth analysis of your own personal numbers that you were born with and will carry through life. The Portrait devotes at least one full page of interpretive text for each number. All of the calculations in the Portrait are performed by our IBM System/34 computer.

Your personal numbers are unique to you. They tell you the lessons you must learn during your life and the spiritual growth and development you can attain. They also reveal the state of consciousness which you have reached and record the growth of your soul. When you begin reading your Numerology Portrait, you'll discover among other things why you are likely to make a lot of

money, why you will enjoy a good marriage, or why you tend to be idealistic.

From your Life Lesson Number, you will find out what you have to learn in this lifetime. This number is extremely significant in your choice of a career. It also represents the cosmic gift you are given in order to accomplish your destiny. Your Soul Number is what you, in your inner secret self, desire to be. This part of your personality is not easily recognized by others unless they know you very well. The Soul Number also indicates what you may have done in previous lifetimes. The Outer Personality Number represents the personality you present to the world. It's the you as others perceive you and is important in understanding how other people react to you. The Path of Destiny Number represents your aim

in life. It shows the path you must walk, what you should accomplish and what you must be.

Your Numerology Portrait encompasses these and other aspects of your personality. It is authoritative and unerringly accurate. Every word, every explanation embodies the work of Faith Javane, one of America's most respected teachers of numerology and her student and co-author Dusty Bunker, a teacher and author of three books on numerology.

Your Numerology Portrait is inexpensive. Of course, we realize that there is no substitute for the one-to-one interchange between a numerologist and his or her client. However, a good numerologist would charge as much as $40 to $50. Compare that to the incredibly low price of $5.00 for the Numerology Portrait. This low price is possible because the text and the mathematical formulas are both stored in our IBM System/34 computer. You pay only for the cost of putting your personal information into the computer, compiling one copy, hand checking it and then sending it. You will receive your copy in approximately two weeks.

Along with your portrait is a money-back guarantee that is unconditional. This means that you can return your Numerology Portrait at any time for any reason and get a full refund. Para Research takes all the risk, not you!

Order today. Your Numerology Portrait just may be the most important picture you ever look at. It will show you aspects of your personality that you may never have thought to exist.

© 1982 Para Research, Inc.

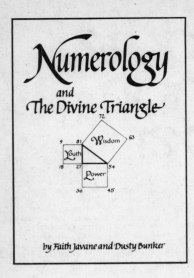

NUMEROLOGY & THE DIVINE TRIANGLE

Faith Javane & Dusty Bunker

Now in its fifth printing, this major work embodies the life's work of Faith Javane, one of America's most respected numerologists, and her student and co-author Dusty Bunker, a teacher and columnist on metaphysical topics.

Part I introduces esoteric numerology. Topics include: the digits 1 through 9; how to derive your personal numbers from your name and date of birth; how to chart your life path; the symbolism of each letter in the alphabet; the life of Edgar Cayce, and more.

Part II delineates the numbers 1 through 78 and, illustrated with the Rider-Waite Tarot deck, synthesizes numerology, astrology and the Tarot. *Numerology & The Divine Triangle* is number one in its field.

ISBN 0-914918-10-9
280 pages, 6½" x 9¼", paper $10.95

NUMEROLOGY AND YOUR FUTURE

Dusty Bunker

In her second book, Dusty Bunker stresses the predictive side of numerology. Personal cycles, including yearly, monthly and even daily numbers are explored as the author presents new techniques for revealing future developments. Knowledge of these cycles will help you make decisions and take actions in your life.

In addition to the extended discussion of personal cycles, the numerological significance of decades is analyzed with emphasis on the particular importance of the 1980s. Looking toward the future, the author presents a series of examples from the past, particularly the historical order of American presidents in relation to keys from the Tarot, to illustrate the power of numbers. Special attention is paid to the twenty-year death cycle of the presidents, as well as several predictions for the presidential elections.

ISBN 0-914918-18-4
235 pages, 6½" x 9¼", paper $9.95